DEPENDENT ACCUMULATION
AND UNDERDEVELOPMENT

D0763599

By the same author

CAPITALISM AND UNDERDEVELOPMENT IN LATIN AMERICA

LATIN AMERICA: UNDERDEVELOPMENT OR REVOLUTION

LUMPENBOURGEOISIE: LUMPENDEVELOPMENT

SOCIOLOGY OF DEVELOPMENT AND UNDER-DEVELOPMENT OF SOCIOLOGY

ON CAPITALIST UNDERDEVELOPMENT

WORLD ACCUMULATION 1492–1789

DEPENDENCE AND UNDERDEVELOPMENT: LATIN AMERICA'S POLITICAL ECONOMY
(with Dale Johnson and James Cockcroft)

MEXICAN AGRICULTURE 1521–1630: TRANSFORMATION OF THE MODE OF PRODUCTION

REFLEXIONES SOBRE LA CRISIS ECONOMICA

ECONOMIC GENOCIDE IN CHILE

AMERICA LATINA: FEUDALISMO O CAPITALISMO?
(with Rodolofo Puiggros and Ernesto Laclau)

ASPECTOS DE LA REALIDAD LATINOAMERICANA
(with Orlando Caputo, Roberto Pizarro and Aníbal Quijano)

QUALE 1984?
(with Samir Amin and Hosea Jaffe)

DEPENDENT ACCUMULATION AND UNDERDEVELOPMENT

Andre Gunder Frank

Monthly Review Press
New York and London

Library of Congress Cataloging in Publication Data
Frank, Andre Gunder, 1929-
  Dependent accumulation and underdevelopment.

  Bibliography: p.209
  Includes index.
  1. Economic history. 2. Capitalism.
3. Saving and investment. 4. Underdeveloped
areas. I. Title.
HC51.F67 1979   330.9'172'4   78-13913
ISBN 0-85345-468-X (cloth)
ISBN 0-85345-492-2 (paper)

Manufactured in the United States of America
10   9   8   7   6   5   4   3   2

To the memory of
my student, friend and comrade in Chile

DAGOBERTO PEREZ VARGAS

who left our theoretical concerns behind
to fight and die heroically to end
accumulation through dependence, underdevelopment and
exploitation

Contents

Preface   xi

Acknowledgements   xviii

1 Introductory Questions   1
  1. The Question of 'Internal' *v.* 'External' Determination   2
  2. The Question of Periodisation   7
  3. Questions of Production and Exchange   10

2 World Capital Accumulation, Trade Patterns and Modes
  of Production, 1500–1770   13
  1. Trade Triangles   14
  2. Differential Transformation of Modes of Production in
     Asia, Africa and Latin America   17

3 On the Roots of Development and Underdevelopment in
  the New World: Smith and Marx *v.* the Weberians   25
  1. On the Weber Thesis   25
     A. Significance of the Weber Thesis   25
     B. The Protestant Ethic and the Spirit of Capitalism   28
     C. Unorthodox Weberian Survivals   30
  2. On Adam Smith and the New World   33
  3. On Karl Marx and Capital Accumulation   38
  4. On World Capital Accumulation, International
     Exchange, and the Diversity of Modes of Production in
     the New World   43
     A. Mining Economies in Mexico and Peru   45
     B. Yeoman Farming in the Spanish Possessions   47
     C. Transformation: The Case of Barbados   50
     D. The Plantation System in the Caribbean and Brazil   52
     E. The U.S. South: Slave Plantations *v.* Farming   55
     F. The U.S. North-east: Farming *v.* Foreign Trade   58
     G. Epilogue – Delayed by Two Centuries   68

4 The Industrial Revolution and Pax Britannica, 1770–
  1870   70
  1. Metropolitan Capital Accumulation and Industrial
     Revolution in Europe   71
  2. Bourgeois Industrial Policy and the New International
     Division of Labour   75
  3. North America   79
  4. Latin America   82
  5. India   87

5 That the Extent of the Internal Market is Limited by the
  International Division of Labour and the Relations of
  Production   92
  1. On Trade   93
     A. On Classicals and Reformers   93
     B. On Comparative Advantage and Free Trade   94
     C. On Deteriorated Terms of Trade   101
     D. On Unequal Exchange   103
  2. On Markets   110
     E. On Dualism   110
     F. On Staple Theory   112
     G. On Linkages   113
     H. On Developing the Internal Market   121
     I. On Infant Industry and Import Substitution   128
     J. On the Division of Labour and Technological Gaps   130
  3. On Production and Accumulation   134
     K. On Economic Sectors and Classes   134

6 Imperialism and the Transformation of Modes of Production in Asia, Africa and Latin America, 1870–1930   140
  1. Rosa Luxemburg on Imperialist Struggle against Nat-
     ural and Peasant Economy   142
  2. Imperialism in Asia   146
  3. Imperialism and the Arab World   154
  4. Imperialism and Africa   157
  5. Imperialism in Latin America   164

7 Multilateral Merchandise Trade Imbalances and Uneven
  Economic Development   172
  1. Patterns of World Trade Imbalances   173

Contents

2. Colonial and Semi-Colonial Capital Contributions to Metropolitan Accumulation and Overseas Investment   189

3. Statistical and Methodological Appendix   199

Bibliography   209

Index   221

Preface

This book is an attempt to approach an explanation of underdevelopment through the analysis of the production and exchange relations of dependence within the world process of capital accumulation. Hence the choice of its title.

We distinguish three main stages or periods in this world embracing process of capital accumulation and capitalist development: mercantilist (1500–1770), industrial capitalist (1770–1870), and imperialist (1870–1930). Each of these periods is examined in a historical chapter that first sets out important developments in the world process of capital accumulation, concentrating especially on the 'exchange' relations between the metropolis and the periphery, and then goes on to analyse the associated transformation of the dependent 'internal' relations of production and the development of underdevelopment in each of the principal regions of Asia, Africa and the Americas. Each of these 'historical' chapters is followed by a 'theoretical' one which discusses an important problem of socio-economic theory (and of historical fact) that arises out of each of these periods: why different parts of the New World of the Americas – specifically the mining and plantation regions on the one hand and the north-eastern colonies in North America on the other – took different paths of underdevelopment and development during the mercantilist period; why the now underdeveloped countries did not experience the development of an internal market similar to that of Western Europe and the new settler regions in North America and Australia during and since the period of industrial capitalism; and how the international division of labour – and specifically the mostly neglected merchandise export surplus from the now underdeveloped regions – contributed to uneven world capitalist development and to capital accumulation in Western Europe and to investment by the latter in the United States, Canada and Australia.

The bulk of the text was written in Chile in 1969/70 and most of the remainder was revised there in 1972/73. The following circumstances influenced its preparation, and the reader should keep them in mind. The author had previously contributed to the development of the 'dependence' approach to underdevelopment with his *Capitalism and Underdevelopment in Latin America* (written in 1963–65 and published in various editions in 1967–71, hereinafter referred to as *Capitalism*) and in other writings. In 1968/69, I sought to extend this 'dependence' approach to the study of other areas as well by preparing/editing with Said A. Shah a bulky Reader on Underdevelopment, emphasising dependence in Asia, Africa, the Arab World and Latin America. The first and second drafts of the present text were written in October 1969 and February 1970 and intended as the theoretical introduction to the first – historical – volume of the Reader (while a second volume on contemporary underdevelopment was in preparation). This emphasis on dependence and its analysis in the historical experience of each of the major regions of the 'third world' still marks this book as published today.

At the same time, the analysis of dependence by the present author and others had become the object of increasing criticism. Critics argued that our approach (1) emphasised 'external' exchange relations to the virtual exclusion of 'internal' modes of production; (2) that it did not take adequate account of the differences in various parts of Latin America and the world or of different stages of development; and (3) that it did not really achieve a dialectical dynamic analysis of the worldwide historical process of capital accumulation in which both metropolitan economic development and dependent peripheral underdevelopment should be analysed as part of a single process. The most common criticism was the first one, which was reiterated in a critique of the second draft of the present text itself by Giovanni Arrighi. Samir Amin, who at the time was writing his own *Accumulation on a World Scale* criticised the second draft as well for failing to differentiate and analyse the major stages of capitalist development adequately (and for 'seeing everything through Latin American eyes'). The third criticism was most particularly the author's own and reflected my conviction, already expressed in the Preface to *Capitalism*, that it is necessary to study the historical development of the single world capitalist system.

These inadequacies and critiques led to the preparation in July 1970 of a third draft (comprising 160 single-spaced pages that incorporated material from the previous drafts), in which I attempted to face all three of the above critiques and challenges simultaneously: (1) To analyse dependence through the 'internal' relations if not the modes of production, accounting for their mutual determination of and relations to the 'external' relations of exchange, particularly though not exclusively with the metropolis; (2) to examine the 'internal' determining dynamic of the historical process of capital accumulation or de-accumulation and its distinguishable stages of development or underdevelopment; and (3) to place all these elements within the single historical process of the development of a single world capitalist system. This meant emphasising the process of capital accumulation but so far as possible examining its different modalities in the various parts of the world simultaneously at each stage of the single world historical process, instead of doing the regional or country histories serially one after the other, each only tangentially related to the process as a whole and not at all related to each other, as I had done in *Capitalism,* in the Reader and in the first two drafts of the present work. In doing so, of course, the original intention to 'introduce' the Reader was left behind; and the length and scope of the present book was qualitatively changed in its 1970 third draft.

This draft, then entitled 'Towards a Theory of Capitalist Underdevelopment', and the resultant present book as well thus represent an attempt to transcend the 'dependence' approach, but without yet abandoning it or the focus on underdevelopment, and to proceed on towards the integration of dependence and underdevelopment within the world process of accumulation. Beginning with the discussion – in part reproduced here in the Introduction – of the theoretical problems posed by this theoretical transition, the third draft sought to proceed historically from one stage of world capitalist development to another and through the analysis of the relationship between production and exchange relations sought to examine on the one hand the differential contributions of each of the major world regions to the world process of capital accumulation during each of its major stages of development, and on the other hand to analyse the underdeveloping consequences of this participation in world accumulation for each of the major regions of the now underdeveloped 'third world'.

This attempt necessarily was only very partially if at all successful (although some readers of the manuscript, for instance Ernest Mandel writing in a 'postface' to a new edition of his *Traité,* regarded it as a great advance – perhaps over this author's previous lag). The intention to revise the third draft to render it minimally satisfactory was frustrated by other concerns in Chile after Allende's electoral victory in September 1970. Later, partial revisions advanced in two different directions. One direction was to expand and deepen the historical analysis by also examining the cycles of accumulation that are apparently identifiable even in pre-industrial times and examining the relations or related simultaneous participation of the various parts of the world at each point in time or at least in each phase of each cycle. This historical work, undertaken mostly in 1973, expanded the twenty-odd pages of the present Chapter 2 into more than 250 pages of new text. This work, which had been intended to reach the present, was cut short by the 1973 coup in Chile and then by lack of the author's research materials; and has now become the book entitled *World Accumulation 1492–1789*.

The other line of revision of the 1970 third draft was to prepare three long articles, each substantially revised in 1972/73 and since, so as to treat certain theoretical problems that had not been satisfactorily resolved in the 1970 manuscript. The first of these, here Chapter 3, 'On the Roots of Development and Underdevelopment in the New World: Smith and Marx *v.* the Weberians' is an attempt to answer why, in colonial times, different New World colonies had already taken off in different directions of development and underdevelopment. By examining successively and comparatively the combinations of 'internal productive relations' and 'external exchange relations' of the mining economies of Mexico and Peru, the yeoman farming areas in the Spanish possessions, the plantation systems in Brazil, the Caribbean and the (later) U.S. South, and New England, the argument emerges that the combination of 'colonial' productive and exchange relations made for the beginnings of the development of underdevelopment and that the absence of these through 'benign neglect' was necessary but not sufficient to permit the development experienced by New England but not by other yeoman societies. What further distinguished New England was its particular 'semi-peripheral' intermediate (as per Wallerstein) or 'proto-subimperialist' insertion and participation in the process of world capital accumulation, associated with its particular role in the triangular trade, which permitted an important merchant capital accumulation and its subsequent investment in industrialisation in the New England and Middle Atlantic colonies. The same chapter also offers a reading of Adam

Smith (as well as of Karl Marx) that supports a major portion of this argument and at the same time rejects or revises the argument, which has been traditional from Smith to the United Nations Commission for Latin America (CEPAL), but including also many historians of the United States, left and right, as well as previous writings of the present author, to the effect that the development of the internal market was related to the relatively equal distribution of income and relative political democracy supposedly existent in yeoman farming societies.

The title of the second theoretical essay (here Chapter 5) is a play on the words of Adam Smith's famous dictum: 'That the Extent of the Internal Market is Limited by the International Division of Labour and the Relations of Production'. This essay also revises the present author's earlier stand (in *Capitalism* and earlier drafts of the present work) about the role of the distribution of income in the development of the internal market and poses the following questions: What, if not the distribution of income, does then determine the development of the internal market, and why did it develop at some times and places and not in others? What are the relations between the production and export of raw materials and the development of an internal market and domestic production of manufactures and capital goods? To answer these questions, I first examine critically some unsatisfactory classical, neo-classical and reformist international trade theses on comparative advantage, free trade, and the terms of trade; then, by discussing the extent and formation of the internal market in terms of the 'dualism' thesis, examine the staple theory, linkages, infant industry and import substitution policies, technological gaps; and finally I examine the relation of sectoral divisions and class interests in the process of capitalist production and accumulation. This discussion of the formation of the internal market transcends the historical account of pre-industrial development and refers as well, indeed principally, to development experiences and problems that have arisen during the nineteenth and twentieth centuries.

The third long theoretical essay, here Chapter 7, on 'Multilateral Merchandise Trade Imbalances and Uneven Economic Development', examines the system of international trade developed under classical imperialism from 1870 to 1930 by focusing not so much on the balance of payments, including service payments, as is more orthodox, but on the pattern of real merchandise trade and how its imbalance – that is how the real export surplus of the now

underdeveloped regions of the world to its now developed ones –
contributed to the development of the latter and the underdevelopment of the former. These three long essays or chapters thus treat
some of the theoretical problems of capital accumulation, dependence and underdevelopment posed in the 1970 manuscript and
reproduced in the introductory Chapter 1 that follows.

The global historical account and the examination of the
transformation of the modes of production in Asia and Africa, and
in Latin America since Independence, does not, however, explicitly
appear in these three essays/chapters. Therefore, each of the above-
mentioned 'theoretical' chapters is preceded by a 'historical' one
(re-incorporating the historical material from the 1970 manuscript), which sets out the general historical context for the
theoretical analysis and relates it to the transformation of the modes
of production in each of the major world regions – including in part
the European metropolis and North America – in each of the major
stages of world capitalist development: the Mercantilist Period,
1500–1800 (Chapter 2), the Industrial Revolution and Pax Britannica (Chapter 4), and the period of Classical Imperialism to 1930
(Chapter 6). These chapters are shorter because part of the
historical material *is* already in the 'theoretical' chapters and
because the revision of the remaining historical material expanded
so much as to become – as noted above – a separate book covering
the first of the above periods alone. I hope that this brief historical
review can none the less serve to re-establish the unity of history and
theory that informed this entire project from its inception.

I gratefully acknowledge the vital contribution of Said Shah to
this book and to extend this acknowledgement also to many others
who contributed their critiques along the way but who probably
would not wish voluntarily to assume or to be saddled with any
responsibility for what is written here. Among these I have already
named Giovanni Arrighi and Samir Amin, and I must add Ernest
Mandel, Paul Sweezy, Harry Magdoff, Urs Müller-Plantenberg,
and particularly my friends and colleagues at the Centro de
Estudios Socio Economicos (CESO) of the University of Chile, Ruy
Mauro Marini, Theotonio dos Santos, Jaime Torres and others, as
well as many of my students in Chile – the still living, whom it is
better not to name under present circumstances, and the others,
particularly my friend Dagoberto Perez, tragically assassinated by
the Junta on 16 October 1975 while fighting heroically to end
accumulation through dependence, exploitation and under-

development. May his cause and his memory live.

The following chapters have previously been published in the same or in a similar version in the following serial publications:

Chapter 3 in the *International Review of Sociology* (Journal of the International Institute of Sociology, Universita degli Studi di Roma) Rome, II Series, Vol. x. No. 2–3, August-December 1974, and in a revised form in *Theory and Society* (Elsevier Scientific Publishing Company) Amsterdam, 2, 1975.

Chapter 5 in the *Economic and Political Weekly*, Bombay, Vol. xi, Nos. 5–7, Annual Number, February 1976.

Chapter 7 in the *Journal of European Economic History* (Banco di Roma) Rome, Vol. 5, No. 2, Fall 1976.

The author gratefully acknowledges the institutional and financial support of the Max Planck Institute in Starnberg, Germany and the German Foundation for Peace and Conflict Research (DGFK), who enabled him to revise earlier manuscript drafts and to prepare them for publication as this book.

Frankfurt   A.G.F.

Acknowledgements

The author and publisher wish to thank the following who have kindly given permission for the use of copyright material:

George Allen & Unwin Limited for a table from *Forty Years of Foreign Trade*, by Paul Lamartine Yates

Augustus M. Kelley Publishers for an extract from *Selections from the Economic History of the United States 1765–1860*, by Guy Steven Callender

Liverpool University Press for an extract from *Studies in British Overseas Trade 1870–1914*, by S. F. Saul

W. W. Norton & Company, Inc., for a diagram from *The Commerce of Nations*, by J. B. Condliffe

Random House, Inc., for an extract from *The Wealth of Nations: An Inquiry into the Nature and Causes of the Wealth of Nations*, by Adam Smith

Routledge & Kegan Paul Limited and Monthly Review Press for an extract from *The Accumulation of Capital*, by Rosa Luxemburg

Peter Smith Publishers, Inc., for an extract from *History of Agriculture in the Southern States to 1860*, by Lewis C. Gray

Epigraph

The discovery of America, the rounding of the Cape, opened up fresh ground for the rising bourgeoisie. The East-Indian and Chinese markets, the colonization of America, trade with the colonies, the increase in the means of exchange and in commodities generally, gave to commerce, to navigation, to industry, an impulse never before known, and thereby to the revolutionary element in the tottering feudal society, a rapid development. . . .

Modern industry has established the world-market, for which the discovery of America paved the way. This market has given an immense development to commerce, to navigation, to communication by land. This development has, in its turn, reacted on the extension of industry; and in the proportion as industry, commerce, navigation, railways extended, in the same proportion the bourgeoisie developed, increased its capital, and pushed into the background every class handed down from the Middle Ages. We see, therefore, how the modern bourgeoisie is itself the product of a long course of development, of a series of revolutions in the modes of production and of exchange. . . .

The bourgeoisie, by the rapid improvement of all instruments of production, by the immensely facilitated means of communication, draws all, even the most barbarian, nations into civilization. The cheap prices of its commodities are the heavy artillery with which it batters down all Chinese walls, with which it forces the barbarians' intensely obstinate hatred of foreigners to capitulate. It compels all nations, on pain of extinction, to adopt the bourgeois mode of production; it compels them to introduce what it calls civilization into their midst, i.e., to become bourgeois themselves. In a word, it creates a world after its own image. . . .

The bourgeoisie cannot exist without constantly revolutionizing the instruments of production, and thereby the relations of production, and with them the whole relations of society. Conservation of the old modes of production in unaltered form was, on the contrary, the first condition of existence for all earlier industrial classes. Constant revolutionizing of production, uninterrupted disturbance of all social conditions, everlasting uncertainty and agitation distinguish the bourgeois epoch from all earlier ones. All fixed, fast-frozen relations, with their train of ancient and venerable prejudices and opinions, are swept away, all new-formed ones become antiquated before they can ossify. All that is solid melts into air, all that is holy is profaned, and man is at last compelled to face with sober senses his real conditions of life, and his relations with his kind. The need of a constantly expanding market for its products chases the bourgeoisie over the whole surface of the globe. It must nestle everywhere, settle everywhere, establish connections everywhere. . . .

Karl Marx & Friedrich Engels
The Communist Manifesto 1848

1 Introductory Questions

This book and these introductory questions to it are an attempt to break out of the vicious circle of 'development theory'. Most contemporary – that is neo-classical – development theorists are caught in a vicious circle of their own making in that they argue that the poor are poor because they are poor – and the rich are rich because they are rich (Myrdal 1957). For some economists the 'low level equilibrium trap' (Leibenstein) manifests itself through a Keynesean demand or market exchange side: since the poor cannot pay, it does not pay the rich to invest, and the poor remain poor. Other economists and most social scientists (in sociology, anthropology, psychology, political science, human geography) are trapped in a vicious circle on the supply or productive side: their theory posits that the poor remain poor because they lack the capital, entrepreneurship and other social, cultural, psychological and political characteristics which these theorists suppose to characterise the industrial capitalist countries and which they therefore suppose to be necessary for investment and development. Trapped in a narrow vicious theoretical circle of their own making, which effectively defines the theoretical limits of their own creativity but does not correspond to the reality of development and under-development, most contemporary theorists are quite unable to explain – and related policy makers are still less able to change – the nature and causes of the poverty and the wealth of nations. To break out of the vicious circle, we propose to return to classical political economy as a point of departure and to attempt to contribute to its extension in the light of later historical and theoretical developments.

To free ourselves from the irrelevance of narrowly limited neo-classical theory for any serious inquiry into the nature and causes of the wealth and poverty of nations, we may take the global historical vision of Adam Smith and the dialectical historical analysis of Karl Marx as points of departure in an attempt to advance toward a whole world encompassing holistic, real-world historical, socially structural (and therefore in fact theoretically dialectical) theory of development and underdevelopment. This task will require the scientific examination of the historical evidence and record of capitalist development and the better rereading (in the sense of Althusser) of Smith and Marx in the light of this evidence – all of which has been deliberately eschewed by neo-classical 'development theory'. With this purpose and in this spirit we review the participation of Asia, Africa and Latin America in this worldwide historical process; and we emphasise the subordinate *dependence* of these areas within the process of world capitalist development as the cause of their development of underdevelopment. The present theoretical essay is an attempt to advance a step beyond the 'dependence' approach and to propose an inquiry into the process of capital accumulation as the determinant nature and cause of the wealth and poverty of nations. Therefore, this book and its 'rereading' of classical political economy also re-examine the established historical record and evidence.

1. The Question of 'Internal' *v.* 'External' Determination

We may examine the question whether development and under-development are determined internally or externally to the social unit undergoing change and whether the determinant realm is that of production or that of exchange – or both.

Marx says, 'the modern mode of production developed only where the conditions for it had taken shape within . . .' and, as Mao Tse-tung puts it, 'a suitable temperature can only change an egg but not a stone into a chicken'. Yet all classical and Marxist political economy, including Smith, Marx and Mao, recognise that the worldwide expansion of capitalism and the concomitant re-lationships of exchange and domination between the capitalist metropolis and its colonies in Asia, Africa and Latin America exerted a determinant influence on the historical development or rather underdevelopment of these regions. Nevertheless, the at-tempt to account for or explain – to understand, let alone to intervene in – this latter part of the world historical process still poses serious theoretical problems. How can our theoretical analysis recognise the primacy of the 'internal' productive process in the colonies and yet reconcile or combine it with the also determinant 'external' exchange and other relations of dependence on the capitalist metropolis? Herein Smith is of only limited help (although we shall draw on his analysis 'Of Colonies' below) since he tends to focus on exchange to the exclusion of production and goes so far as to suggest at one point that the misfortunes of the colonies 'seem to have arisen rather from accident'. Marx's preoccupation with the productive process in the metropolis leads him to relegate our problems to a volume of *Capital* that he never came to write, while in the meantime regarding these consequences of international trade as 'really beyond the scope of our (his) analysis' and closing his short (ten-page) chapter XXXIII on 'The Modern Theory of Colonisation' in Vol. I by acknowledging: 'However, we are not concerned here with the condition of the colonies. The only thing that interests us is the secret discovered in the new world by the Political Economy of the old world . . . that the capitalist mode of production and accumulation . . . have for their fundamental condition . . . the expropriation of the labourer' (Marx I, 774).

The question of internal *v.* external determination has been posed and answered by others. Mao Tse-tung has written in 'On Contradiction':

As opposed to the metaphysical world outlook, the world outlook of materialist dialectics holds that in order to understand the development of a thing we should study it internally and in its relations with other things . . . The fundamental cause of the development of a thing is not external but internal; it lies in the contradictoriness within the thing . . . its interrelations with other things are secondary causes. Thus materialist dialectics effectively combats the theory of external causes, or of an external motive force, advanced by metaphysical mechanical materialism and vulgar evolutionism . . . Does materialist dialectics exclude external causes? Not at all. It holds that external causes are the condition of change and internal causes are the basis of change, and that external causes become operative through internal causes. In a suitable temperature an egg changes into a chicken, but no temperature can change a stone into a chicken, because each has a different basis.

Addressing himself specifically to our problem, Palloix writes in the same vein: 'For my part, I think that one should begin with the (internal) exigency of the dominant economies in order to see at the other end of the chain—through unequal exchange—its effect on the development of the others. Unequal exchange is a relay, a link, and not an end in itself' (Palloix 1969a, 221).

But with respect to the underdeveloped countries themselves, Palloix continues elsewhere: 'The external dynamic never leads to an internal dynamic, but on the contrary follows it; it is never autonomous, but induced by the internal dynamic. Beyond that, what is called the external dynamic is nothing other than the external manifestation of the problems raised by the internal dynamic' (Palloix 1969b, 21).

Bettelheim argues similarly that

> the 'exploitation' of the poor countries by the rich . . . is tied at the same time to the important fact of the 'penetration' of the capitalist mode of production in the dominated countries and to the changes in structure that the *capital movements* provoke in the heart of the world capitalist economy. . . . Therefore, it is necessary to regard each 'country' as constituting a social formation characterized by a specific structure, and notably by the existence of *classes* with contradictory interests. It is this structure which determines the mode of the insertion of each social formation in the international relations of production. Here we again find this fundamental proposition: Relations of exploitation cannot constitute themselves at 'the level of exchanges'; they must necessarily be rooted at the level of *production*, without which the exchanges could not renew themselves. (Bettelheim in Emmanuel 1969, 325; emphasis in the original)

These considerations present us with a formidable problem: ideally, we should attempt a historical theoretical analysis of the entire process of capitalist accumulation in the world as a whole and of the changes in the modes of production associated therewith throughout the world. But the analysis and the development of theory necessary for this task are beyond the scope of this essay and the book it introduces. This imposes severe limitations on the adequacy of the theory of underdevelopment that can be developed within that scope. But the development of theory adequate for the analysis of capitalist accumulation and development – and thus of underdevelopment – on a world scale remains beyond our capacity: Since Lenin, and after Baran and Sweezy nearly half a century later, works that promise a major breakthrough toward such a global theory have been very few and recent – and also oriented primarily toward the underdeveloped part of the world capitalist system: the studies of *Problèmes de la croissance en économie ouverte* by Palloix (1969), of *L'échange Inégal* by Emmanuel (1969) and the most ambitious 'Théorie de l'accumulation capitaliste à l'échelle mondiale' by Amin (unpublished at the time of writing). The virtual limitation of our inquiry into underdevelopment primarily to the underdeveloped countries and their dependence on the developed one is therefore not arbitrary but rather necessary.

This limitation in turn presents us with an additional theoretical and expository problem of its own. Marxist analysis of capitalist development has examined primarily the mode of production and capital accumulation in the capitalist metropolis. Can we simply transpose the Marxist categories from the interior of the metropolis to the interior of the colonies? No, the would-be Marxists who have done so have only achieved scientifically and politically disastrous results. (For critiques see Frank 1969, Vitale 1968.) Can we simply regard the colonies as nations that are innocently victimised (or saved) by external forces emanating from the metropolis? No, the self-styled 'structuralists', such as those associated with the United Nations Economic Commission for Latin America who have done so, have managed a merely superficial image of some symptoms of dependence, which distract our attention from the fundamental internal nature or causes of 'external dependence' (for critiques see Ramirez 1966, dos Santos 1969, Frank 1969). How then can we analyse the 'internal' mode of production and accumulation or non-accumulation in the colonies and still take due account of colonial dependence on the 'external' relations of exchange and capital flows between the colony and its metropolis?

To follow this dialectical procedure in our own analysis, as Palloix and Bettelheim are forced to observe, inevitably, leads us back to the examination of the internal contradictions of the world capitalist system as a whole and of its metropolis within it. Moreover, to be adequate by these standards our analysis would have to be syncronically and dynamically dialectical on a world scale: it would be necessary to analyse the simultaneous mutual interactions of all parts of the world system at each point in historical time and to examine how their contradictions generated their nature and interaction at each succeeding point in time. This is still beyond our capacity here, but is (later) attempted in Frank, *World Accumulation 1492–1789* and in Wallerstein, *The Modern World System*.

In this book, on the other hand, we devote – still very inadequate – attention to the internal dynamics of world capitalist and metropolitan capital (ist) accumulation and development; and we attempt a step towards a synchronic analysis by trying to identify three main historical stages in world capitalist accumulation and development until recently; and we examine how the principal contradiction among the worldwide relationships within each stage led to the development of the next stage. Particularly, for the underdeveloped part of the world capitalist system, we seek to emphasise the main internal contradictions that characterise its modes of production. None the less despite our best intentions, our limitations in this regard may be not merely quantitative but also qualitative.

In commenting on an earlier draft of this same essay, our friend Giovanni Arrighi has correctly observed: 'I now come to the more fundamental question. Throughout this introduction, as in your previous works, the analysis of the internal structure is always subordinated to that of the external conditions. You adopt, that is, what Mao in his "On Contradictions" calls the "metaphysical outlook." Explanations of the development of things are not *first of all* looked for in their internal structure and contradictions, analysing, once these have been identified, their dialectical interaction with external conditions. You tend instead to look for external determination of both phenomena and internal structures and contradictions . . . I do not think, in other words, that you keep up with your pledge to analyse *dialectically* the interrelations between unequal exchange and the limitations imposed on the factors of production by the social conditions of production. The main *aspect* of this tendency is the subordination of class analysis to the analysis of the colonial structure. The two can and must be combined. . . . The difference between Mao's approach and yours is that in the former the colonial structure is "built-in" in a class analysis whereas in your work it is the analysis of the class structure (when it is made) that is "built-in" in the analysis of the colonial structure. Though the conclusions are often similar, the two approaches differ in two momentous aspects: (*a*) . . . Your approach tends to prevent the identification of the historical forces and contradictions which can beget revolutionary structural changes . . . (*b*) More fundamentally, your approach favours generalization (which, contrary to abstraction, is quite alien to the Marxist method) and therefore discourages the concrete analyses of concrete situations which is the essence of Marxism (and this notwithstanding the fact that your conclusions stem from concrete analyses): Politically, generalizations are, of course, very dangerous as they lead to actions often unrelated to the inner contradictions of that to be changed . . .' (Arrighi, personal communication, 23 March 1970. An extended version of this same argument was subsequently published in two articles, Arrighi 1970, 1972.)

Here our intention, of course, is to avoid the errors Arrighi mentions. But our quantitative limitations sometimes exclude the analysis of 'external' factors as contradictions internal to world or metropolitan capitalism, and our qualitative limitations lead us to displace internal contradictions in the colonies from their rightful place in an attempt to analyse the dependent external causes, which Mao does not exclude but which many Marxists – to say nothing of neo-classical theorists – have neglected in their examination of underdevelopment. Our attempt is not to generalise from specific concrete experience, but to abstract the general principles which underlie and govern this concrete reality so that these principles may be more effectively used to change concrete reality in each time and place.

2. The Question of Periodisation

The problem of periodisation has been faced by other students of the problem with purposes similar though not quite the same as ours. Among these we may mention Preobazhensky, Mandel and Amin. In his discussion of primitive accumulation, Preobazhensky wrote in the 1920s:

We must distinguish three periods in the history of the exploitation by capitalism of pre-capitalist forms on an economic basis. There was a period of youthful capitalism, with theoretically free competition but *de facto monopoly* . . . After this period follows a period of free competition . . . Finally comes a third period, the period of monopoly capitalism. In this period, thanks to the establishment of a system of national-capitalist organisms . . . we see, on the one hand, a tendency on the part of each large capitalist colonial power to extend to the colonies its monopolization of the internal market and to defend this right by force of arms. On the other hand, thanks to the export of capital to the colonies, surplus profit from the colonies more and more takes the form of surplus profit from enterprises with the same level of technique but lower wages. This gradual shifting from one kind of exploitation to another . . . (Preobazhensky, 94–5)

Mandel distinguishes similar periods and emphasises the typical exchange relations between metropolis and colonies in each:

In the light of Marxist economic theory, the historical process of the origin and the appropriation of surplus value constitutes, therefore, a dialectic unity with three different moments: unequal exchange on the basis of unequal values, equal exchange on the basis of equal values; unequal exchange on the basis of equal values. Only the consideration of these three historical moments permits an answer to the question about how capital in the Western world originated, how it has been able to grow, and how it has been able to expand over a large part of the globe. This preliminary review thus already confronts us with two moments – the unequal exchange of the pre-capitalist epoch; the unequal exchange at the heart of contemporary world commerce – with a specific relation between western capital and the so called developing countries . . . (Mandel, 'L'accumulation primitive et l'industrialisation du tiers-monde'. Translation into English from the French original and the Spanish translation by *Pensamiento Crítico*, Havana, No. 36, taking account of the omission, due to typographical error, of two of the three moments in the French original but which are included in the Spanish version; pp. 146 and 117, respectively.)

Each of Mandel's stages corresponds roughly in historical time to the classical ones of Preobazhensky, but as we will note below the three types of exchange relationships between the metropolis and its colonies were not always experienced at exactly the same time by each of the colonies.

Samir Amin, whose interest in the capitalist development of structural underdevelopment resembles our own but whose work in preparation on 'L'accumulation du capital à l'échelle mondiale' far exceeds ours in scope, distinguishes similar stages in this latter work. He pays greater attention to the different roles or functions of the colonies in the process of world, that is metropolitan, capital accumulation in each of the three stages; and he relates the same to the particular processes and kinds of structural underdevelopment that particular colonies or groups of colonies experienced in consequence. Amin summarises (in a personal letter – not intended for publication – in comment on an earlier draft of the present essay):

> I distinguish 3 periods: (1) mercantilist, (2) developed (*achevé*) capitalist (post industrial revolution, pre monopolist) and (3) imperialism. To each of these periods there correspond specific functions of the periphery at the service of the essential needs of accumulation at the center. In stage (1) the essential function of the periphery (principally American, supplementarily African which supplied the former with slaves) is to permit the accumulation of money wealth by the Atlantic merchant bourgeoisie, wealth which transforms itself in real (*achevé*) capital after the industrial revolution. Hence the system of plantations (after the pillage of the mines) around which all of America turns from the XVI to the XVIII centuries. This function loses its importance with the industrial revolution when the centre of gravity of capital moves from commerce to industry. The new function of the periphery thus becomes to lower (*a*) the value of labor power (through the provision of agricultural products of mass consumption) and (*b*) the value of the constituent elements of constant capital (by providing raw materials). In other words, the periphery permits fighting against the tendential decline in the rate of profit [as Marx observed as well – AGF]. To achieve this during period (2), capital has only one means at its disposal: commerce. During period (3) on the other hand, capital also has the very efficient means of the export of capital. Hence and only from then on does true unequal exchange appear, and not before.

The 'true', we may presume, here refers to what Mandel calls 'unequal exchange on the basis of equal values' and which Preobazhensky associated with 'surplus profit from enterprises with the same level of technique but lower wages' and which is the principal type of exchange that Emmanuel analyses under the title 'L'Echange Inégal', and which are problems of analysis and periodisation to which we will return in our discussion of the nineteenth century. Amin would be the last to deny the prior dominance of what Mandel calls 'unequal exchange on the basis of unequal values' in the mercantilist period, during which this less refined type of exploitation played a major role in world capital accumulation, the development of the metropolis, and the under-development of most colonies, as already observed by Smith and Marx. This first period and especially the internal structural transformations in the colonies during this period is examined in our own analysis of the development of underdevelopment in Chapters 2 and 3.

3. Questions of Production and Exchange

We may note that in terms of our theoretical problematique, each of these schemes of the historical process of capitalist accumulation and development emphasises a different aspect (though this emphasis in the above-quoted brief passages does not necessarily characterise the major work of any of the three authors): in the first scheme, the distinction between stages is primarily derived from differences in the structure of production in the metropolis. In the second scheme these differences are implicitly related to associated differences in the kinds of exchange relations between the metropolis and the colonies. Amin is more explicit about the function of these kinds of exchange in the metropolitan process of accumulation and production, and emphasises the determination of the former by the latter. In view of the afore-mentioned scope and limitations of the present essay, our own attention will be devoted primarily to the structural transformation within the colonies in this process and to an attempt to examine how the function of the colonies in each stage of the process of – world capitalist accumu-lation is related to the productive – and importantly to the non-accumulative – process and its organisation through the mode of production in the colonies. Briefly, we will suggest that in the first stage the colonies were severely decapitalised and their structural capacity for development was severely weakened though not eliminated. During the second stage, which was not exactly contemporaneous in all the colonies, the weak social forces of capitalist development unsuccessfully struggled for survival (except in the new transplanted settler colonies) against the metropolitan industrial bourgeoisie and its allies in the colonies themselves. And during the third monopoly capitalist or imperialist stage the economic basis of a developmentist national bourgeois class in these colonies was entirely eliminated or prevented from forming at all, thus precluding further or future development under capitalism and consolidating the further development of underdevelopment in the colonies short of socialist revolution, while generating the contradictions and struggle of the present stage of neo-imperialism and socialist revolution. Throughout this analysis, due to our limitations, we will face the above-mentioned problem of 'external' exchange *v.* 'internal' productive or class determinacy.

The principal purpose of our examination of the historical experience of the stage of capitalist accumulation and development is to abstract out the essentials of the then contemporary mode of production in those colonies that participated in this process most intimately and importantly. But the (first) mercantile capitalist stage became the basis, directly and indirectly through their mutual relations, of the second and third stages in both the metropolis and the colonies. Therefore, our examination of the first stage must also include the analysis of the historical roots of processes that did not bear their most important fruit until later.

In our examination of the first stage, the following three questions arise: (1) Why did most European colonies suffer underdevelopment and others achieve development; and specifically why did most of the New World underdevelop and only parts of the United States and Canada escape this fate? (2) How determinant in this process was concentration in the monoproduction of raw material for export? (3) What is the historical origin and explanation of the differences in wage levels between underdeveloping and (really) developing countries?

These three questions and the answers to them are intimately related to each other and to the process of world capital accumulation, capitalist development and underdevelopment. Without going into details, some of which are examined later in this book (Chapter 5), we may provisionally make the following observations. Capitalist development and industrialisation have prospered in Western Europe (though not in its Mediterranean areas) and in its white settler colonies overseas, specifically the United States, Canada, Australia and New Zealand. Partial development has occurred in South Africa, Rhodesia and Palestine, which are occupied by white European immigrants and the indigenous population. The remaining colonies (and semi-, neo- and ex-colonies) comprising the vast majority of mankind became under-developed. These latter colonies concentrated on and became specialised in the monoproduction of un- or hardly processed raw materials for export to the metropolis, although some of the settler colonies also concentrated on raw material exports at some times of their history. Emmanuel, and more recently Amin and Martinez (in still unpublished studies), deny that specialisation in raw materials production is *per se* determined for underdevelopment (though for different reasons than neo-classical economists or the Canadian 'staple' theory of growth school) and claim that the apparent determinant relationship is an 'optical illusion' (Emmanuel 49–50) and its emphasis a 'mystification' (Amin).

Instead the principal analyst of unequal exchange, Emmanuel, as well as Palloix and Amin, argue that unequal exchange (of equal values) between the metropolis and the colonies, at least since the nineteenth century, is determined by unequal wage levels between the same. Like Marx and Preobazhensky, they argue that trade between high-wage and low-wage countries results in unequal exchange of equal values (or market prices that overvalue high-wage-produced goods and undervalue low-wage-produced goods) and thereby contributes to the capital accumulation and development of the former at the expense of the decapitalisation and underdevelopment of the latter. Emmanuel also observes that the underdeveloped countries all have low wage levels and that high wage levels and development are to be found precisely in Western Europe and its afore-mentioned overseas settlements, and he goes on to argue that 'development thus appears not as the cause but as the consequence of high wages' (Emmanuel, 161). Leaving aside for the moment the merits (further examined below in Chapter 5) of this argument, we may here only observe what Emmanuel himself recognises about his own analysis: the wage level thus becomes *the* independent variable in the whole analysis of Emmanuel, who makes no effort to explain the origin of the original wage levels and their differences between the trading countries, except for a few side (and largely erroneous) observations that we shall examine below. But this means that, with Bettelheim and Amin, we must ask the third question posed above: what initiates and accounts for the original differences in wage levels between the metropolis plus its overseas settlements and the bulk of the colonial countries of Asia, Africa and Latin America? This problem is examined in the chapters that follow.

2 World Capital Accumulation, Trade Patterns and Modes of Production, 1500–1770

We may review the first major period or stage of world capital accumulation, capitalist development and underdevelopment by briefly summarising the international division of labour and pattern of trade between roughly 1500 and 1770 and examining the concomitant transformation of the modes of production in the colonial areas. The associated capital accumulation and capitalist development in the European metropolis is examined as part of the second stage of this historical process in Chapter 4.

The three-centuries-long mercantilist stage of world capital accumulation was dominated by a marked and irreversible increase of European commercial or mercantile activity and the growth of colonial production for export, which was in turn stimulated, controlled and exploited by European metropolitan commerce. This characterization is not meant to deny the importance of European production or its transformation during the period (of whose importance we also take account), but to contrast this European mercantile vs. colonial productive relationship and its associated unequal exchange on the basis of unequal values (see Mandel quote above) with the second and third periods' productive dominance of Europe and the concomitant adaptive transformation of colonial production and of the essential character of their relationship of unequal exchange on the basis of equal values. In the words of Woytinsky and Woytinsky in their authoritative *World Commerce and Governments* (p. 9), 'New times required a radical revision of foreign trade policy. The emphasis shifted from the search for foreign products – the mainsprings of foreign trade until the sixteenth century [and in part later we would add] – to the search for outlets for domestic merchandise . . . [this] brought a remarkable change in the colonial policy of the seafaring European nations.'

It should perhaps be specifically noted (since in our analysis this factor does not receive the attention it deserves), that, as Marx observed, though, force is the midwife of all important changes, the use of force backed up by the power of the growing national state was perhaps especially essential at this stage of capital accumulation, during which the European metropolis had relatively little elase with which to extract production or exact tribute from the colonies. In the words of the editors of the *Cambridge Economic History of Europe* (Vol. iv, p. xix), 'the technological advantages of the sixteenth-century Europeans, combined with their adventurous outlook, would go far to explain why they secured immediate dominance. But the long-term subservience to the markets of Europe in which the colonial economies were maintained was the result not only of economic conditions but also of the military power exercised by the white races at the moment of impact and during the period of consolidation,' though notably it is precisely where for a long time the Europeans lacked this military dominance, that is in Asia, that metropolitan domination and colonial transformation of the mode of production was long delayed compared to America and Africa.

1. Trade Triangles

The world division of labour and the pattern or flow of trade may be divided into two major triangles, the Asian or Oriental and the Atlantic, which for a long time remained fundamentally different from each other precisely because they were so intimately connected through metropolitan Europe. The Oriental trade triangle and its major East-West axis had grown up in the centuries before the Discovery of America (and had relied heavily on the intervention of the Near Eastern Muslims whose importance is largely neglected in the present analysis). This 'spice' trade involved fundamentally the export of Oriental spices *and* (mostly textile) *manufactures* to Europe and their payment in bullion of European origin. With the incorporation in the sixteenth century of parts of Africa and the New World into the expanding mercantile capitalist system, part of the Oriental exports were re-exported by Europe to

Africa and America (though physically some of them were shipped directly across the Pacific on the 'Manila' galleons); and an increasing part of the Oriental goods was paid for by Europe with American silver. As was noted above and is again emphasised below, the consequences of this trade for changes in the mode of production in Asia were for a long time relatively moderate.

The Atlantic triangle, which soon grew to occupy much more shipping and to transport much more merchandise (including human merchandise) than the Oriental one, has been summarised (though he largely omits the place of the Spanish colonies) by Eric Williams:

> In this triangular trade England – France and colonial America equally – supplied the exports and the ships; Africa the human merchandise; the plantations the colonial raw materials. The slave ships sailed from the home country with a cargo of manufactured goods. These were exchanged at a profit on the coast of Africa for Negroes, who were traded on the plantations, at another profit, in exchange for a cargo of colonial produce to be taken back to the home country. As the volume of trade increased, the triangular trade was supplemented, but never supplanted, by direct trade between home country and the West Indies (or other colonialized regions), exchanging home (and Oriental) manufactures directly for colonial produce. The triangular trade thereby gave a triple stimulus to British industry. The Negroes were purchased with British (and Oriental) man-ufactures; transported to the plantations, they produced sugar, cotton, indigo, molasses, and other tropical products, the process-ing of which created new industries in England; while the maintenance of the Negroes and their owners on the plantations provided another market for British industry, New England agriculture and the Newfoundland fisheries. By 1750 there was hardly a trading or manufacturing town in England which was not in some way connected with the triangular or direct colonial trade. The profits obtained provided one of the main streams of that accumulation of capital in England which financed the Industrial Revolution. (Williams, 51–2)

To this major triangle must be added the smaller one cited above by Mannix, which involved African slaves, Caribbean sugar and New England rum; the North Atlantic triangle centred on the fisheries of

Newfoundland (Brebner); and of course the Spanish and later Portuguese American gold and silver trade, which fed the Oriental trade, and increasingly imported British and Oriental manufactures sold by the British in the Spanish and Portuguese colonies (and mother countries).

The nexus of this international division of labour and its related interlocking triangles of trade was European commerce (Italian, Iberian, Dutch, British, more or less in that chronological order of dominance), which exacted the major share of the profit from this colonial (and for a time also metropolitan) production on each of the legs of the various triangles. In this connection two related mechanisms perhaps deserve special mention since they have received less attention than the oft-named monopoly merchant trading companies: re-exports and multilateral settlement of payments. Both are summarised, with respect to Britain, by Saul:

> Re-exports of goods imported from the new areas of trade, insignificant in the middle of the seventeenth century, constituted 30 per cent of total exports fifty years later . . . Re-exports consisted mainly of textiles, tobacco and sugar . . . The multilateral financing of trade was already important. In general, Britain used a large surplus with Western Europe to pay for her deficits elsewhere. The size of these indirect settlements was due in part to the re-export trade, but even if re-exports are omitted the pattern remains the same in its basic essentials . . . the importance of the Portuguese trade (in the mid eighteenth century when Brazil became a major gold supplier) should not be underestimated. It contributed towards the establishment of London as the world's bullion market, and these same bullion supplies provided the essential link in the chain by which Britain expanded trade with the East and purchased military supplies in the North . . . The West Indies and her southern American colonies had become by the middle of the eighteenth century perhaps the most vital part of Britain's trade connections. The West Indies alone were supplying a quarter of her imports, and together with the American colonies took about a fifth of her exports . . . , however, the trade patterns of the two groups of colonies were entirely different. The West Indies almost always had a favourable balance with Britain, and in fact re-exported to the colonial territories of other countries much that was imported from Britain. The balance was settled indirectly in two main

ways: through the 'slave triangle,' whereby Britain sent consumer goods to West Africa and slaves were transported across the Atlantic, and secondly through an import surplus from the North American colonies, who supplied the West Indies with foodstuffs, live animals, timber, etc . . . A second channel of settlement for them [the American colonies] lay in the export of fish, wheat, flour, and rice to Southern Europe. (Saul, 3–8)

This commercial exchange, especially of colonial products, colonial labour and colonial bullion produced through modes of production that relied substantially on physical force and violence, and their re-export and multilateral payment, involved very largely the unequal exchange on the basis of unequal values, which exploited the producers, especially in the colonies, and benefited the merchants, especially in the metropolis. Though this unequal exchange may have been different from that which came to prevail in the nineteenth and twentieth centuries (analysed by Emmanuel), it certainly generated an important flow of capital from the productive colonies to the metropolis which accumulated this capital and channelled it into its own development, as we will see below, when we examine important changes both in the source and the use of this capital accumulation after about 1760/80.

2. Differential Transformation of Modes of Production in Asia, Africa and Latin America

The modes of production associated with this process of world and metropolitan capital accumulation differed from one set of colonies to another according to their respective places and functions in that stage of the development of the worldwide mercantile capitalist system. The most important colonial participant, the New World, experienced the deepest and most far-reaching transformation of its modes of production and the greatest development of underdevelopment. Africa occupied an intermediate place in both the degree of its incorporation into that stage of the historical process and the transformation of its mode of production; and Asia, by and large, participated and changed least.

Asia, in general, sold its agricultural and manufactured products to European traders who called and/or established themselves on coastal enclaves and paid in gold and silver. Europe had little else to offer civilised Asians and still lacked or could not finance sufficient military power to enforce trade or production on them. The Woytinskys recall and quote: 'At the time, Europe lagged behind Asia in industrial skill. In exchange for silk, cotton, sugar and spices, Europe could export only small arms, which were hardly any better than those made in the East . . . The superiority of commerce, handicraft and administration in China in comparison with Italian cities was the theme of the fascinating story Marco Polo told . . . His story relates to the end of the thirteenth century, but there is no indication that Europe was catching up with China in the following century and a half . . . After having landed in 1498 at Calicut, on the Malabar coast of India, Vasco da Gama returned to Europe with a friendly letter from the Raja of Malabar to the King of Portugal. "In my kingdom there is abundance . . . What I seek from thy country is gold, silver, coral and scarlet." ' (Woytinsky 8, 649) As late as 1793 the Emperor of China wrote the King of Britain, George III: 'As your Ambassador can see for himself, we possess all things. I set no value on objects strange or ingenious, and have no use for your country's manufactures.' The British answer, half a century later, of course was to stimulate Chinese appetites for British goods by sending them opium grown in her Indian colony. Though Asian production of commodities for export to Europe (and re-export to Africa and America) no doubt intervened in the autonomous transformation of modes of production in Asia, it did not substantially redirect this development until much later, except in particular limited instances. The earliest relatively far-reaching transformations of the modes of production occurred in parts of South-east Asia where Islamic, Portuguese and Dutch rivalries and political intervention in local rivalries began to extend local incorporation in the expansion of mercantile capitalism from simple trade to production for export. (The various stages of this process and the accompanying development of underdevelopment are analysed in Geertz and Wertheim. Also see, for instance, *Cambridge History of Europe*, Vol. IV, xxiii-xxix and 368–71.) Perhaps, ironically the Western influence also began to spread in Japan, but there led to its 'closing' for two centuries until Comodore Perry 'opened' it again in 1853. In terms of the accumulation of capital on a world scale, the exchange of Asian products for American silver produced by forced labour represented an 'unequal exchange' which benefited the Europeans at the expense of the Asians (and of course Latin Americans); and it was so perceived by the contemporary mercantilists and merchants who found that the American silver fetched the best price in Asia, measured in surplus realisable in Europe. Both the degree and the amount of unequal exchange or exploitation of Asians by Europeans changed quantitatively in the mid-eighteenth century. Major transformations of Asian society, especially in India, accelerated after the Battle of Plassey in 1757 (for a review see Chapter 4 below and for more detailed discussion see Mukherjee and Sen as well as Frank, *World Accumulation 1492–1789*, Chapter 4).

None the less, during the mercantilist stage of capitalist development before the industrial revolution and on the basis of simple commercial trade, the Europeans had no product of their own to offer the industrially more advanced and self-sufficient Chinese and Indians. The only European possibility to expand the trade with the East was to pay with silver from the West. This circumstance had several connected consequences: it permitted Europe through simple trade to realise and accumulate part of the value of Asian labour, which remained organised substantially by the pre-existing mode of production for nearly two centuries, before it underwent profound transformations in a later stage of world capitalist development. But this temporary tranquillity in Asia or the historical delay in the wholesale transformation of its society was only compatible with world capitalist development thanks to the simultaneous violent total transformation of the mode of production which was necessary in the other extremity of the worldwide mercantile capitalist system in order to produce there the silver needed for the relatively peaceful Oriental trade. Finally, this trade with both extremities of the 'old' world profoundly conditioned Europe's own transformation and development – and thereby the history of all the world.

The expansion of the world capitalist system and the establishment of the colonial relationship with Latin America, the Caribbean, and the South of the United States also drew large parts of Africa into this system in the seventeenth and eighteenth centuries.

The development of plantation economies in the New World, which were dependent on imported slave labour as their principal productive power, brought large parts of Africa, inland from Dakar to the Congo, into the historical process of world capitalist development. Although the South Europeans had already imported some Africans to work on sugar plantations in Mediterranean and Atlantic islands before the discovery of America in the fifteenth century, the recourse to African labour increased in the sixteenth century when they were shipped to Spanish America. It grew to much greater proportions still during the seventeenth, eighteenth, and first half of the nineteenth centuries, when African labour was shipped by the metropolitan powers to supply the large majority of the labour needed particularly in their colonies in Brazil, the Caribbean, and the South of the United States. It was estimated that during this time 100 million Africans left their homes in that continent, although not nearly that many survived the slave wars and 'middle passage' to land on the opposite shores of the Atlantic. Later careful calculations by Philip Curtin reduce this earlier estimate very substantially. Thus, Africa became an integral part of the development of world capitalism. In order to supply the single-product colonialised export economies of the New World with the labour that produced all this wealth for the metropolis, Africa was also converted into a single-product export economy, and that product was its most precious patrimony: its own people, and among them the most productive ones.

Like the silver, sugar, and cotton of the New World, the 'production' and export of slaves from Africa had to be organised; for the Africans were not standing on the seashore waiting to be bound into slavery overseas. Although there had been indigenous slavery in Africa before, this slavery was economically and socially different from that which was to develop as part of world capitalist development; and neither the mode of production nor the social organisation already existent in any part of Africa was adequate to supplying millions of slaves for world capitalist development. Accordingly, as Rodney, Hargreaves, and Davidson show, this process of development also had to transform the mode of production and social organisation of large parts of Africa substantially. For the long run, more important still than its loss of manpower and economic surplus, was the transformation of African society as a result of the 'recruitment' of slaves in the interior through warfare and trade organised by the coastal tribes who sold these slaves to the metropolitan traders that anchored off shore: between the coastal tribes and the interior ones, and between both of them and the metropolitan slave traders, substantially the same single-product export economy developed as in the Latin American and Caribbean countries. In Africa the colonial relationship with the metropolis transformed the class structure and generated the mutual economic self-interest of the metropolis and the local rulers in the pursuit of an underdevelopment policy for the masses of the people, not only for those that were shipped away in slavery but also for the majority of those that remained. Thus, the development of world capitalism and of the metropolis in Western Europe (and later also in North America) laid the productive and social foundations of a self-sustaining process of development of underdevelopment in Latin America and Africa.

Africa exported labour in 'exchange' for a few manufactures that originated in Europe or Asia, and most particularly and significantly – as would be the case again in the same and other colonies in the nineteenth and twentieth centuries, albeit with the instruments appropriate to these stages – received precisely those foreign products that were most instrumental for transforming the mode of production of the importing economy and for generating its export products: rum and guns. These imports were demanded and used by the Africans – and not just or even primarily by foreigners – who were most active in and who benefited most from the transformation of the mode of production appropriate to supplying the African export product demanded by the 'world market' at that stage of world capital accumulation and capitalist development. At the turn of the eighteenth-nineteenth century the British metropolis became increasingly interested in exporting its own textiles to Africa. While the economic importance and political power of the West India interests declined before the demand for cotton from the slaves for the United States South grew, declining British interest in Africa as a source of slaves began to be replaced by her growing interest in Africa as a market for British textile manufactures. As to the question of the equality or inequality of 'exchange' of millions of Africa's most productive people for rum, guns and textiles, it is hard to calculate the answer, though by posing the question the answer rather speaks for itself.

Of the three continents that underdeveloped as part of the process of world capital accumulation and capitalist development, during the first stage of this process the 'new world' of the Americas undoubtedly made the largest contribution and suffered the greatest development of underdevelopment. America exported the gold, silver, dyes, tobacco, sugar and other products – and through them much of the value – that were absorbed in the simultaneous transformation of the mode of production and process of accumulation in the European metropolis. In 'exchange' the colonialised regions of America imported the labour, capital goods and consumer goods that were necessary to fuel or direct their process of production and consumption in relation to metropolitan needs. It proved to be impossible to organise and develop this process of production and exchange through the pre-existing mode of production in the high-civilisation densely populated silver-producing regions of Mexico and Peru, or to create metropolitan enclaves in these regions that would divide them into dual economies or societies in part of which the pre-existing mode of production would persist. Excepting in some marginal regions (including one where marginality was replaced by semi-metropolitan status: New England), a relatively 'independent' mode of production centred on independent small-scale farmers proved to be unprofitable and unattractive for the investment of capital or the migration of labour whose passage was paid by others in most of the remaining areas of the New World. In these capital and labour were inserted and the productive process organised through the implantation and expansion of a plantation economy. The modes of production and class structure in both the major mining and the plantation regions did not (as we observe in Chapters 3 and 5) encourage the accumulation of capital and the diversification of production in these regions themselves. Rather, they initiated the capitalist development of structural underdevelopment and generated strong local vested class interests in policies that would further develop underdevelopment in the nineteenth and twentieth centuries. None the less, excepting perhaps in the Caribbean sugar plantations which represented the extreme form of this mode of producing underdevelopment, this colonial and class structure did not totally preclude the growth of manufacturing and other productive processes and interests, and these latter sought to defend their economic interests and to promote relatively autonomous capitalist development in the beginning of the nineteenth century. If their ambitions – and with them the possibilities of capitalist development, particularly in Latin America – were frustrated, it was because they were economically and politically too weak to resist the offensive of the opposing raw materials productive and commercial export and import interests on the domestic front, and because these latter were again strengthened by the new economic and political forces that the industrial revolution generated on the international front of the nineteenth century. This trend made itself increasingly visible in Latin America as well after the 1770s. In the meantime, three centuries of unequal exchange on the basis of unequal values had drained most of the 'new' world's colonies and colonialised peoples of vast amounts of capital that the European metropolis invested in the economic development, which in the nineteenth century was, in turn, to consolidate Latin America's underdevelopment.

An examination of the location of the most ultra-underdeveloped 'depressed' regions in the New World today, regions characterised not only by exceptional poverty, but oppressive social institutions, extreme catholic clericalism or protestant fundamentalism, illiberal political organisation, etc., reveals that they are all regions in which an earlier period of primary products production for export from the region has given way to decadence after their mines, soil, timber, or market were exhausted in the course of world capitalist development. This is the case not only of the (ex) mining regions, Minas Gerais in Brazil, the 'little' and the 'great' north of Chile, the highlands of Bolivia and Peru, the centre of Mexico, but also West Virginia and parts of the Rocky Mountain area in the United States and of Quebec in Canada; the former major agricultural or fishing export regions of the Caribbean, the North-east of Brazil, parts of Central America and Southern Mexico, the cotton South or 'Tobacco Road' in the United States, the Maritime Provinces and the Gatsby Peninsula in Canada; and the indigenous labour export areas adjacent to many of these export-productive regions. Though their present poverty is in part due to the exhaustion of their natural resources and/or to the dense settlement and erosion of inadequate agricultural lands in moutainous mining regions, the principal source of their present ultra-underdevelopment is not so much physical as it is the social structure they have inherited from their 'golden years' of export boom, and which is still reflected in their 'archaic customs'. Inspection of the most poverty-stricken regions in Asia and Africa will reveal essentially the same pattern of exceptionally severe double colonial and class exploitation in the mining regions of Central Africa and their sources of labour supply; in the cotton-export Nile Valley; in Bengal and the southern plantation states of Madras and Kerala in India; in Central Java; etc.

Historical and comparative analysis thus leads to a revealing apparently paradoxical observation that was foreshadowed by Smith and systematised by Marx: the rich became poor and the poor became rich. The apparent paradox disappears if we examine the dialectic of world capital accumulation and capitalist development that underlines it. The capitalist division of labour has exploited the riches of human and natural resources of some regions through a mode of production and unequal exchange that have condemned these regions to the development of underdevelopment while permitting the accumulation of the capital generated by these and other riches. And the poverty not only of New England, Australia, New Zealand, but in important respects of Western Europe and Japan as well, has permitted the growth of a mode of production, wage level and benefits from unequal exchange (as we will further observe in the nineteenth and twentieth centuries) that has generated economic development. Therefore, we propose the distinction between colonialisation, whose mode of production, low wage level and colonial unequal exchange spell out a sub-ordinate dependence within the process of world capital accumu-lation that has condemned them to necessary development of underdevelopment, and colonisation by transplanted settlers whose mode of production, relatively high wage level and at least partial protection against (if not immediate benefit from) external unequal exchange has permitted them to achieve economic development. Woytinsky and Woytinsky (678) make a similar distinction between 'settlement colonies' and 'exploitation colonies'. The different forms and functions of colonialisation and colonisation and the 'internal' modes of production and 'external' relations of exchange associated with them in the New World during the mercantilist period are analysed in detail in the following Chapter 3; and for other regions as well during the industrial and imperialist period they are examined in the succeeding chapters.

3 On the Roots of Development and Underdevelopment in the New World: Smith and Marx *v*. the Weberians

1. On the Weber Thesis

A. Significance of the Weber Thesis

An important alternative interpretation to the analysis of capitalist development and underdevelopment by Marxists and the present writer is the interpretation by Max Weber, his followers and his perverters, which has attained dominance in the United States from where it has in turn been re-exported to its cultural neo-colonies. Karl Mannheim (cited by Shapiro, 225) referred to Max Weber as the Marx of the bourgeoisie; and his widow and biographer, Marianne Weber, said that his principal work was an attempt to replace historical materialism as an interpretation. Such otherwise diverse writers as Kautsky, H. M. Robertson, Sorokin, Aron, Bastide, Gerth and Mills, Marcuse, Parsons, Bendix, and Gouldner agree that Max Weber's work represented an attempt to replace or at least seriously to amend the Marxist theory of economic infrastructural dominance over the superstructure and to lend instead particular importance to psycho-cultural factors and religion to account for the rise of capitalism. Of course, this ambition obliged Weber to devote considerable attention to the work and working methods of Marx, whom Weber respected as an opponent. Philosophically, in distinction to the optimism of Smith and Marx, Weber was a pessimist in regard to human nature (Stark, 203); and politically, though 'progressive' on some social issues, Weber was

25

downright reactionary on major political issues of his day, whole-heartedly supporting German bourgeois nationalism and imperi-alism (Mommsen, Shapiro) and totally opposing the Soviet re-volution of 1917 and the Communist revolutionary movement in his own Germany in 1918 (Shapiro, Gerth and Mills). It is difficult to accept the argument of Jozyr-Kowalski in the *Polish Sociological Bulletin* that Weber's intellectual respect for Marx, his assimilation of some Marxist analysis and historical partial explanations would seem to negate Weber's opposition to Marx. Weber's own re-cognition (Gabel, 175) in his study of Chinese religion that the latter was not an obstacle to the rise of capitalism in China and Rodinson's recent demonstration that Islam has not been incompatible with capitalist development either are, rather, inevitable weaknesses in the Weberian argument. In any case, Weber's American followers, principally but not only Parsons and his school, have disregarded not only the weaknesses in Weber's comparative historical method, but increasingly also the relative strengths it still had in Weber's hands. To use Max Weber for the ideological purposes of 'modern sociological analysis' as Parsons calls it, his contemporary American followers have had to scientifically castrate Weber.

Gouldner observes:

Weber's position was, in large part, a polemic against the Marxist conception that ideologies were a 'superstructural' adaptation to the economic 'infrastructures' . . . His *Protestant Ethic* was directed against the Marxian hypothesis that Pro-testantism was the result of the emergence of capitalism; more generally, Weber opposed the Marxist conception that values and ideas are 'superstructural' elements that depend, in the last analysis, upon prior changes in the economic foundation; Weber, rather, sought to demonstrate that the development of modern European capitalism was itself contingent upon the Protestant Ethic. (Gouldner, 121, 179–80)

The anti-Marxist offensive was carried further by Weber's leading disciple in the United States, Talcott Parsons, who in doing so established himself as the still unchallenged dean and most influential exponent of American (or, as Gouldner calls it, 'acad-emic') sociology.

It was Parsons who had changed. What happened, in short,

was that with the Depression [of the 1930s] and the growing salience of Marxism in the United States, there was greater pressure to develop and fortify the intellectual alternatives to Marxism and *to expel Marxism from consideration* as a sociology . . . (Gouldner, 188–9, italics by AGF.)

Parsons himself evidently thinks that he and his followers succeeded, for he claimed in 1965:

> In conclusion, it must be emphasized that the anti-Marxian position on this crucial issue – that of the status of cultural factors – has in the last generation been immensely strengthened by developments, theoretical and empirical . . . they rather support Weber against both Marx and Hegel . . . The basic conclusion seems almost obvious . . . In sociology today, to be a Marxian . . . is not a tenable position. (Parsons 1967, 134–5)

Yet these American ideologists are not content and strive for further 'developments': Birnbaum concludes his comparison of Marx and Weber by suggesting:

> Weber's concern with the independent effects of ideology on social development, then, originated in his polemical encounter with Marxism . . . In similar fashion, Weber himself may be amended. We have said that he gave the ideological variable an explicit independent status in the analysis of social change . . . Perhaps we can say that the insertion of a viable psychological theory in the analysis of social process is the next step for systematic social theory: if so, this is well underway. (Birnbaum in Smelser [ed.] 1967, 15–16)

Moreover, as Gouldner observes,

> though functionalism in the United States is involved in a crisis, its world career is far from at an end. Indeed, the career of functionalism, and of academic sociology more broadly, is now just beginning in Eastern Europe and in the Soviet Union . . . Many Marxists, in the Soviet bloc as elsewhere, manifest a growing attraction to academic sociology, including functionalism and even Parsons himself. (Gouldner, 447, 449)

These 'developments' have been elsewhere critically examined by
the author under the titles 'Functionalism and Dialectics' and with
special reference to the next psychological step, in 'Sociology of
Development and Underdevelopment of Sociology' (reprinted in
Frank 1969). This is not the occasion to pursue this question in
general, other than to keep it in mind in so far as it constitutes the
theoretical and ideological context of the more specific question
posed here and in other parts of this book, to which we may now
turn.

B. *The Protestant Ethic and the Spirit of Capitalism*

What are the origins of the differences – development in the North
and underdevelopment in the South – now observable in the New
World of the Americas, and how can they be accounted for and
explained? The best known and most widely accepted answers to
this question are those of Weber and his conscious or unconscious
followers. Yet these answers and the theory behind them are far
from satisfactory in that they are inconsistent with historical
evidence, theoretically limited and untenable, and politically
reactionary. Rejecting then the Weberian and neo-Weberian
interpretations, we propose to return to the classical tradition
reaching from Marx back to Smith and to seek to approach an
explanation that is at once consistent with the historical evidence
and with our theoretical approach to the analysis of the process of
world capital accumulation and the transformation of modes of
production advanced throughout this book.

The Weber thesis, developed by him in his *The Protestant Ethic and
the Spirit of Capitalism* and his comparative studies of world religions,
is summarised and applied to the New World in Weber's last work,
General Economic History:

> It is pertinent to inquire into the significance which the
> acquisition and exploitation of the great non-European regions
> had for the development of modern capitalism . . . The acqui-
> sition of colonies by the European States led to a gigantic
> acquisition of wealth in Europe for all of them . . . This
> accumulation of wealth brought about through colonial trade
> has been of little significance for the development of modern
> capitalism – a fact which must be emphasized in opposition to
> Werner Sombart . . . Sombart has assumed that the standard-

ized mass provision for war is among the decisive conditions affecting the development of modern capitalism. This theory must be reduced to its proper proportions . . . In the last resort, the factor which produced capitalism is the rational permanent enterprise, rational accounting, rational technology, and rational law, but again not these alone. Necessary complementary factors were the rational spirit, the rationalization of the conduct of life in general, and a rationalistic economic ethic . . . Two main types of exploitation are met with: the feudal type in the Spanish and Portuguese colonies, the capitalistic in the Dutch and English . . . A religious motive also played a part in the shape of the traditional repugnance of the Puritans to feudalism of any sort. (Weber, *History*, 298, 300, 308, 354, 298, 301)

Weber's own disclaimer in the concluding paragraph of his *The Protestant Ethic and the Spirit of Capitalism* – 'but it is, of course, not my aim to substitute for a one-sided materialistic an equally one-sided spiritualistic causal interpretation of culture and of history' – has been largely forgotten by his followers or has gone unobserved in their practice as they have been spinning psychological threads and weaving institutional fabrics in an attempt to obscure the structure and development of the underlying worldwide economic system of capitalism. The essence of their arguments has been several times graphically summarised by cartoonists, who, sharing the scholars' ideological convictions though not their scientific pretensions, depict a lazy Mexican taking a long siesta in the tropical sun while leaning against the (Catholic) church wall. That is underdevelopment; if only he had the Puritan spirit, his country would be developed like theirs!, so runs the argument. (For a critique, see the above cited and other essays in Frank, 1969, Part 2.)

The Weberian thesis, and still more its latter-day Parsonian and other corruptions (see Frank, 1969, chapter 2), is totally untenable in the light of the evidence. With respect to the rise of European capitalism, the Weber thesis has long since been challenged by Tawney and disposed of by H. M. Robertson and others and recently by Kurt Samuelsson. As Smith and Marx already observed, capitalism was born in Catholic Italy, Spain and Portugal; and it flourished in Catholic Belgium and among Catholic entrepreneurs in Amsterdam before it developed in Protestant Britain. As for the New World, the historical evidence shows exhaustively and the present essay more summarily that European

institutions were not simply transplanted from the Old World to the
New World. Yet even without this exhaustive evidence, it is clear
upon simple inspection that the Weber thesis could not account for
the underdevelopment of the Caribbean – and later African and
Asian – colonies that were also blessed with British capitalism and
which underdeveloped far more than the Spanish Caribbean before
the latter was also converted into an export plantation. Nor can the
Weber thesis account for the differences between the North and the
South of British North Amercia. After examining the historical
evidence, Bruchey concludes, 'in sum, it is necessary to conclude
that to a significant extent mercantile success was not so much
owing to Puritanism as achieved at its expense' (Bruchey, 48);
Gabriel Kolko argues that 'had the alliance between the religious
conceptions of the Puritans and the merchant class been as real as
Weber assumed it to be, the conflict [between puritanism and
business] might not have occurred so quickly' (quoted in Bruchey,
47); and Samuelsson summarises, 'thus our conclusion is that,
whether we start from the doctrines of Puritanism and "capitalism"
or from the actual concept of a correlation between religion and
economic action, we can find no support for Weber's theories.
Almost all the evidence contradicts them' (Samuelsson, 154).
Moreover, even to the limited extent to which Old World
differences among migrants may have played a role in the New
World a coherent theory of underdevelopment (or of development)
would have to explain why different kinds of people went to
different places and behaved differently in the New World. And the
answer to these questions must be sought not in the personality
characteristics of the migrants but in the socio-economic structure
and mode of production of the societies they emigrated from and
integrated themselves into, and in the relations between these
societies.

C. *Unorthodox Weberian Survivals*

None the less, the spirit of the Weber thesis or its ghost is pervasive.
Apart from the new orthodoxy of academic sociology and its recent
conquests abroad, the Weberian ghost also haunts heretics like the
economist A. Emmanuel and the anthropologist Darcy Ribeiro, to
name no more, whose work is consciously and explicitly dedicated
to challenge orthodoxy with new analyses inspired, as they claim,
by the old Marx. In Emmanuel's analysis of unequal exchange
(*L'Echange Inégal*, discussed in Chapter 5) the central argument is

that differences in wage levels between countries *cause* unequal exchange between them and that this in turn is a major reason for the observed differences in development. The wage rate, thus, is the independent and unexplained variable in his analysis. Explicitly recognising the same, Emmanuel none the less dedicates some brief attention, which is marginal to his central argument, to 'the institutional factors which determine the equilibrium wage in the first place [and which] are not exogenous accidents to human society' (Emmanuel, 163). He then (pp. 164–5 and again 354) supposes or claims that the *initial* high wage level in the United States, relative to other parts of the world and especially to Latin America, was 'in the last analysis' due to a higher or 'different subsistence wage and the "demands" of the people who settled the United States' (p. 164). That is, Emmanuel like the neo-Weberians believes that the people who settled in the United States were somehow 'different' and that this difference 'in the last analysis' accounts for the subsequent development of the United States, which then only snowballed thanks to unequal exchange and other factors. Latin America, Emmanuel holds on the contrary, started its development with a 'relative handicap' because of the 'starting level of living of the immigrants' and 'the transplantation to the colonies of the clerico-feudal structures of the metropolis' (Emmanuel, 164). It was this starting handicap with respect to the United States and Europe which 'in the last analysis' of Emmanuel explains why Latin America has never been able to catch up, inasmuch as the mechanism of unequal exchange could only widen the initial gap. Beyond the validity or adequacy of Emmanuel's central argument about unequal exchange (which is discussed elsewhere in this study), this last analysis is quite unacceptable in that it contravenes historical fact, is theoretically inadequate *per se* because it would still leave unexplained why different kinds of people and institutions settled in different parts of the New World, and because so weak a theoretical foundation calls into question the adequacy of any analysis – of unequal exchange or any other – which builds upon or otherwise incorporates it. This argument is sustained by the discussion of the Weber thesis and the alternative explanation below.

Our problem has recently also been considered, and to some extent clarified, by the anthropologist Darcy Ribeiro (in various books, more summarily in his 'Culture-Historical Configurations of the American Peoples', cited here:

Although there are many contributing factors, the perfor-
mance of the Transplanted Peoples (principally of North America) in comparison with the others (of most of the remainder of
the Americas) can be explained principally in terms of the
difference between self-colonization and external domination . . . Other factors that explain differences . . . stem from
the more maturely capitalistic nature of societies from which the
Transplanted Peoples came. Outstanding among these is the
more equilitarian nature of the Transplanted society (at least in
the north) . . . and in the integrative capacity of their social
structure . . . Their basic characteristics are (1) cultural homogeneity . . . (2) considerable equalitarianism, based on de-
mocratic institutions . . . and (3) 'modernity' . . . The
Transplanted Peoples grew out of immigrant colonies, dedicated
to small farming, crafts, and small-scale trade. All of them
experienced long periods of penury . . . It is of course no
coincidence that these Transplanted Peoples are to be found in
temperate zones . . . The European immigrant is more comfor-
table in temperate climates and avoids tropical areas whenever
possible. The converse is true of peoples adapted to the tropics . . . There is a degree of parallelism between these attitudes
toward work and certain Catholic and Protestant views on the
subject. This does not mean that these religions played an
important causal role in implanting the attitudes, but only that
both of them supported the *status quo* of the societies in which they
predominated: more maturely capitalistic ones in the Protestant
case and more backward aristocratic ones in the Catholic case.
The importance of this support should not be underestimated . . . (Ribeiro 10–12)

This wealth of explanatory factors adduced by Ribeiro really
reflects, we believe, considerable poverty in the explanatory power
of his argument: the reference to climatic factors to explain
migratory differences is inconsistent with the evidence of voluntary
European worldwide migration from and to a large variety of
climates and with the fact of forced migration of Asian, African and
Latin American Indian labour from one climate to another; and in
so far as climate is adduced as explanatory of development or
underdevelopment it would be inadmissible to accept the long-since
scientifically discredited arguments of Huntington, and it would be
necessary to relate climatic and geological factors to the associated

modes of production, which Ribeiro does not do. The reference to religious factors echoes Weberian arguments that are contradicted by the evidence examined by the authors cited above. The reference to the maturely capitalistic source of transplanted people is not explanatory unless it is related to the differences in the functional contribution of the recipient societies in the different stages of the process of world capital accumulation and capitalist development, and unless this relation could account for the differences in the contribution of historically contemporaneous European migrants to the development and underdevelopment of, say, New Zealand and New Guinea or Australia and Algeria. And the reference, echoing Adam Smith, to small farming and small trade society and its reflection in cultural homogeneity, equalitarianism and democracy – in so far as they are historically accurate, which as we have observed is by no means absolutely so – would, as for Emmanuel also, only become explanatory in so far as their own origin or cause can be explained and related to the reasons for 'the difference between self-colonization and domination' – which Ribeiro calls the 'principal' explanatory factor, but which he does not attempt to explain or account for. Ribeiro's reference to 'many contributing factors' thus still leaves us with much explaining to do.

2. On Adam Smith and the New World

We may begin our own explanation by reading Adam Smith's *Inquiry into the Nature and Causes of the Wealth of Nations*, published in 1776:

> The discovery of America, and that of the passage to the East Indies by the Cape of Good Hope, are the two greatest events recorded in the history of mankind. Their consequences have already been very great (590) . . . In the cargoes, therefore, of the greater part of European ships which sail to India, silver has generally been one of the most valuable articles. It is the most valuable article in the Acapulco ships which sail to Manila. The silver of the new continent seems in this manner to be one of the principal commodities by which the commerce between the two extremities of the old one is carried on, and it is by means of it, in a great measure, that those distant parts of the world are connected with one another (207) . . . By opening a new and inexhaustible

market to all the commodities of Europe, it gave occasion to new divisions of labour and improvements of art, which in the narrow circle of ancient commerce, could never have taken place for want of a market to take off the greater part of their produce. The productive powers of labour were improved, and its produce increased in all different countries of Europe, and together with it the real revenue and wealth of the inhabitants (416) . . . In the meantime one of the principal effects of these discoveries has been to raise the mercantile system to a degree of splendour and glory which it could never otherwise have attained to. It is the object of that system to enrich a great nation rather by trade and manufacturers than by the improvement and cultivation of the land, rather by the industry of the towns than by that of the country. But, in consequence of those discoveries, the commercial towns of Europe, instead of being the manufacturers and carriers for but a very small part of the numerous and thriving cultivators of America and the carriers, and in some respects manufacturers too, for almost all the different nations of Asia, Africa and America [591 – this, we may recall, was written *before* the industrial revolution!] . . . A new set of exchanges, therefore, began to take place which had never been thought of before, and which should naturally have proved as advantageous to the new, as it certainly did to the old continent. The savage injustice of the Europeans rendered an event, which ought to have been beneficial to all, ruinous and destructive to several of those unfortunate countries (416) . . . By uniting, in some measure, the most distant parts of the world, by enabling them to relieve one another's wants, to increase one another's enjoyments, and to encourage one another's industry, their general tendency would seem to be beneficial. To the natives, however, both of the East and West Indies, all the commercial benefits which can have resulted from those events have been sunk and lost in the dreadful misfortunes which they have occasioned (590) . . . In the short period of between two and three centuries which has elapsed since these discoveries were made, it is impossible that the whole extent of their consequences can have been seen. What benefits, or what misfortunes to mankind may hereafter result from those great events, no human wisdom can foresee . . . (590)

How right, we may now observe with two additional centuries of hindsight, Smith was in finding it impossible to foresee the whole extent of the future consequences of these events. But his own observation permitted him to see the dreadful misfortunes that had resulted from those events in the past; and Smith had the wisdom to foresee at least the possibility that, as well as benefits, further misfortunes for mankind could also result from this new set of exchanges and mercantile system, which Smith's neo-classical followers since then, however much they claim to be guided by his vision, cannot yet see even with the aid of hindsight.

Regarding the motivations or ambitions of the early European colonisers of the various parts of the New World and the different rewards that they encountered, Smith wrote:

> In consequence of the representations of Columbus, the Council of Castile determined to take possession of countries of which the inhabitants were plainly incapable of defending themselves. The pious purpose of converting them to Christianity sanctified the injustice of the project. But the hope of finding treasures of gold there, was the sole motive which prompted them to undertake it . . . All the other enterprises of the Spaniards in the new world subsequent to those of Columbus, seem to have been prompted by the same motive. It was the thirst for gold . . . (528–9). Every Spaniard who sailed to America expected to find an Eldorado. Fortune too did upon this what she had done upon very few other occasions. She realized in some measure the extravagant hopes of her votaries, and in the discovery of Mexico and Peru . . . she presented them with something not very unlike that profusion of the precious metals which they sought for . . . The first adventurers of all the other nations of Europe, who attempted to make settlements in America, were animated by the like chimerical views; but they were not equally successful . . . In the English, French, Dutch and Danish colonies, none have ever yet been discovered; at least none that are at present supposed to be worth the working. The first English settlers in North America, however, offered a fifth of all the gold and silver which should be found there to the king, as a motive for granting them their patents. In the patents to Sir Walter Raleigh, to the London and Plymouth companies, to the council of Plymouth, &c. this fifth was accordingly reserved to the crown. To the expectation of finding gold and silver mines, those first settlers too joined that of discovering a north-west passage to the East Indies. They have hitherto been disappointed in both. (531)

This rather casts some doubt on the latter-day 'puritan' theses about the protestant ethic in North as against the licentious but lazy greed in South America; and it represents an important first step toward establishing the objective differences in the material base of these parts of the New World.

Smith also began to offer explanations of why the different parts of the New World had already experienced differing fortunes of development:

> The Spanish colonies, therefore, from the moment of their first establishment, attracted very much the attention of their mother country; while those of the other European nations were for a long time a great measure neglected [until the exigencies of capitalist development attracted greater European, other than Spanish, attention to the Caribbean – though not more than the continuing Spanish attention to the Mainland]. The former did not perhaps thrive better in consequence of this attention; nor the latter worse in consequence of this neglect. (534)

Elsewhere Smith observes additionally,

> in the disposal of their surplus produce, or what is over and above their own consumption, the English colonies have been favoured, and have been allowed a more extensive market [and, one may add, to invest the domestic productive and international trade surplus in their own development], than those of any other European nation. Every European nation has endeavoured more or less to monopolize to itself the commerce of its colonies . . . but the manner in which this monopoly has been exercized in different nations has been very different. (541–2).

This distinction by Smith between different manners of exercising monopoly and between different degrees of 'attention' and his observation about their consequences, on how different colonies 'thrive', may appear to lead merely to an explanation of under-development in terms of 'external' factors. But though it recognises important differences in the 'disposal of their surplus' or the degree of equality or exploitation in the 'external' exchange associated with different kinds of metropolitan-colonial relationships, Smith's observation also points to the necessarily related differences in the 'internal' modes of production between colonies that are neglected but thrive, and colonies that attract attention but do not thrive.

In examining the 'Causes of the Prosperity of the new Colonies', Smith observed in 1776, the year the colonies declared their independence, about parts of North America:

> Every colonist gets more land than he can possibly cultivate. He has no rent, scarce any taxes to pay, no landlord shares with him in its produce, and the share of the sovereign is commonly but a trifle. He has every motive to render as great as possible a produce, which is thus to be almost entirely his own . . . He is eager, therefore, to collect labourers from all quarters, and to reward them with the most liberal wages. But those liberal wages, joined with the plenty and cheapness of land, soon make those labourers leave him, in order to become landlords themselves . . . wages are high . . . In other countries, rent and profits eat up wages, and the two superior orders of people oppress the inferior one. But in new colonies, the interest of the two superior orders obliges them to treat the inferior one with more generosity and humanity: at least, where the inferior one is not in a state of slavery. (532)

And in the British North American colonies even slaves were exploited less than they were in the British or French Caribbean colonies.

Thus Adam Smith, the 'father' of modern economics, or rather of classical political economy, has more to offer to the serious student of *The Nature and Causes of the Wealth of Nations* than the first three (out of thirty-two) chapters on the division of labour, which is about as far as any ill-advised modern reader is likely to get in the book. (That *is* as far as we got in Frank Knight's course on the history of economic thought at the University of Chicago. Knight's disciple — and by way of Herbert Simon his inheritor — Milton Friedman all but abandoned Smith altogether, preferring to replace him by Alfred Marshall as the father of economic 'analysis', which Friedman instructed us to learn from the *footnotes* of Marshall's *Principles of Economics* (1890) and to relegate virtually the entire empirically rich text and appendixes to oblivion.) Thus, to pursue the ideological objectives of the beneficiaries' capitalism, *marginal* economics is employed to divert attention from the core of the worldwide systemic nature and the historical causes of the dreadful misfortunes, as Smith called them, also engendered by the division of labour, whose systemic and historical dimension was an important though now largely forgotten part of the classical political economy of Smith.

3. On Karl Marx and Capital Accumulation

Marx recognised his debt to Smith and Ricardo in the analysis of market exchange and distribution and, without abandoning but rather deepening the system-wide historical perspective of classical political economy, Marx extended it to the analysis of the process of production and capital accumulation. In the expansion and development of mercantile capitalism the various parts of the New World participated in the system with different modes of production and contributed differently to the process of capital accumulation.

A century after Smith, Karl Marx observed the same historical process and developed theoretical tools to extend the analysis from market exchange to the mode of production in capitalist accumulation and development:

> Although we come across the first beginnings of capitalist production as early as the 14th or 15th century, sporadically, in certain towns of the Mediterranean, the capitalistic era dates from the 16th century . . . The modern history of capital dates from the creation in the 16th century of a world-embracing commerce and a world-embracing market . . . The colonies secured a market for the budding manufactures, and, through the monopoly of the market, an increasing accumulation. The treasures captured outside Europe by undisguised looting, enslavement, and murder, floated back to the mother-country and were turned into capital . . . As a matter of fact, the methods of primitive accumulation is anything but idyllic . . . In actual history it is notorious that conquest, enslavement, robbery, murder, briefly force, play the great part . . .
>
> The discovery of gold and silver in America, the extirpation, enslavement and entombment in mines of the aboriginal population, the beginning of the conquest and looting of the East Indies, the turning of Africa into a warren for the commercial hunting of black-skins, signalized the rosy dawn of the era of capitalist production. These idyllic proceedings are the chief momenta of primitive accumulation. On their heels treads the

commercial war of the European nations, with the globe for its theatre . . . The different momenta of primitive accumulation . . . arrive at a systematical combination, embracing the colonies, the national debt, the modern mode of taxation, and the protectionist system. But they all employ the power of the State, the concentrated and organized force of society, to hasten, hothouse fashion, the process of transformation . . . Force is the midwife of every old society pregnant with a new one. It is itself an economic power . . . Liverpool waxed fat on the slave trade. This was its method of primitive accumulation . . . In fact, the veiled slavery of the wage workers in Europe needed, for its pedestal, slavery pure and simple in the new world . . . Capital comes [into the world] dripping from head to foot, from every pore, with blood and dirt. (Marx, I, 715, 146, 753–4, 714, 751, 759–60)

In volume III of *Capital* Marx goes on to argue that, beyond relying on the aforementioned methods of 'primitive accumulation', the process of capitalist accumulation and development in the metropolis also benefits from the resulting subsequent forces of market exchange through foreign trade with the colonies:

Since foreign trade partly cheapens the elements of constant capital, and partly the necessities of life for which the variable capital is exchanged, it tends to raise the rate of profit by increasing the rate of surplus-value and lowering the value of constant capital. It acts generally in this direction by permitting the expansion of production. It thereby hastens the process of accumulation, on the one hand, but causes the variable capital to shrink in relation to the constant capital, on the other, and thus hastens a fall in the rate of profit. In the same way, the expansion of foreign trade, although the basis of the capitalist mode of production in its infancy, has become its own product, however, with the further mode of production, through the innate necessity of this mode of production, its need for an ever-expanding market. (Ricardo has entirely overlooked this side of foreign trade.) Another question – really beyond the scope of our analysis because of its special nature – is this: Is the general rate of profit raised by the higher rate of profit produced by capital invested in foreign, and particularly colonial, trade? Capitals invested in foreign trade can yield a higher rate of profit, because, in the first place, there is competition with commodities produced in other countries with inferior production facilities, so that the more advanced country sells its goods above their value even though cheaper than the competing countries . . . The favoured (advanced) country recovers more labour in exchange for less labour, although this difference is pocketed, as in any exchange between labour and capital, by a certain class. Since the rate of profit is higher, therefore, because it is generally higher in a colonial country, it may, provided natural conditions are favourable, go hand in hand with low commodity prices. A levelling takes place but not the levelling to the old level, as Ricardo feels. (Marx, I, 232–3)

This observation about the function of international trade in the nineteenth century, was quoted and developed in his discussion of primitive accumulation by Preobazhensky in the 1920s and foreshadows the analysis of unequal exchange (*L'Echange Inégal*) published by Emmanuel in 1969, and we shall return to it in our own discussion of international exchange in the nineteenth and twentieth centuries.

Returning to the beginnings of capitalist development and underdevelopment, Marx emphasises the relation between market exchange and mode of production in capitalist accumulation and development in his summary in volume III of *Capital* of 'Historical Facts about Merchant's Capital'.

There is no doubt – and it is precisely this fact which has led to wholly erroneous conceptions – that in the 16th and 17th centuries the great revolutions, which took place in commerce with the geographical discoveries and speeded the development of merchant's capital, constitute one of the principal elements in furthering the transition from feudal to capitalist mode of production. The sudden expansion of the world-market, the multiplication of circulating commodities, the competitive zeal of the European nations to possess themselves of the products of Asia and the treasures of America, and the colonial system – all contributed materially toward destroying the feudal fetters on production. However, in its first period – the manufacturing period – the modern mode of production developed only where the conditions for it had taken shape within the Middle Ages. Compare, for instance, Holland with Portugal. And when in the 16th, and partially the 17th century the sudden expansion of

commerce and the emergence of a new world-market over-
whelmingly contributed to the fall of the old mode of production
and the rise of capitalist production, this was accomplished
conversely on the basis of the already existing capitalist mode of
production. The world-market itself forms the basis for this mode
of production. On the other hand, the immanent necessity of this
mode of production to produce on an ever-enlarged scale tends to
extend the world-market continually, so that it is not commerce
in this case which revolutionizes industry, but industry which
constantly revolutionizes commerce. Commercial supremacy
itself is now linked with the prevalence to a greater or lesser
degree of conditions for a large industry. Compare for instance,
England and Holland . . . There is, consequently, a threefold
transition. *First*, the merchant becomes directly an industrial
capitalist . . . *Second*, the merchant turns the small masters into
his middlemen, or buys directly from the independent producer,
leaving him nominally independent and his mode of production
unchanged. *Third*, the industrialist becomes merchant and
produces directly for the wholesale market. (Marx, III, 327–30)

Sweezy, Dobb and Takahashi have further analysed the relative
priority of exchange (*first* and *second* above) and production (*third*
above) in this process in Europe but have left the same question
almost entirely unasked, let alone answered, for the colonial parts of
the capitalist system. Sweezy concludes the discussion by asking,

Why was feudalism succeeded by capitalism? If one agrees
with Dobb, as I do, that the period from the fourteenth century to
the end of the sixteenth century was one in which feudalism was
in full decay and yet in which there were no more than the first
beginnings of capitalism, this is a genuinely puzzling question . . . True, the decline of feudalism was accompanied (I
would say 'caused') by the generalization of commodity production, and, as Marx repeatedly emphasized, 'commodity
production and developed commodity circulation, trade, form
the historical preconditions under which it (capital) arises'
(*Capital*, I, p. 163). But historical preconditions do not in
themselves provide a sufficient explanation. (Sweezy, 63)

Again, Sweezy's question refers to Europe (a few lines later he asks
for more research on the origins of the industrial bourgeoisie),

though the question might also be taken to refer to the capitalist system as a whole. But the question does not refer particularly to colonies, which is our specific interest and question. Whatever the difficulty in answering Sweezy's question, the answer to our question – once it is posed – is to be found in the evidence and analysis presented below.

Finally, Marx ends the same chapter by drawing the following conclusions and guides, beyond those of Adam Smith, for theoretical analysis:

> The first theoretical treatment of the modern mode of production – the mercantile system – proceeded necessarily from the superficial phenomena of the circulation process as individualized in the movements of merchant's capital, and therefore grasped only the appearance of matters . . . The real science of modern economy only begins when the theoretical analysis passes from the process of circulation (exchange) to the process of production . . . (Marx, III, 331)

Commenting on Marx's *Grundrisse*, a recent writer emphasises,

> Marx's . . . rejection, on grounds of superficiality, of the thesis that the market mechanism is a motivating, causal, or fundamental factor; and its recognition that the market is merely a device to coordinate the various individual moments of a process far more fundamental than exchange . . . the hidden but essential core-processes of capitalist production and accumulation. (Nicolaus, 45–6)

Marx treats problems of production and accumulation in settlement areas of the United States and elsewhere in his chapter on 'The Modern Theory of Colonization' dedicated to the critique of Wakefield's colonisation scheme in Australia. 'We treat here of real Colonies, virgin soils, colonised by free immigrants. The United States are, speaking economically, still only a Colony of Europe' (Marx, I, 765n) in the sense of being an area that absorbs its colonists. 'The essence of a free Colony . . . consists in this – that the bulk of the soil is still public property, and every settler on it therefore can turn part of it into his private property and individual means of production . . . So long, therefore, as the labourer can accumulate for himself – and this he can do so long as he remains possessor of the means of production – capitalist accumulation and the capitalistic mode of production are impossible. The class of wage-labourers, essential to these, is wanting.' As Wakefield had noted, a Mr Peel, who had taken 3000 people to the Swan River colony in Australia 'was left without a servant to make his bed or fetch him water' as long as they had free access to land. Hence Wakefield's 'systematic colonization' scheme which should do for Australia what land monopolisation, servitude and slavery had done for plantation colonies in the New World (Marx, I, 766–8).

4. On World Capital Accumulation, International Exchange, and the Diversity of Modes of Production in the New World

Any serious inquiry, then, into the differences in the origins of the historical experiences and subsequent development paths of the various regions of the New World must begin with an examination of the historical process of capital accumulation on a world scale, since that was the driving force of the various processes in the New World which were integral parts of the world process, and go on to consider how it was mediated through differing modes of production in the various parts of that World which corresponded to the differing – though related – roles these regions played in that worldwide process. Differences in colonial policies and experiences in the New World were much less due to – and still less explicable by – supposed differences among colonisers as the Weberians claim than they were accounted and accountable by the differing circumstances the colonists found in the New World and by the relations of these to the metropolitan needs, as Smith had suggested. Or more explicitly, as Gray argues in his classic study of *Agriculture in the Southern United States to 1860*, 'the record of the experience of European nations that established colonies in the New World confirms the observation of Paul Leroy-Beaulieu, that the policies of colonization must conform to the conditions encountered. Sharp contrasts in colonial policy and accomplishment were due partly to economic and political differences in the colonizing nations but even more to wide differences in the natural environment and native populations of the countries colonized' (Gray, II, 303).

Why then did these differences in colonial exchange relations, modes of production and wage levels arise and give rise to different – though mutually related – paths of development and underdevelopment? Why did the Spaniards devote preferential exploitative attention to Mexico and Peru, and produce a mode of production, wage level, and unequal exchange of treasures for virtually nothing at all, inhibiting domestic capital accumulation and directing it into the development of underdevelopment? Because they found gold and silver there – and an already existing socially organised labour force and technological knowledge, whose exploitation through *less than subsistence wages* in the colonies, to permit the expansion of trade and the accumulation of capital in the European metropolis, required a certain mode of production and under historically changing circumstances varying institutional forms in these colonies. Why did the Spaniards not do likewise in the Caribbean and some parts of the mainland, neglecting to impose as exploitative a mode of production there as the British did in some of their colonies? Because these regions did not offer the same exploitative possibilities to low investment as those which occupied Spanish attention in Mexico and Peru. Why did the British who went to North America not follow the Spanish example of exploiting indigenous labour to produce gold and silver? As Smith rightly observed, not because they did not want to, but because these factors were not to be found there. Why did the Portuguese, British, French, Dutch, Germans and later Spaniards and North Americans implant dependent single-crop plantation export economies worked by 'low-wage' (but despite a 'useful' life of about seven years in Brazil perhaps not as far below subsistence wage as in Mexico and Peru) slave labour, thereby implanting a mode of production and colonial exchange relationship which, not fundamentally unlike the Spanish Mexican or Peruvian ones, generated the development of underdevelopment in Brazil, the Caribbean and then the South (but not the North) of the United States? Because these regions offered the potential for this kind of labour exploitation and capital accumulation, albeit only with an initial investment of capital and importation of labour that could and would not have been justified without the resulting profit and the necessary degree and kind of exploitation.

Then why did the British 'neglect' and fail to devote the same 'attention' to their New England and Middle Atlantic colonies – and the French to New France (today Quebec, which did not begin to underdevelop until after its colonialisation by the British after 1763)? Only because these regions lacked all the conditions necessary to attract that kind of attention – and to impose a manner of monopolising and extracting the surplus through low wages and unequal exchange, and to develop a mode of production that would develop underdevelopment like elsewhere in the New World. This is the fundamental explanation of why some parts of the New World had the necessary and sufficient conditions to begin the development of underdevelopment, while others did not. This does not, perhaps, constitute an adequate explanation as well of the sufficient conditions for development, but the mode of production in 'colonial' New England and its exploitative exchange relation to the Caribbean and the American South, with their respective 'peculiar institution', undoubtedly contains the explanation, which is beyond the scope of this essay.

We may review these differing modes of production in turn and inquire into their varying causes or explanations in somewhat greater detail.

A. *Mining Economies in Mexico and Peru*

After the conquest of Mexico in 1520, the Spaniards first imposed slavery on the part of the indigenous population that they immediately controlled. But slavery was abolished by 1533, and it was replaced as the predominant organisational form by the *encomienda* of service and tribute. This institution assigned the Indians of designated communities to particular Spaniards, who did not receive ownership of their persons, lands or other property, but were authorised to exact tribute in personal services, goods and money from them. This tribute was the principal source of the Spaniards' capital, and the *encomenderos* invested it in a variety of mining, agricultural, commercial and other enterprises, such as further conquests, that permitted the realisation of this tribute for shipment abroad and for further capital accumulation in Mexico itself. The mode of production through which the indigenous population generated the goods they paid in tribute to the Spaniards and the products they consumed themselves was initially the small-scale communal production of pre-conquest times. In 1548, though tribute in goods or money was maintained, tribute in the form of labour services was prohibited and replaced by the *repartimiento* (or distribution), an institution which in Mexico was called the *catequil* and in Peru the *mita*. Between 1545 and 1548 Mexico experienced an epidemic that wiped out one third of the indigenous population (estimated at 11 million and more recently at 25 million at the time of the conquest), which greatly reduced the labour supply, especially in particular communities or places. At the same time, the first great silver mine at Zacatecas was discovered in 1548; and this significantly increased the Spanish demand for Indian labour. Therefore, the *encomienda* was no longer a suitable institution for organising the allocation of the labour supply; and it was replaced by the *repartimiento*, which was a more flexible form of organisation in that a certain number of man-days of labour were assigned to particular Spaniards by a state official, called *juez repartidor*.

Moreover, the beneficiary of this forced-labour assignment, similar to that still used with prison labour, now had to pay the labourers an officially fixed wage. The number of man-days exacted from Indian communities by the *repartimiento* and their pay scale differed from one region and one time to another in Spanish America, depending on Spanish need and local supply. Indeed, in Chile for instance, the labour service *encomienda* survived for two centuries and the *repartimiento* was never instituted. The reason is that the much less developed mining economy of Chile (for lack of major mines) and the lower labour supply, combined with the indigenous Indians' less developed social organisation (compared to the Incas and the Aztecs) rendered the labour *encomienda* possible and the *repartimiento* inappropriate. In Mexico, the *repartimiento* lasted until 1632, but in agriculture it ceased to be the dominant organisational form after 1580. In the mid-sixteenth century large landowners had already begun to hire labour in addition to what they were assigned by the *repartimiento*, for which they had to compete with the more favoured mines, and paid this labour a 'free market' wage that was about double the official *repartimiento* wage. Soon, however, especially as Spanish agriculture expanded in competition with the indigenous one, the landowners found that wage payments were not enough to assure themselves of the needed labour supply, and they began to tie labour to the farm through debt and other means. After 1580, the now traditional *hacienda* became the dominant form of labour organisation in Mexican agriculture. Another epidemic in 1575–8 had again wiped out one half of the indigenous population. At the same time, in part due to decreased indigenous supply and increased urban demand, agricultural prices rose sharply and mining production declined as exhaustion of the most accessible veins and higher taxes raised production costs. As a result, mining became both absolutely and relatively less profitable for nearly a century, while large-scale Spanish agriculture increased in profitability and attracted capital and labour into this sector, both of which were in part transferred out of the mining sector. In Chile, the same form of *hacienda* organisation did not become dominant until more than a century later, after 1700, when the opening of the Lima market for Chilean wheat stimulated the conversion of labour-extensive livestock ranches into labour-intensive wheat farms for export production.

Thus, in the mining regions of Mexico, Peru and to a lesser extent Chile and other parts of the Spanish empire, it was precisely the exploitation of the mines – or more accurately of the labour necessary to work the mines – which determined the dominant relations of production, not only in the mines themselves but in much of the agricultural and service sectors that were subservient to the mining economy. The fluctuating needs for labour to produce the gold and silver (as well as the mercury used in the silver smelting process) demanded by the metropolis and increasingly used for the expansion of its trade with the Orient, combined with the ever-declining local supply of labour and the diminishing capacity of the surviving pre-Colombian socio-political institutions to organise the continued supply of this labour and of the foodstuffs and other inputs required by the mining economy and its local administrators and beneficiaries, determined the dominant mode of production and its historical transformation in these regions.

B. *Yeoman Farming in the Spanish Possessions*

But not all the New World had the same experience. Notably, of all the islands in the Caribbean, those that remained Spanish enjoyed by far the most benign rule compared to the French, English and Dutch sugar colonies – or compared, as well, to the major Spanish colonies on the mainland. The Spaniards sought and found gold in the islands; and, before the Mexican and Peruvian mines started to pour forth their treasures, the Spaniards decimated virtually the entire indigenous population of the Caribbean within fifty years of Columbus' arrival (Sauer). But once the vastly greater treasures of the mainland began to attract Spanish attention, capital and migrants (including many from the Caribbean islands themselves), the by then largely Spanish population remaining in the islands was substantially left to fend for itself. As a result, as Guerra y Sánchez observes:

The process of the allotment and division of Cuban land during the sixteenth, seventeenth, and eighteenth centuries led to the creation of a class of large-scale and small-scale proprietors who were descendents from the first settlers and who were deeply attached to their native soil. Mainly poor, rough people who lived in isolation from the outside world because of the strict laws forbidding any trade or commerce with foreigners, they raised livestock, cultivated small subsistence plots, and occasionally traded hides, salted or cured meat, and other agricultural products with the ships that called at Havana once or twice a year . . . but in Cuba the foundations were laid for a new and original nationhood, the fruit of three centuries of settlement. The different systems of allotment and utilization of the land determined the different destinies of the British and the Spanish Antilles. For the one, decline; for the other, progress, slow but constant. (Guerra y Sánchez, 35–6)

Only after 1760, and still more after 1898, economic and political changes in the world and in Cuba itself transformed Cuba into the world's principal sugar plantation. Other Spanish islands, like Santo Domingo and Puerto Rico, had a similar history.

Thus, the Spanish possessions produced no more than 2 per cent of Caribbean sugar in 1741–5 and less than 1.5 per cent of the production in the New World. In 1766–70, following Cuba's take-off into sugar production after 1760, the share of the Spanish possessions had risen to 3 per cent and 1.5 per cent respectively (Sheridan, 22–3). It would not become significant until after the slave rebellion in French St Dominique (Haiti) virtually took them, by far the largest Caribbean and New World producer, out of the market.

Throughout the 17th and 18th centuries . . . another Spanish possession in the Caribbean, Trinidad, languished, a colony in name . . . Thus did Trinidad and the West Indies live under Spanish colonialism – disregard . . . No Spanish ships for trade, no Spanish soldiers for defence. And there were no Spanish settlers for economic development . . . There being no gold (or silver), Spain was not impressed, and Spaniards were not interested . . . this is the explanation of the metropolitan failure to send ships, the metropolitan failure to send soldiers, the unwillingness of Spaniards to settle in Trinidad. (Williams 1964, 11, 20–21)

On the Spanish-American mainland as well, the areas that lacked either densely populated and highly civilised Indian population or precious metals, or both, had similar experiences at least until the mid-nineteenth century. In Colombia

> until the middle of the last century the manufactures and the rich agriculture of the East contrasted with the poverty of the West and the misery of the Central region, Departments of Boyaca and Cundinamarca. The West was mining . . . in Boyaca and Cundinamarca reigned . . . the latifundium. . . . In the East the situation was very different . . . There are no latifundios, there could not be any. No gold or silver mines were found. Therefore, no negroes are brought in . . . Manufactures arise . . . The economy of the Colombian East, during this time, was not oriented toward the foreign market. (Nieto Arteta, 79–80)

Similarly in Central America,

> Costa Rica, the poorest and most isolated region of that time . . . had a more homogeneous social structure based almost exclusively on the descendants of the Spanish. (Torres, 16)

These regions did not fall into step and adopt the dominant pattern of Latin America until they were converted into producers of coffee for the world market of the nineteenth century. The most important exception to the dominant mode of production in Latin America was the southern and most isolated cone of the continent, and particularly the La Plata region (Argentina), which had a relatively more diversified productive and egalitarian social structure until after the industrial revolution when European demand for wool, wheat, and meat and the supply of steam and refrigerated ships and railroads to transport them combined with the transformation of the class structure to determine the course of this region's (under) development since then.

These regions of Latin America and the Caribbean, thus, did not suffer the same fate as the major regions of colonial exploitation and – excepting those to whom this fate befell in an extreme degree in the nineteenth century – they are not among the most depressed areas today. Yet, though some of these regions developed some manufacturing for both the local and the export market during colonial times, they none the less were not able to take off into self-sustained development in the nineteenth or twentieth centuries, and in some cases on the contrary suffered the development of underdevelopment during the last century. Though their colonial history did not mark them with the necessary and sufficient conditions for the development of underdevelopment, it also did not leave them with the conditions sufficient for development – at least within the capitalist framework of the last century.

Our thesis is further confirmed by the experience of other Caribbean islands which began as settler colonies but were later converted into sugar plantations.

Initially, the settlement patterns, productive activity and organisation, and in general the kind of society installed in some non- or ex-Spanish Caribbean islands was essentially similar to that of the Spanish islands, quite independently of the nationality, culture or 'spirit' of the European settlers. The British and also the French – though these less so because of the smaller pressure to emigrate from their homeland – established settler colonies with small-scale yeoman farmers largely dedicated to subsistence farming and some indentured servants employed in minor but diversified export agriculture. But beginning at the mid-seventeenth century, one by one these early settler colonies were converted into exploitation colonies as well and integrated into the process of world capitalist development as specialised monoproducers of sugar – and as generators and suppliers of capital for the process of capital accumulation in the metropolis. The leading commercial nation of the world at the time, the Dutch, after their expulsion from Brazil, took advantage of the economic and political dislocations produced by the Cromwellian revolution of 1640 in England to begin the process in Barbados.

C. *Transformation: The Case of Barbados*

Contemporary observers, as quoted and interpreted by Harlow in his *History of Barbados 1625–1685* (published in 1926), graphically recorded the beginning of the process:

> In the days when a variety of small crops were grown, the land was occupied in small holdings by a large number of tenants. This

system, usual in most young British colonies [and, as we noted above, also in those Spanish ones that did not offer civilised Indians and mines], was partly the result of the original grants of small allotments to the first settlers . . . In this way the island was possessed of a numerous and sturdy 'yeoman' class, who were indeed the backbone of the colony. With the advent of the sugar industry this healthy condition of affairs was altered. Sugar planting to be successful requires large acres of land and a plentiful supply of cheap labour: the Dutch system of long credits provided the more affluent with the means to obtain both. But the small planter with his few acres and little capital could not face the considerable initial expense of setting up a sugar factory. The land in consequence fell more and more into the hands of a coterie of magnates . . . An example of the process was to be found in Captain Waterman's estate, comprising 800 acres, which at one time had been split up among no less than forty proprietors. Emphasizing the same fact Ligon instances the land value of 500 acres belonging to Major Hilliard. Before the introduction of the new manufacture the plantation was worth £400; yet in 1648 one half of it was sold for £7,000. 'And it is evident all the land here, which has been employed to that work, hath found the like improvement' . . . Already in 1667, this substitution of the negro slave for the white servant had reached an advanced stage. In that year Major Scott stated that after examining all the Barbadian records he found that since 1643 no less than 12,000 'good men' had left the island for other [places], and that the number of land owners had decreased from 11,200 smallholders in 1645 to 745 owners of large estates in 1667; while during the same period the negroes had increased from 5,680 to 82,023. Finally he summed up the situation by saying that in 1667 the island 'was not halfe soe strong, and forty times as rich as in the yeare 1645' . . .

This two-fold process – comments Harlow – whereby a sturdy English colony was converted into little more than a sugar factory, owned by a few absentee proprietors and worked by a mass of alien labour, constitutes the main feature of Barbadian history (Harlow, 10–44, 306–10) and of Caribbean history as a whole, except that the Spanish islands joined this history much later and initially under local ownership.

D. *The Plantation System in the Caribbean and Brazil*

The 'plantation system' came to dominate the North-east of Brazil, most of the Caribbean, and subsequently the South of the United States, as well as scattered other regions in the New World. Lacking substantial mines and dense populations, to say nothing of high civilisations, these lowland tropical areas evidently did not permit the kind of exploitation that the Spaniards imposed in Mexico and Peru. But their geographical and climatic characteristics did permit their participation in and substantial contribution to the process of capital accumulation during the commercial revolution if their natural resources could be suitably combined with the labour, capital and organisation necessary to make them produce at a profit. It was these circumstances which initiated the mode of production that has determined the historical fate of most of these regions until this day.

Gray summarises:

The plantation system had its genesis in the economic organization of the early joint-stock company . . . The plantation system was the natural successor of the colonizing company. With quasi-public functions of colonial foundation accomplished and the functions of government taken over by public agencies (after the initial private colonizing investments had largely proved to be commercial failures), the remaining task was to finance immigration and settlement. The plantation system afforded a convenient method of uniting capital and labor in the business of production. It would have been impracticable for the European capitalist to advance to each laborer the necessary expenses of emigration and settlement, leaving him to work out his own success and to repay the debt at will. The planter was the effective agent through whom European capital might be so employed, and the plantation was the agency of colonial expansion which brought together and combined three separate factors in utilizing the natural resources of the New World; the labor of the industrial servant or the slave, the capital furnished by the European merchant, and the directive activity of the planters. In some instances, of course, the planters themselves furnished part or all of the capital . . . (Gray, II, 312, 311) [Frequently] the establishment of private plantations followed as a third stage, favored by the fact that the new enterprises were not compelled to assume the expenses and responsibilities of initial colonization, had the advantage of experience with the new environment and the opportunity in some cases to acquire at small cost the lands, improvements, and equipment of the unsuccessful colonizing agencies. With the development of regular trade the latter was provided not only with market outlets for his products, but also a means of procuring on credit the requisite servants, slaves, and equipment. (Gray, II, 341)

Elsewhere Gray specifies:

The most characteristic institution of the plantation colony was the plantation system, which may be formally defined as follows: *The plantation was a capitalistic type of agricultural organization in which a considerable number of unfree labourers were employed under unified direction and control in the production of a staple crop* . . . The definition implies also that (1) the functions of laborer and employer were sharply distinct; (2) the system was based on commercial agriculture, except in periods of depression; (3) the system represented a capitalistic stage of agricultural development, since the value of slaves, land, and equipment necessitated the investment of money capital, often of large amount and frequently borrowed, and there was a strong tendency for the planter to assume the attitude of the business man in testing success by ratio of net money income to capital invested; and (4) there was a strong tendency towards specialization – the production of a single crop for market. It is significant that three of the characteristics developed in manufacturing by the Industrial Revolution—commercialism, capitalism, and specialization—were attained in Southern agriculture as early as the first half of the seventeenth century through the establishment of the plantation system. (Gray, II, 302, emphasis in original)

Though referring specifically to the Caribbean, the economic, social and political consequences of the implantation of the plantation system in the New World is summarised by Mintz:

Caribbean regional commonality is expressed in terms of nine major features as follows: (1) lowland, sub-tropical, insular ecology; (2) the swift extirpation of native populations; (3) the early definition of the islands as a sphere of European overseas agricultural capitalism, based primarily on the sugar-cane, African slaves, and the plantation system; (4) the concomitant development of insular social structures in which internally differentiated local community organization was slight, the national class groupings usually took a bipolar form, sustained by overseas domination, sharply differentiated access to land, wealth, and political power, and the use of physical differences as status markers; (5) the continuous interplay of plantations and small-scale yeoman agriculture, with accompanying social-structural effects . . . the distinction between coastal plain and rugged highland foretold a sharp divergence of enterprise that has typically marked Caribbean (and other plantation regions') agriculture with plantations concentrated on the coasts and in inland valleys, and small-scale enterprise and some hacienda forms occurring in mountainous sectors. (Mintz, 915, 917)

As was observed and emphasised already by Smith and Marx, and of course by the planters and slaves themselves, under the initial conditions of plentitude of land (subject to some restriction only in the Caribbean by the small size of some of the islands, which on the other hand constituted impediments to escape) and scarcity of labour, the plantation enterprise could only operate with profitable low-cost labour if the latter was subject to force in the form of indenture or slavery. Ultimately, indenture became unmanageable because of reduced supplies coming from Europe and increased difficulties of enforcement in the colonies – and negro slavery became the dominant, though never the only, source and form of plantation labour.

Each plantation and region had a tendency to specialise in a single crop, especially in periods of rising prices, and to engage in extensive agriculture that was none the less exhaustive of the soil and the lives of the labourers. Referring to the United States, George Washington explained, 'the aim of the farmers of this country, if they can be called farmers, is, not to make the most they can from the land, which is, or has been cheap, but the most of the labour which is dear' and he referred to Jefferson, who explained similarly that 'where land is cheap and rich and labour dear, the same labour spread in a slighter culture over one hundred acres, will produce more profit than if concentrated by the highest degree of cultivation on a small portion of the lands' (quoted in Gray, ii, 449).

A large share of the profit of the plantation enterprise, both in the supply of labour through the slave trade and in the sale of sugar and its by-products of molasses and rum was retained by merchants and financiers in the European metropolis (and New England-Middle Atlantic States sub-metropolis) or remitted to absentee owners residing abroad.

E. The U.S. South: Slave Plantations v. Farming

Another region of the New World which did not offer the Europeans any of the characteristics they had encountered in Mexico and Peru was the south of what was to become the United States. The colonists found no mines; the population was sparse and uncivilised. All of North America, including Canada, is estimated to have contained no more than 1,000,000 native inhabitants, of whom only about 200,000 lived in the area east of the Appalachian mountains where European colonisation was directed before the Independence of the United States (Aptheker 1959, 15). But the southern – as distinct from the northern and even Middle Atlantic – part of this region did offer agricultural and climatic conditions similar to those in the plantation regions of the Antilles and Brazil, though less exclusively so than the latter. These circumstances would become crucial in the determination of the historical future of the region. Gray observes:

> In climate and in social organization the Southern Colonies belong midway between the two extremes . . . best typified by the British West Indies and New England. (302)

After beginning slowly in the early seventeenth century with colonisation companies and indentured servants similar to those in the West Indies, the development of the South came to combine commercial and self-sufficient subsistence agriculture.

> The commercial planter produced a market crop under competitive conditions, investing capital, much of it borrowed, and incurring money expenses . . . the self-sufficient farmer was not seeking profits, but a living. He incurred but little money expenses, invested little capital, and assumed no regular financial obligations. Yet, complete self-sufficiency was exceedingly irksome . . . therefore the self-sufficing farmer constantly sought a marketable product . . . the relative extent of self-sufficiency and

commercialism in plantation areas varied from period to period and from region to region . . . In the general course of economic evolution a significant phenomenon was the tendency of slavery and the plantation system, under favourable conditions, to supplant other types of economy. This process was repeated over and over again. Where conditions favoured commercial production of staples, the small farmers found themselves unable to resist the competitive power of slave labour organized under the plantation system. Gradually they were compelled either to become great planters – and many did not possess sufficient ability and command over capital to accomplish this – or to re-establish a regime of rude self-sufficing economy in a region less favourable for commercial agriculture. (Gray, II, 451, 453)

On the one hand, as would be the pattern in much of agricultural expansion and development in the United States and elsewhere (such as Brazil today), the 'self-sufficient' small farmer, who invests little capital, first *creates* capital through his pioneering settlement of the land which he 'improves', and then contributes to the accumulation and concentration of capital when he is displaced by the large capitalist planter who is thereby spared this initial investment.

From another standpoint, however, the tendency may be regarded as a process of geographic specialization whereby the plantation system triumphed in regions most suitable to production of staples, while the self-sufficing or intermediate types of economy developed and survived in regions geographically adapted to them, although unfavourable to a plantation economy. . . . (Gray, II, 444) [or vice versa.]

In plantation areas commercial agriculture was characterized by a tendency to specialize in production of a single market crop . . .

The same conditions, therefore, which favoured commercialism also favoured the tendency to concentrate upon the production of a single staple . . . In the sugar and rice regions the tendency to specialization was even greater, for the desire to employ the limited labour force most profitably was intensified by the fact that regions of the South suitable for production of these crops were more severely limited . . . Fundamentally, however, the one-crop system was a result of the selective influence of economic competition leading to world-wide specialization. (Gray, II, 458–9)

Bruchey summarises in his *The Roots of American Economic Growth 1607–1871,* referring to the colonial era:

Numerous specialized farms or plantations devoted large parts of their resources to the production of one or two crops for foreign markets. In this category fall the tobacco farms and plantations of tidewater Maryland, Virginia, North Carolina, and Georgia, and large grain farms of Pennsylvania, western Maryland and the Valley of Virginia. Other familiar staples are the indigo of the Carolinas and the rice of South Carolina, which accounted for one-half to two-thirds of the value of the colony's exports during the eighteenth century. (Bruchey, 28–9)

Later, of course, cotton was to become king.

But this development had an additional consequence. Gray observes:

In the South, on the other hand, westward expansion brought inevitable depression to the older regions, a depression to be distinguished from the temporary periods of low prices that periodically affected the prosperity of new, as well as old, plantation regions. The unfortunate effects of westward expansion, as we have noted, began to be felt in Virginia and Maryland before the Revolution. From this time forward the history of the older South was marked by a continual widening of the area in which planting had ceased to be profitable. (II, 445).

These areas had a tendency to become depressed regions, agriculturally, economically and socially exhausted, though the older regions of the South for a time maintained themselves with the aid of a new export: slaves, born and reared in the eastern Old South to be sold to the New South farther west.

Thus, though indenture was in the beginning far more important than negro slavery and sometimes accounted for 40 per cent of the population in some regions, slavery developed far more rapidly in the eighteenth century. By the time of the American Revolution in 1776, the slave population numbered about 500,000 and accounted for nearly 40 per cent of the population of the South and nearly 20 per cent of the approximately 2,800,000 population of the North American colonies (Aptheker, 39, 41). In 1780 the total population of the thirteen colonies was 2,780,000, of whom 575,000 were negroes and all but about 40,000 of these in the South (*Historical Statistics of the United States*, 756).

F. The U.S. North-east: Farming v. Foreign Trade

The North-east of the United States, especially New England and to a lesser degree the Middle Atlantic provinces of New York and Pennsylvania (which with respect to the South were in an intermediate position socio-economically as well as geographically), offered circumstances that were significantly different from those encountered anywhere else in the New World – and it is this north-eastern region which later took off into the capitalist development associated with the United States. What were these differences, and how do they account for this capitalist development?

A widely accepted answer to this question is the 'Weber thesis' in its crude form or in its latter-day pseudo-social-scientific embellishments. But, as this entire analysis suggests, this thesis is unacceptable on theoretical and empirical grounds. We must agree with others, like Kurt Samuelsson in his *Religion and Economic Action* and Stuart Bruchey in *Roots of American Economic Growth,* who also reject the Weber thesis as an explanation of New England's development:

> In New England too, despite a correlation that certainly appears superficially strong, we have been unable to find anything suggesting the existence of a connection, in the deeper meaning of the word, between Puritanism and capitalism; the Puritan South – for it has long been much more Puritan than the states of the North—is economically 'under-developed' (Samuelsson, 120–1); [and] in sum, it is necessary to conclude that to a significant extent mercantile success was not so much owing to Puritanism as achieved at its expense (Bruchey 1965, 48).

Indeed, even in so far as such cultural factors among immigrants are or appear related to capitalist development, it would be necessary to explain why certain kinds of people migrated to particular places and not to others. And if the Yankees were by nature so enterprising, why did they not go to the South or the Caribbean to exercise their entrepreneurial talents where the export trade offered more opportunities? Thus, to have any explanatory value, any possibly important cultural factors would still have to be related to the socio-economic relations in the regions to (not from) which people migrated and to how these regions were inserted in the expanding world mercantile capitalist system.

Another attempt to explain development in the North-east of the United States takes account of certain socio-economic factors, though often without abandoning the Weber thesis. These socio-economic factors and the supposed explanation built on them are symbolised by the independent self-sufficient yeoman subsistence farmer and may be summarised by factors such as exceptionally equal and great economic opportunity due to access to land, relative equality of income distribution, both of which supposedly generated the development of an internal market, substantial political democracy and ethno-racial homogeneity. These factors were emphasised by such classical observers as Smith (as quoted above) and de Tocqueville in his *Democracy in America* (published between 1835 and 1840), and they find echo also in such contemporary anti-liberal writers as Ribeiro (quoted above). Of course, with varying emphasis by historians, economists, sociologists, political scientists, etc., these factors form essential parts of the ideological fabric woven by contemporary North American social science to 'explain' U.S. development and justify its now reactionery political policy (e.g. *America: The First New Nation* by Seymour Lipset).

The evidence with regard to the existence of some of these socio-economic characteristics, and their greatest concentration in New England (Bruchey 1965, 30) is summarised by Bruchey:

Despite the existence of wide inequality in the sizes of holdings and of some leasehold tenures in all the colonies, it seems that relatively few people who wished land were unable to obtain it . . . the price of land was 'not too high for the settler' . . . Fundamentally, it was the favourable land-man ratio that made possible in all the colonies a wide distribution of individually owned and privately operated farms . . . It is pertinent here to cite the judgement of Carl Bridenbaugh that pauperism in the 'more rural communities [was] almost nonexistent' in the seventeenth century. (25–6) [Bruchey goes on to inquire] considerations of these kinds raise the question whether the structure of colonial society was favorable to growth. How rigid were its class lines . . . [and to answer] . . . yet probably in few societies in history have the means of subsistence been so widely distributed among the mass of the people as in colonial America. (57–9)

To account for capitalist economic development in the North-east in terms essentially of these and related socio-economic characteristics, it would still be necessary to explain why and how (if at all) they permitted or generated such development in this region – and why other regions with similar characteristics in the New World or elsewhere, such as La Plata, São Paulo and other settler regions surveyed above (pp. 47-50), did not also experience the development of the north-eastern United States. Any attempt to do so reveals that the insertion, participation and function of the North-east in the expanding system of mercantile capitalism and the process of world capital accumulation was significantly different from that of other regions and that other factors, peculiar to the North-east, were also crucially determinant in its development.

Adam Smith already offered some explanations to account for the socio-economic and political differences between the North and the South and other colonies. The settlement pattern and distribution of land-ownership in the North, as well as the relatively high wage level associated with the non-wage opportunities that these offered (as Marx also observed), cannot be simply explained by the physical availability of land, since it was initially greater in the South and elsewhere. On the contrary, it was the relative *poverty* of the land and climate, as well as of course the non-existence of mines, in the North-east which explains why access to land was less foreclosed than it was in the South and elsewhere. Determinant in differentiating these regions was the possibility of extracting a profit from the land in the South – essentially through production for export – much more than in New England even in the grain regions of the Middle Atlantic States. But this profit was possible in the South, as in the Carribean, only if free access to land was limited by its monopolisation in the best areas and by further restrictions on the mobility of labour through servitude or slavery, which were not profitable in the North.

These different profit possibilities also explain, as Smith observed, the reasons for the British 'neglect' of the North relative to the 'attention' devoted by the British (and French) to the South and to the Sugar Islands in the Caribbean and by the Spanish to their mining, though not their Caribbean and other possessions. If this attention did not make the colonies 'thrive' better, as Smith remarked, it was of course because the political and economic controls and institutions of this 'attention' were designed precisely to exploit and develop the profit possibilities more efficiently – while the 'neglect' of the northern colonies left these more nearly to fend for themselves. 'British capital had little interest' in New England, observes Bruchey (49); and Nettels (in W. A. Williams, 10) argues that 'the policies that affected the Middle Colonies and New England differed materially in character and effect from the policies that were applied to the South'. The same may perhaps be said of some other 'neglected' regions of the New World which, like New England, did not then have the mode of production and the exploitative colonialties of the mining and plantation regions and which were not therefore already condemned to underdevelopment during mercantile capitalist times. But these other regions did not also share the peculiarly privileged participation of New England in mercantile capitalist development.

The North-eastern colonies came to occupy a position in the expanding world mercantile capitalist system and in the process of capital accumulation which permitted them to share in the latter as a sub-metropolis of Western Europe in the exploitation of the South, the West Indies, and indeed of Africa and indirectly of the mining regions and the Orient. This privileged position – not shared by others in the New World – must be considered as contributing crucially to the economic development of the North-east during colonial times and to its successful political policy of Independence and further development thereafter. This privileged position and role impinged on northern transport, mercantile and financial participation in southern and western export (and import) trade, the North-east's advantageous participation in the West India trade, the slave trade and indeed world trade; north-eastern manufacturing development, largely for export; and in the associated capital accumulation and concentration in northern cities.

Manufacturing already developed more in the North than in the South during colonial times, although the difference was far less than it would become in the nineteenth century. This difference has sometimes been attributed to a difference in the growth of the internal market, greater in the North than in the South, which is attributed in turn to the relatively more equal distribution of income in the North and to the South's specialisation in agricultural production for export, reliance on slave labour, etc. The question of production for the internal or external market and their relation to capitalist development and that of economic development in the United States and other settler regions in the nineteenth century are further examined inChapter 5 of this book. Here it will suffice to observe that, whatever the theoretical merit or weaknesses of this argument, colonial and especially eighteenth-century manufacturing development in the north-eastern United States was heavily dependent on the *external* export market.

In his study of *The Economic Growth of the United States 1790–1860*, Douglass North remarks, referring to 1790:

> Whatever proportion of the rural population is assumed to have been part of the domestic market, it is impossible to escape the conclusion that this market was small and not heavily concentrated, since a small fraction of the population constituted a market for commercial production. It is not surprising that the domestic demand for goods and services did not result in a rapid shift of people into the market, nor did the market exist on a scale that made possible any but household manufacturing. Had the United States of 1790 been a closed system, the possibilities for growth would have been limited indeed. (18)

The first U.S. Secretary of the Treasury, Alexander Hamilton listed a wide variety of manufactures, divided into 17 categories in his famous 1791 'Report on Manufactures'. However, in 1772 nearly one third of North American iron production had been exported (Bruchey, 22), and much manufacturing which was not directly exported was none the less indirectly dependent on the export and carrying trade:

> Most commercial manufacturing was closely articulated with the needs of foreign trade, consisting of naval stores manufactories, ropewalks, canvas and sailmaking shops, sugar and salt refineries, anchor and chain forges, cooperage establishments, lumberyards, breweries and distilleries, gistmills, blacksmiths, shoe and carpenter shops, cargo warehouses, and shipbuilding yards. (Bruchey, 22)

Of these, the last-named were of particular importance in New England's development. The British Navigation Act of 1661 had had a discernible effect on American development:

It stimulated the shipbuilding and shipping industries in New England and the Middle Colonies. It did not, however, create those industries. But the English Government drove the Dutch from the trade of English America before English shipping could meet the full needs of the colonies . . . New England shipowners could employ their American-built vessels in the trade of the whole empire. New England benefited directly from the expulsion of the Dutch from the trade of English America. (Nettels, 9–10)

It has been estimated that by the time Independence was declared in 1776, one third of the British merchant fleet had been built in the colonies (Harper, 46).

British mercantilist attempts to prohibit or even to restrict other manufacturing in the northern colonies were largely unsuccessful. The British programme to produce naval stores in the northern colonies for colonial export to Britain did not attain its objectives and rather supported American development. And the regulations controlling the shipment or transhipment of certain enumerated products of the colonial trade between the New World and the European metropolis, though they adversely affected the agricultural export regions of the Caribbean and the South, did not hinder and in some ways – even if unintentionally – aided northern development and manufacturing. Until 1764, despite the unenforced Molasses Act of 1733, this was true of the molasses trade, which importantly generated northern distilleries of rum which in turn developed into an important item or link in the whole pattern of northern overseas trade and local capital accumulation (of which more below). There is now substantial agreement, e.g., by Harper (in Schreiber, 41) with Beard and with Schlesinger (19–20) that laws against manufacturing did not adversely affect the northern colonies and that trade regulations did not seriously affect their interests before 1763. Only after the Peace of Paris of that year, after having incurred large debts in the preceding Seven Years' War but having eliminated the French threat from North America (as well as India), did the British impose new onerous revenue-generating regulations on their American colonies, which these writers and others argue interfered with the normal good business especially of the dominant merchants in the North and impelled them to an alliance with indebted southern planters and to the Declaration of Independence in 1776. (For a fuller examination of this period see my *World Accumulation 1492–1789*, Chapter 5.)

Thus, yeoman 'subsistence' farming and manufacturing for the 'internal' or domestic market was by no means the principal motor of northern development or the significant source of its capital accumulation in the colonial period. On the contrary, as Samuelsson observes,

> in New England one had to go outside agriculture to attain wealth, or indeed even a slightly above-average livelihood. The fur trade, fishing, maritime carrying and the slave trade soon became the most important branches of economic life. And these were occupations in which, because they yielded larger profits than could be had from other trades, a surplus was created that could be made available for new and more ambitious projects. (114)

Beyond the increasing participation of northern coastwide and even overseas shipping, merchandising, and financing in the commerce with the staple export economy of the South, the North became an ever more essential link in the colonial and slave trade that made profitable production of sugar possible in the West Indies (including the French ones). This participation in the mercantile capitalist system in turn became an essential factor in capital accumulation and capitalist development in the North itself.

> His Majesty's Collonys in these [West Indian] parts cannot in tyme of peace prosper, nor in time of War subsist, without a correspondence with the people of New England. (William Lord Willoughby to the Privy Council, 18 December 1667, quoted in Harlow, 268).

The production of sugar for European consumption and capital accumulation by the Caribbean plantation economy meant that:

> there is no island the British possess in the West Indies that is capable of subsistence without the assistance of the [American] Continent, for to them we transport their bread, drink and all the necessaryes of humane life, their cattle and horses for cultivating their plantations, lumber and staves of all sorts to make casks for their rumm sugar and molasses, without which they could have none, ships to transport their goods to the European markets,

nay, in short, the very houses they inhabitt are carried over in frames, together with shingles that cover them, in so much that their being, much more their well being, depends almost entirely upon the Continent. (Vetch in 1708, quoted in Williams, 111)

Though the North American producers and merchants did not replace the British in the Caribbean trade, their productive capacity, lower transportation costs and, particularly in time of war, their access to the West Indian sugar islands (English, French, and when the Spanish increased production at the end of the eighteenth century the latter as well) gave the North Americans an important competitive advantage – and made their own development dependent on this external market:

> The only articles produced in the colony [Rhode Island] suitable for remittance to Europe consists of . . . the whole amounting to about £5000 per annum . . . all of which bears but a very inconsiderable proportion of the debt contracted for British goods. It can therefore be nothing but commerce which enables us to pay it. As there is no commodity in the colony suitable for the European market, but the few afore-mentioned; and as the other goods raised for exportation, will answer no market but in the West Indies, it necessarily follows that the trade thither must be the foundation of all our commerce; and it is undoubtedly true, that solely from the prosecution of this trade with other branches that are pursued in consequence of it, arises the ability to pay for such quantities of British goods. (Remonstrance to the Board of Trade, passed by the Rhode Island Legislature, 24, January 1764, in Stavarianos, ed., 118)

Not just Rhode Island, but all the North-east and particularly New England were heavily dependent on the trade with the West Indies and the market that their mode of production generated:

> In 1770 the continental colonies sent to the West Indies nearly one-third of their exports of dried fish and almost all their pickled fish; seven-eights of their oats, seven-tenths of their corn, almost all their peas and beans, half their flour, all their butter and cheese, over one-quarter of their rice, almost all their onions; five sixths of their pine, oak and cedar boards, over half their staves,

nearly all their hoops; all their horses, sheep, hogs and poultry; almost all their soap and candles. As Professor Pitman has told us, 'It was the wealth accumulated from the West Indian trade which more than anything else underlay the prosperity and civilization of New England and the Middle Colonies.' (Williams, 108)

Moreover, New England capital accumulation was substantially based on its own corner of the larger triangular trade (examined in Chapter 2 above and in my *World Accumulation 1492–1789*).

By the middle of the eighteenth century the New England slave trade was three-cornered, like the Liverpool trade, but it was simpler and even more symmetrical. Essentially it was based on three commodities: rum, slaves and molasses. At its home port the vessel would take on a cargo consisting chiefly or entirely of rum . . . In Africa the rum would be exchanged for as many slaves as it would buy, often at the rate of two hundred gallons per slave. The black cargo would be sold to the West Indies, and part of the proceeds invested in molasses, usually purchased in the French or Spanish Islands, where it was cheaper. On the final leg of the voyage, the vessel would carry the molasses back to New England, to be distilled into more rum, to buy more slaves. (Mannix, 159–60).

Benjamin Franklin, testifying to a committee of the British House of Commons in 1766, explained further how his Pennsylvania could import £500,000 worth of goods from Britain each year while exporting only £40,000 to her, as he answered the question put to him 'How then do you pay the balance?' Franklin replied:

The balance is paid by our produce carried to the West Indies, and sold in our own islands, or to the French, Spaniards, Danes and Dutch; by the same carried to the other colonies in North-America, as to New England, Nova Scotia, Newfoundland, Carolina and Georgia, by the same carried to different parts of Europe, as Spain, Portugal and Italy. In all which places we receive either money, bills of exchange, or commodities that suit for remittance to Britain; which together with all the profits on the industry of our merchants and mariners, arising in those circuitous voyages, and the freights made by their ships, center finally in Britain, to discharge the balance, and pay for British manufactures continually used in the province, or sold to foreigners by our traders. (quoted in Faulkner, 80–1).

John Adams, one of the fathers of North American independence and freedom, noted the divine wisdom and benevolence of this whole mercantile capitalist system and development:

> The commerce of the West Indian Islands is part of the American system of commerce. They can neither do without us, nor we without them. The Creator has placed us upon the globe in such a situation that we have occasion for each other. (quoted in Williams, 121)

We may observe that the Creator also took good care to place on the same globe the black labour force, which both the American and the Caribbean (as well as the European) capitalists had occasion for and without which neither could have done as they did: contribute to the development of England and New England and to the underdevelopment of most of the New World and Africa, and later of Asia as well.

The importance of the triangular trade, at least as far as the routing of particular ships was concerned, has, however, been recently challenged by G. M. Walton ('New Evidence on Colonial Commerce'), who argues that the vast bulk of shipping engaged in simple shuttle voyages between two ports. Moreover, Walton belittles the importance of the North American direct trade with Africa, which he claims amounted to less than 1 per cent of the total.

On the other hand, James F. Shepherd and G. M. Walton emphasise the importance of invisible and especially shipping earnings for the North American colonies:

> Historians have generally recognized that 'invisible' earnings were probably important in paying for the deficits in the British trade [of North America] . . . Shipping earnings were unquestionably the largest source of earnings from the sale of services for the colonies . . . When the relatively large 'invisible' earnings are considered, the overall deficits in the commodity trade of New England and the middle colonies are substantially reduced, and the balances of the southern colonies are transformed into surpluses. The importance of the West Indian and

southern European trades to the New England and middle colonies is apparent . . . From 1768 through 1772, shipping earnings rank second only to tobacco [and are followed by bread and flour, rice, fish and indigo in that order]. The sale of shipping services to overseas buyers was a major part of colonial market activity, particularly that of New England which earned 54 per cent of all colonial shipping earnings. This fact has frequently been overlooked, or at least not properly stressed, by economic historians . . . Capital inflows into New England and the southern colonies were small . . . a growing capital stock in these colonies would have been due almost entirely to colonial saving and not to foreign investment. (Shepherd and Walton, 234, 235, 255–6, 258, 261)

It was not in this sense that the colonial situation of the North American colonies was beneficial to their economic development. But neither was their accumulation of capital, particularly in New England, simply derived from the expansion of the internal market or the effective demand and savings on yeoman farmers. It was derived from these colonies' particular place and participation in the colonial world!

G. Epilogue – Delayed by Two Centuries

The commerce of the British Northern Colonies in America, is so peculiarly circumstanced, and from permanent causes, so perplexed and embarrassed, that it is a business of great difficulty to investigate it, and put it in any tolerable point of light, so that it may be understood; this perhaps may be the cause why so little hath been attempted, and still less effected, in this intricate but very interesting enquiry.

That which most particularly and unhappily distinguishes most of these Northern British Colonies from all others, either British or any other nation, is, that the soil and climate of them is incapable of producing almost anything which will serve to send directly home to the Mother Country. Yet notwithstanding this fatal disadvantage, their situation and circumstances are such, as to be obliged to take off, and consume greater quantities of British Manufactures, than any other Colonies; their long cold winters call for much clothing, but their deep and lasting snows make it impossible to keep sheep, and thereby procure wool to supply that demand. Again, the same long winters prevent the labour of slaves being of any advantage in the Colonies; this, together with almost endless countries lying back yet to be settled with inhabitants, makes hands so scarce, and labour so dear, that no kind of manufactures can be set up and supported in these Colonies: and thus it appears on one hand, that the inhabitants are obliged by necessity to take great quantities of goods from the Mother Country; so on the other, it is no less evident that nature hath denied them the means of returning anything directly thither to pay for those goods.

When these singular circumstances are fully known, and duly considered, it will easily be found what the cause is, that a much greater number of ships and smaller vessels are employed by the people of these Colonies, than of any others in the world: unable to make remittances in a direct way they are obliged to do it by a circuity of commerce unpractised by and unnecessary in any other Colony. The commodities shipped off by them are generally of such a nature, that they must be consumed in the country where first sold, and will not bear to be reshipped from thence to any other; from hence it happens that no one market will take off any great quantity; this obliges these people to look out for markets in every part of the world within their reach, where they can sell their goods for any tolerable price, and procure such things in return, as may serve immediately, or by severale commercial exchanges, to make a remittance home. ('An Essay on the Trade of Northern Colonies of Great Britain in North America' (1764), cited in Callender, 51–2)

4 The Industrial Revolution and Pax Britannica, 1770—1870

The industrial revolution, first in Britain and later in other metropolitan countries, of course involved far-reaching transformations of the metropolitan economy, polity, society and culture that are beyond our scope. The associated technological revolution and innovation, which has received so much attention, cannot be realistically understood in isolation from this process of capital accumulation and market expansion. 'Whatever the British advance was due to, it was not scientific and technological superiority', notes Hobsbawm (47); and it is at least symbolic that, as Williams (102–3) recalls, 'it was the capital accumulated in the West Indian trade that financed James Watt and the steam engine. Boulton and Watt received advances from Lowe, Vere, Williams and Jennings', and Boulton wrote Watt, 'Lowe, Vere and Company may yet be saved, if ye West Indian fleet arrives safe from ye French fleet . . . as many of their securities depend on it.'

An adequate explanation of the internal dynamics of metropolitan transformation within the context of world capitalist development remains a prerequisite for any really adequate analysis of both the 'external' and the 'internal' dynamics of the development of underdevelopment in the colonies. But an extensive examination of the concomitant economic, social and political transformation of the European (and later other) metropolitan economies is beyond the scope of this book (but see my *World Accumulation 1492–1789*). Therefore, we shall have to limit our present inquiry into a brief examination (as distinct from analysis) of certain changes in the metropolitan economy that were closely associated with its relation to the colonies, so that we may then pursue our inquiry into the resultant transformations in the mode of production and exchange relations of the colonies during the second and third stages of world capitalist development. Since the essential internal dynamics of the metropolis is beyond our scope, we may for purposes of expository convenience review in turn the colonial contribution to metropolitan capital accumulation and the importance of the colonial market in the early phases of the industrial revolution, some changes in metropolitan political economic structure and policy – especially free trade – related to the industrial revolution, the most important resulting changes in the international division of labour and relations of exchange, and finally the concomitant changes in the economic and political structure of the colonies (and North America) during the second stage of world capitalist development until the mid-nineteenth century.

1. Metropolitan Capital Accumulation and Industrial Revolution in Europe

Beyond the already quoted observations by Marx and others, the contribution (hardly through 'equal' or 'equivalent' exchange) by the colonies to capital accumulation, market expansion and capitalist development is recognised by the *Cambridge Economic History of Europe*:

> The third group of structural changes which are inevitably associated with industrialization and growth is concerned with the nation's relationship with the rest of the world. . . . The close integration of the international economy is paralleled by a corresponding integration at the national level. This generally involves an increase in the share of incomes from foreign trade in the total national income . . . The British case is the classic prototype of an industrial revolution based on overseas trade. Gregory King's estimate for 1688 put English exports at 5 or 6 per cent of the value of national income. A century later the proportion had risen to 15 per cent. Roughly another century later they had reached an all-time peak of about 36 per cent in the early 1880's. The growth of English commerce in the eighteenth century provided a large part of the accumulated wealth necessary to finance nascent industry in the last quarter of the century. The opportunity to buy raw materials and sell finished products in foreign markets vastly extended the range of economic opportunitity open to British industry . . . (IV, 51)

The role of the West Indies in this process (as quoted from Williams and Saul in the discussion of 'trade triangles' in Chapter 2, pp. 14–17) was already attested to even by Adam Smith, who so vehemently denounced and combatted this colonial trade: 'The profits of a sugar plantation in any of our West Indian colonies are generally much greater than those of any other cultivation that is known either in Europe or America' (Smith, 366). Williams has examined the matter further and, beyond the already cited observations about the triangular trade, concludes:

> The profits obtained provided one of the main streams of that accumulation of capital in England which financed the Industrial Revolution . . . The development of the triangular trade and of shipping and shipbuilding led to the growth of the great seaport towns. Bristol, Liverpool and Glasgow occupied, as seaport and trading centers, the position in the age of trade that Manchester, Birmingham and Sheffield occupied later in the age of industry . . . What the West Indian trade did for Bristol, the slave trade did for Liverpool . . . What the building of ships for the transport of slaves did for the eighteenth century Liverpool, the manufacture of cotton goods for the purchase of slaves did for eighteenth century Manchester. The first stimulus to the growth of cotton monopolies came from the African and West Indian markets . . . It was this tremendous dependence on the triangular trade that made Manchester. (52, 60, 68).

But in the second half of the eighteenth century, the capital contribution of the East Indian trade, and particularly of India itself, also increased quantitatively and qualitatively. The definitive victory of the British against the Indians at the Battle of Plassey in 1757, the displacement of the French after the Peace Treaty of 1763, and the political (perhaps more than economic) shock of American Independence after 1776 were contributing, if not determinant, factors in increasingly shifting (to use Adam Smith's words) the 'attention' of the British from one 'extremity' of the world to another. In this regard Brooks Adams observed: 'Very soon after Plassey the Bengal Plunder began to arrive in London, and the effect appears to have been instantaneous, for all authorities agree that the "industrial revolution", the event that has divided the nineteenth century from all antecedent time, began with the year

1760 . . . At once, in 1759, the bank [of England] issued £10 and £15 notes [for the first time]' (quoted in Mandel, 444).

The contribution of colonial exploitation to the process of world capital accumulation in its first three-centuries-long stage and its concentration in the European metropolis is estimated and summarised by Mandel:

> It can be stated unhesitatingly that the contribution made by this stolen capital was decisive for the accumulation of the commercial and money capital which, between 1500 and 1750, created the conditions which proved propitious for the industrial revolution. It is difficult to calculate the total amount involved, but if one takes into account only the most substantial contributions these add up to a staggering sum . . . The total amount comes to over a billion pounds sterling, or more than the capital of all the industrial enterprises operated by steam which existed in Europe around 1800 . . . It can be concluded without exaggeration that for the period 1760–1780 the profits from India and the West Indies alone *more than doubled* the accumulation money available for rising industry [in Britain]. (Mandel, 1970, 443–5, emphasis in original. On the same topic see, also, Mandel, 1968).

The other side of the question is posed and answered rather equivocally by David Landes in his essay devoted to 'Technological Change and Industrial Development in Western Europe, 1750–1914' and contributed to the *Cambridge Economic History of Europe*: 'How much of the increase in demand and the trend toward mass production of cheaper articles is to be attributed to the expansion of home as against foreign markets is probably impossible to say.' But Landes continues on the same page, 'One may perhaps attempt this kind of comparison for the wool industry: at the end of the seventeenth century English exports of wool cloth probably accounted for upwards of 30 per cent of the output of the industry; by 1740, the proportion had apparently risen, possibly to over half, and in 1771–2, something under a half. In this important branch, then, the major impetus seems to have come from the export trade, and the most active exporting area in the industry . . . Yet the answer is not so simple . . .' (*Cambridge* VI, Part I, 287–8). But later Landes continues, 'The commercial frontier of Britain lay overseas – in America, Africa, south and east Asia. The first was by far the most important: the West Indies and mainland colonies together bought 10 per cent of English domestic exports in 1700–1, 37 per cent in 1772–3, about 57 per cent in 1797–8. Wool had played a big part in these gains: the sale of cloth in the new Atlantic market (America and Africa) grew sixfold from the beginning of the century to the eve of the American Revolution. Now it was cotton's turn . . .' (ibid., 313–14).

For the earlier part of the period, Adam Smith (as quoted above) and Mantoux had already stressed the importance of foreign trade and markets; and Hobsbawm (52) summarises his observations by suggesting that 'the cotton industry was thus launched, like a glider, by the pull of the colonial trade to which it was attached.' But perhaps the most important recent research into the question is that of Deane and Cole (who also contributed the opening chapter on 'The Growth of National Incomes' to the above cited Vol. VI of the *Cambridge Economic History of Europe*) on *British Economic Growth 1688–1959*. Their findings may be briefly summarised in tabular form (Deane and Cole, 78, reproduced for other years as well in Palloix 1969a, 186):

Years	Export Industries	Internal Market Industries	Agricultural Production	National Income
1700	100	100	100	100
1760	222	114	115	147
1780	246	123	126	167
1800	544	152	143	251

On the basis of these and other data Palloix concludes:

One of the fundamental lessons to be drawn from these facts is the marked acceleration of the rate of growth from 1780 to 1800 – 4.6% for exports, 2.1% for national product – at a time when 70% of British exports went to the third world, defined here as the territories that were politically and economically dominated. . . . We may note . . . for the period 1780–1800 the particularly high annual growth rate of cotton goods (14.1%), iron and steel (5.1%), and other metal working (5% on the average). Recourse only to the internal – at that time agricultural – market would not have allowed such a development of the productive forces. This constraint imposed by the internal market is visible in Table 3 [partially reproduced above] where the growth rate of agricultural production effectively limits the growth rate of industries working only for the internal market. (Palloix 1969b, 183)

2. Bourgeois Industrial Policy and the New International Division of Labour

Of particular importance for our analysis of underdevelopment are the changes in metropolitan economic policy – and political ideology to justify them – that resulted from the ever more victorious economic/political struggle of the growing industrial interests against the relatively declining agricultural and mercantile ones that had given them their birth and nurtured them to adulthood. Though Britain had been re-exporting Asian cotton textiles – the famous calicoes – for a long time, these cottons were prohibited in England itself to protect the woollen goods industry and the owners of 'enclosed' lands that supplied its raw material. But in 1774, two years before the publication of Adam Smith's book, the prohibition was repealed. This was a significant step, in representation of the growing new industrial interests, in the direction that culminated in the free trade policy. In 1807 important blows were struck against the sacrosanct trinity of the West Indian Planter Class, the East India Company, and the slave traders: the British slave trade was formally forbidden and the monopoly privileges of the East Indian Company were severely curtailed. In 1846 came the repeal of the Corn Laws, that protected British landowners at the expense of the new industrialists; and 1849 witnessed the final blow against the Navigation Acts of the seventeenth century that had done so much to promote British capital accumulation and protect British capitalist development in its infancy. British industrialists had won the battle to institute free trade – and to enshrine it as a natural scientific law. The explanation was advanced by two German contemporaries: Friedrich List and Karl Marx. A realistic American contemporary President, Ulysses S. Grant, later ratified their judgement and predicted that, as soon as it was ready, his own country would switch from protection to free trade as well.

In his "Discourse on Free Trade" Marx said in 1848:

We are told, for example, that free trade will give rise to an international division of labour that will assign each country a production that is in harmony with its natural advantages. You may think, Gentlemen, that the production of coffee and sugar is the natural destiny of the West Indies. Two centuries earlier, nature, which is unaware of commerce, had not placed either coffee trees or sugar cane there. And perhaps a half-century will not pass, and you will no longer find either coffee or sugar there, given that the East Indies have already, by their lower cost production, victoriously combated this supposed natural destiny of the West Indies. And these West Indies with their natural gifts are already as heavy a burden for the English as the weavers of Dacca, who had also been destined to weave by hand since the beginning of time. There is one more thing that should never be lost sight of, and that is even when everything has become a monopoly, today there are also some branches of industry that dominate all the others and that assure to the people that most exploit them *the empire* on the market of the universe. Thus it is that in international trade cotton alone has a greater commercial value than all the other raw materials used for the fabrication of clothing put together. And it is really ridiculous to see the free traders make some specialities in each industrial branch stand out to put them in the balance with the goods of common usage that are produced more cheaply in the countries where industry is the most developed. If the free traders cannot understand how one country can enrich itself at the expense of another, we should not be surprised, since these same gentlemen do not want to understand either that within a country one class can enrich itself at the expense of another. (*The Misery of Philosophy*, translated from French edition, 1950)

The second (and third) stages of world capital accumulation and capitalist development involved a vast expansion of world trade, important changes in the international division of labour, and the most far-reaching as well as deep-going changes in the modes of production in both the metropolis and Asia, Africa and Latin America. According to Ferrer (83), international trade had tripled between 1700 and 1820, quintupled between 1820 and 1870 and soared still more later. Woytinsky estimates world exports at US$ 500 to 600 million in 1820, about $ 5000 million in 1867–68, about $ 20,000 million in 1913, and $ 35,000 million in 1929 before the world depression. 'The growth of world trade slowed down in the 1870's and 1880's but quickened again at the end of the century and, especially, after 1900. The annual increase averaged 1.3 per cent in 1865–1900 and 5.0 per cent from 1805 to 1912–13. The uneven growth of the value of world trade was due partly to fluctuations in prices . . . With rough correction for changes in prices, where the volume of world trade in 1913 equals 100, the index numbers for 1867–68 are 20–25 and for 1880, 35–40' (Woytinsky, 38–9). But the value of world trade, as well as its fluctuation, as measured in these data is due not only to 'fluctuations' of prices but to the kind of prices as well. In so far as 'world market' prices undervalue the exports of the colonial primary goods producers and overvalue the metropolitan manufactured exports, and thus permit unequal exchange based on equal values (as argued in Chapter 5), the growth in the real value of world trade is different from the probably greater than its measure in terms of world market prices.

Foreign trade data for the nineteenth century's principal trading country, Britain, are more exact, albeit equally limited by their reference to market prices as distinct from real values. According to Schlote (42–3), British foreign trade grew approximately 1.8 per cent per annum between 1700 and 1800 but 3.4 per cent per annum between 1800 and 1913. But the growth rate was not even. Between 1781 and 1801, imports increased 2.5 times, domestic exports 2.8 times and re-exports 3.4 times (*Cambridge* VI, 1, 8). For the half-century 1825–70 the growth rate averaged 4 per cent per annum and between 1840 and 1860 it reached 5 per cent per year (Schlote, 42–3).

The fundamental changes in the international division of labour and the transformation of the modes of production in Asia, Africa and Latin America, associated with this expansion of world trade, require and receive much closer attention below. In brief, the change in the international division of labour was, as already noted above, partly summarised by Woytinsky, who notes the earlier beginning of this change but emphasises its nineteenth-century acceleration: '. . . the emphasis shifted from the search for foreign products . . . to the search for outlets for domestic manufactures . . . Europe began to export manufactured goods, mainly textiles (at first), in exchange for tropical and semitropical products supplied by colonial plantations' (Woytinsky, 8). But this change in the division of labour also involved important changes in the relationships of exchange between the trading 'partners': changes in the terms of trade (first against Britain and then against the colonies) and the passage, in Mandel's above-quoted words, from unequal exchange on the basis of unequal values, through equal change on the basis of unequal values, through equal exchange on the basis of equal values, to unequal exchange on the basis of equal values. These same shifts in turn are related to the monopoly capitalist and imperialist transformation of the metropolitan economy and its increasing supplement of international trade by foreign investment, the development of its overseas settler societies, and the transformation of the modes of production – the mode of producing underdevelopment – in Asia, Africa and Latin America, without which this world capitalist development could not have occurred as it did.

None the less, particularly during the second stage of this world capital accumulation and capitalist development, the same transformations did not everywhere take place simultaneously. On the contrary, the prior transformation of some regions (and the changes of its relations with third regions) conditioned and accelerated the subsequent similar transformation of a second set of regions. The industrial revolution in Britain preceeded that of Continental Europe and the United States. The growth of raw materials exports from Latin America at the end of the eighteenth century, and the simultaneous increase in imports of manufactures as well as the resulting destruction of Latin American manufacturing for local and regional markets occurred at a time when India was still exporting large quantities of textiles *and was achieved in part by British re-export of these Oriental textiles to Latin America* – and to Africa, where they paid for slaves used to increase raw materials export production in the Americas – (see quote from the Spanish Viceroy in Mexico, p. 83 below). On the other hand, the displacement of Spain and France by Britain during this period and its own industrial development then led to the de-industrialisation of India and its transformation into an importer of manufactures and then an exporter of raw materials in the first half of the nineteenth century. At the same time Latin America – and North America as well – experienced a relative respite from the onslaught of British textiles and of course of the Oriental textiles that the British had previously re-exported but were now destroying. The growth of the British cotton textile industry, largely at the expense of the Indian one (as we will observe below), during the first half of the nineteenth century in turn stimulated (or permitted?) the development of the iron, steel and machinery industries in Britain.

This metropolitan economic development evoked the renewed metropolitan offensive in the second half of the nineteenth century, whose associated transformation of the mode of production in the colonial raw materials suppliers definitively made impossible any contemporary or future self-generated and self-sustaining economic development within the capitalist mode of production in Latin America, Asia, the Middle East, and Africa.

3. North America

Though a theoretical historical analysis of North America is beyond our scope, we may briefly review some aspects of its experience during this period that are particularly relevant to our inquiry into underdevelopment in other parts of America and elsewhere. According to Bruchey (86–7), 'we may summarize this brief survey of scholarly viewpoints concerning industrialization and economic growth in the pre-Civil War period by pointing out that Martin would emphasize the 1850's, Gallman the 1840's, North the 1830's, and Fogel the 1820's. But why stop here? . . . The importance of manufactures at the earlier date is emphasized by Secretary of the Treasury Albert Gallatin's 1810 Report on Manufactures . . .' North (53) summarises the earlier part of the period: 'Contemporary accounts amply attest to the prosperity of the period. It is logically ascribable to: (1) the importance of the export sector in the total economy; (2) the five-fold (or more) expansion of this sector during the period; (3) the equally large increase in imports for consumption at favourable import prices; (4) the expansion in the domestic economy induced by the increase in income from the export sector.' North goes on to point out that 'throughout the whole period the secular movement of the terms of trade became increasingly favourable' (70) and 'there was increased capital inflow when the terms of trade became more favourable and decreased inflow or actual outflow when they became relatively less favourable' (94).

Manufactures were a slightly declining percentage of exports in the 1830's and thereafter showed a modest gain. Cotton, of course, dominated the export trade. It constituted 39 per cent of the value of exports from 1816 to 1820, and increased to 63 per cent of total export values from 1836 to 1840. Thereafter it dropped somewhat, but the level continued high – over half of the value of exports for the remaining years to the Civil War . . . After exports, the next most important credit in the balance of payments was shipping earnings . . . The funds that immigrants brought with them were an important credit in the last fifteen years of the period under study, when the first great wave of immigration occurred. (North, 75–7)

As all students of U.S. history have noted, these developments were by no means uniform. They were marked by important regional differences – and relationships. Bruchey (159) summarises:

There did tend to develop a marked degree of regional specialization, with the Northwest concentrating its resources on the production of foodstuffs (largely on family farms), Southwest on cotton (dominantly on slave plantations), and Northeast on manufacturing. Income received from exports of cotton, mainly via New York City, played a leading part in making regional interdependence possible. This income enabled the South to pay Northeast for its various marketing services and for manufactured goods, and it enabled that region also to pay the West for foodstuffs exported to the South; finally, it permitted the West to pay the Northeast for manufactured goods. The great increase in population, the settlement of the West, the phenomenal improvements in transportation, and increases in incomes per capita had made possible a territorial specialization which raised to new levels of efficiency the interdependent working of the economy as a whole.

But this 'efficiency' of 'the economy as a whole', to say nothing of the place of its slave-produced cotton exports in British textile and economic development, did not generate economic development for all regions alike. We may briefly examine the experience of the North-east and the South in turn. As to the former (including the Middle Atlantic states) 'the region as a whole shifted from commerce and trade to become a manufacturing region between 1815 and 1860', and the North-east accounted for 75 per cent and 71 per cent of U.S. manufacturing by 1850 and 1860 respectively, with textiles playing the leading role (North, 156, 159–60). In New England, as in England itself, textile manufacturing stimulated 'backward linkages' into the production of textile machinery, and from there to machine building, railroads, iron and steel and heavy industry in general (North 162). North's and others' attempts to explain this development are examined in our discussion of 'On Developing the Internal Market' in Chapter 5, Section H.

Without aspiring to an adequate analysis of northern development and southern underdevelopment in the United States, it is necessary to add a few words on the *political* economy associated with these developments. In his epilogue, Bruchey notes,

> if growth depended on industrialization, the latter depended on the national market, and a national market upon large capital sums for improved transportation. If these are valid assessments, I cannot see how a place of central importance in American economic growth can be denied the role of government, because of its contribution to the formation of a national market and the national credit. . . . This is one reason I have emphasized the 'American Revolution' which permitted the development of an independent national state that could further national capitalist development.' (Bruchey 1965, 213)

But the importance and role of the achievement and use of state power by the American, and particularly North-eastern, bourgeoisie – Bruchey would agree – goes beyond that. Indeed, the very achievement of that state power through the Revolution and its consolidation after the War of 1812 against Britain were already related to, if not determined by, peculiarities of the pre-revolutionary mode of production and class structure and the exploitation of temporary opportunities for international political manoeuvres and gains from foreign trade during the Napoleonic era that were not equally present or available in other parts of the New World. Moreover, the 'efficient' relationship between Northern finance, commerce and manufacturing, Southern cotton, and Western agriculture which permitted the development of the North at the expense of the underdevelopment of the South itself generated a growing crisis as a result of the development of northern productive forces: the Civil War. The immediate cause of this war between the manufacturing North and the cotton South was which of the two would prevail in their competitive expansion into the West. The victory of the North, albeit hard-won, must be attributed to the greater economic and particularly industrial power that it had already been able to develop. And this military victory opened the way to the continued, or renewed, westward expansion and development of industrial capitalism in the United States. The long-standing 'tariff question' between the protectionist North and the free-trade South (and its British ally) was definitively answered in favour of nationalist industrial development protected by increasingly high tariffs. And 'the South did not become less, but more heavily dependent on outside capital . . . it became even more a colony of the North than it had been before the Civil War' (Douglas Dowd, 1956, in Woodman, ed., 251).

4. Latin America

In Latin America the contemporary historical development was far different, although the productive forces and interests in conflict were not so different – but with their relative economic and political power in opposite proportions to those of North America. In 1824 the British Foreign Secretary Canning wrote, 'The nail is driven. Spanish America is free, and if we do not mismanage our affairs sadly she is English.' Four years later, the Liberator of Latin America, Simon Bolivar, prophesied, 'the United States seem destined by providence to plague [Latin] America with misery in the name of liberty.' The first statement was not merely a vain hope, or the second an idle threat. Both Canning and Bolivar were giving expression to the historical process that, if not providence, world capitalist development held in destiny for Latin America, where with regional variations and in temporal sequence both prophecies were to be realised in the nineteenth and twentieth centuries. Moreover, the very social group that had fought for Latin America's formal political independence from Spain and Portugal, and their economic-social-political-ideological descendants of later generations, were for very good reasons of economic self-interest to be the willing instruments of the consolidation of the development of underdevelopment in Latin America that these prophesies implied.

During the eighteenth century, British, and to a lesser degree French, manufacturing development had increasingly displaced Spanish (and Portuguese) exports and local manufactures in Latin America. This penetration was achieved in part through contraband trade, in part through legal trade privileges exacted from the Iberian countries, and in part through a combination of both. The economic and political renaissance of Spain under the

Bourbons and the growing threat and loss of revenue represented by British trade prompted the Spaniards to liberalise the trade privileges of their colonies, especially after 1778, and to extend these still further to Britain's benefit during the wars with France. These developments had far-reaching effects on manufacturing and raw materials production in Latin America at the end of the eighteenth century. The contemporary Spanish Viceroy in New Spain (Mexico) recorded both in 1794:

> Even without any help, and without any direct protection of the government, a certain kind of manufactures, principally cotton textiles, have advanced too much and to a degree that elicits admiration. Coarse wool also provides raw materials for many factories . . . It is very difficult to prohibit the major part of the things that are made in these kingdoms . . . The only way to destroy the factories of the kingdom is that the same or equivalent goods come from Europe at lower prices. This is what has happened . . . The decadence of this commerce was very natural in the changes that have occurred, the progress that the European factories have had and the lower price that the Asiatic textiles generally fetch . . . It turns out that since the year [17]89 the textiles and goods that have been introduced have constantly risen. (Revilla Gigedo, 191–2, 200, 203)

It may be observed in passing that the Viceroy made special mention of the Indian textiles re-exported to Mexico by Britain, which he found increasingly replaced by British-produced goods, although some modern researchers think that at that time even the import of Asian textiles was still rising (e.g. Florescano). The Chilean historian Hernán Ramírez observes, 'it is all important to emphasize that the [same] phenomenon analyzed [by himself for the case of Chile] appeared in various [Latin] American countries. "Trade liberalization," writes the Peruvian historian Deustua Pimentel, "brought with it the destruction of the new flourishing factories by completely overwhelming the [Latin] American markets with merchandise" . . . Referring to the situation that arose in the River Plate provinces, Ricardo Levene notes: "In fact it was the trade initiated by the regulations of 1778 that was the cause of the decline of the first national industries."' (Ramírez, 85)

In his same 1794 report, the Viceroy in Mexico also noted the complementary changes in the production and export of raw materials:

> Far from having declined, in the years of trade liberalization there has been a considerable increase in the quantity of goods imported as well as in the agricultural and other products exported in turn . . . [which] have almost tripled . . . In recent years the output of the mines has grown considerably . . . The causes of this increase are not that there have been greater bonanzas or better ores; it is due principally to the greater number of people working in the mines . . . Many earlier merchants . . . to make greater profits, turned [their capital] to agriculture and mining. (Revilla Gigedo, 198, 202, 205, 209, 210)

This relative shift in production from manufactures to raw materials for export from Latin America at the end of the eighteenth century, that is before Independence, had far-reaching economic and political consequences and indeed was determinant in promoting the political movement for Independence and in channelling its post-Independence economies in a particular direction: still greater expansion of raw materials production for export. The major agricultural and mining producers and exporters were economically and politically fortified by the trade liberalisation before the turn of the nineteenth century and their appetite was whetted by this development while their annoyance grew with the remaining Spanish interference in and toll-taking from their business. These producers and merchants became the principal promoters and financers of the political movement for Independence from Spain in order to achieve state power and to be free to expand the raw materials export business – and thereby to increase Latin American economic dependence on the European, albeit now British, metropolis still more. (See Vitale, Kaplan, Halperin Donghi, and Frank 1972.)

None the less, as the history of Argentina in particular clearly shows, this further transformation of Latin America into raw materials export economies was not instantaneous, automatic or politically easy, despite the British Foreign Secretary's desires and prediction. For in the words of Guizot to the French Parliament, 'there are two big parties in South America, the European party and the American party. The European party, which is smaller, includes the most enlightened men, those most familiarized with the ideas of European civilization. The other party, which is more tied to the soil and impregnated with purely American ideas, is that of the countryside [provinces]. The party wishes that the society develop by itself, in its own way, without loans, without relations with Europe . . .' (quoted in Astesano, 15). Sarmiento, a contemporary Argentinian statesman, and an evidently enlightened member of the 'European' party, summarised the conflict still more succinctly if no less graphically (at least in so far as his own ideology was concerned): it was a question of 'civilisation' or 'barbarism'. The Latin 'Americans' or 'barbarians' from the provinces were those who sought to defend and develop the still remaining manufacturing industry and to promote Latin America's own development without the loans and other subordinating dependency relations with Europe, which the Europeans regarded as 'enlightened' and which their Latin American economic partners and political allies among the raw materials export production interests perceived as the essence of 'civilization'. While Britain was systematically de-industrialising India, these rival economic and political forces still had several decades to fight this and other issues out in a series of bloody civil wars. In distinction to the United States, in Latin America these civil wars always ended with the final victory of the stronger of the two parties, which – thanks to the prior development of the Latin American raw materials productive forces and interests and then the development of metropolitan manufacturing – always turned out to be the raw materials producers and exporters.

In consequence, these industrial efforts were all doomed to subsequent annihilation by the political-military and economic onslaught of the export-oriented interests and their metropolitan allies. This happened for instance in Mexico, where the most modern textile machinery was installed even in an area without previous industrial experience; in the manufacturing centres of Antioquia in Colombia and the inland cities of Mendoza, Tucuman and others in Argentina (as recalled by Artesano and Rosa, for instance); and most particularly the Bismarckian or Japanese national development efforts of landlocked Paraguay, whose development of national industry and a railroad for internal use was financed by national capital and accompanied by near universal primary education, as reported by Box and Cardoso.

All these Latin American national development efforts of the second third of the nineteenth century were then replaced by the underdevelopment policies of the export interests and Great Britain, foremost among which was the policy of free trade.

Thus, though many Latin Americans knew that free trade would accelerate the development of underdevelopment, as is evidenced by many parliamentary debates and documents such as the Mexican *Brief in Favour of Spinners and Weavers*, the primary products producers and exporters imposed free trade because it was in their interest as Ferrer shows for Argentina: 'The merchants and livestock owners, who were the dynamic forces in the development of the Litoral, were chiefly interested in the expansion of exports. Free trade thus became the philosophy and practical policy of these groups . . . Free exports also meant freedom to import' (Ferrer, 56). Since these exporters earned sterling or dollars, it was, as Ferrer argues, equally in their interest to supplement their free trade policy with the underdevelopment policy of repeated national currency devaluations, which gave them more purchasing power at home for the foreign exchange they earned, while rendering imports more expensive for others, and thus regressively redistributing national income in their favour and restricting the internal market still more, to accelerate the development of underdevelopment still further.

In Latin American, then, the first part of this (second) 'industrial' stage of world capital accumulation and capitalist development gave rise to a quantitative decrease in manufacturing and a quantitative increase in export raw materials production. Though these did not involve an immediate qualitative transformation of the modes of production, in combination with the political crisis in the European metropolis they led to the formal independence of Brazil and of virtually all Spanish colonies in the Americas (except Cuba and Puerto Rico). During the second part of this second stage of world capitalist development in the first half of the nineteenth century, the struggle for state power and its use to promote either nationalist industrialisation policies or further expansion of the raw materials export sector in Latin America, combined with the British cotton textile industry's expansion and concentration of demand for raw materials (particularly cotton, which few parts of Latin America were then able to produce), seems to have hindered the expansion (and particularly in Mexican and Bolivian mining to have occasioned a contraction) of raw materials production and export until the mid-nineteenth century. None the less, Latin American manufactures already suffered during this period, despite various (but always challenged and therefore unstable) attempts at protection and development. Moreover, the previously Spanish and even many Latin American merchants were displaced by British (and to a much lesser extent French and U. S.) shipping, finance, wholesaling and in many cases even retailing, which then converted most of Latin America into commercial neo-colonies of Britain and in part paved the way for the emergence of a fully neo-colonial mode of production in Latin America during the second half of the nineneenth century. Already during the first half of the nineneenth century, metropolitan financial and commercial control, in alliance with Latin American raw materials export interests, limited the extension of nationalist policies and national development. Moreover these foreign transportation, financial and commercial 'invisible' services served as instruments to drain capital out of Latin America at a time when the commodity terms of trade were apparently moving in its favour; and, as Halperin Donghi (151–2) has suggested, some 'invisible' reinvestment of these foreign earnings on service account may have helped finance the importation of metropolitan manufactures (or, we might observe, metropolitan export penetration) into Latin America during a stage of world capitalist and Latin American development, when the latter's raw materials exports were not expanding.

5. India

During the second stage of world capital accumulation and capitalist development, the most important transformations in the modes of production in the colonies and in the exchange relations between them and the metropolis undoubtedly took place in North America (in the North and South), perhaps in Indonesia, and most especially in India. Here only a brief review of the facets of Indian history that are most important to our inquiry into the second stage of world capitalist development and underdevelopment is possible. As was observed above, during the first stage of world capitalist development the participation of India did not involve important qualitative changes in the mode of production that was developing under the Mogul emperors (who in turn had largely exacted their tribute from India without substantially modifying the pre-existing mode of production). None the less, the growth of Indian trading interests (particularly in Bengal) tied to the British and the (in part related) increase in political instability and rivalry among Indian rulers paved part of the way to the British victory at Plassey in 1757 and the rapid domination and transformation of India thereafter – at a time when China, for instance, was still firmly under Chinese imperial rule and remained relatively impenetrable to the European metropolis.

After Plassey, the operations of the British East India Company rapidly changed from trade to plunder. During this first, as distinct from the second, part of the second period of world capital accumulation and capitalist development, according to the *Parliamentary Report on the East India Company* of 1813, 'the importance of that immense Empire to this country is rather to be estimated by the great annual addition it makes to the wealth and capital of the Kingdom, than by any eminent advantage which the manufactures of the country can derive from the consumption of the natives of India' (quoted in Clairmonte, 80). Nevertheless we may recall that British manufactures received an indirect advantage from the Indian manufactures, which through re-export Britain used to destroy local manufacturing and then to create a market for British manufacturing elsewhere in the world. The annual addition to the wealth and capital of Britain that India made in direct tribute payments alone through the East India Company approximated £1 million in some years (Mukerjee, 193); and Digby estimated the total British plunder of India between Plassey (1757) and Waterloo (1815) at £1000 million, which he compared to the English national debt in 1815, that is after all the Napoleonic Wars, of £861 million (Clairmonte, 79–80).

After the Napoleonic wars, that is during the second part of the second period of world capital accumulation and – especially British – capitalist development, the 'exchange' relationship with India and the latter's mode of production were importantly and still more drastically transformed.

For the development of underdevelopment in India, more important still was the destruction of industry and of the socio-economic nexus between manufacturing and agriculture in the countryside. The latter had assured India a certain degree of social equilibrium not only in pre-British but even in East India Company times. As analysed by Marx, capitalist development has everywhere destroyed this equilibrium, as it also did in Britain, at the cost of considerable human suffering by those whose livelihood and way of life was displaced by this capitalist development. The resulting development of underdevelopment in India and elsewhere cannot therefore be attributed to the simple destruction of the pre-capitalist social fabric. An essentially similar destructively process permitted the development of development in Britain and in other metropolitan countries, while it required the development of underdevelopment in India and other colonialized countries. The explanation for this difference must be sought in the fact that this destructive process took place as the mutually interrelated parts of the single process of world capitalist development. Given the colonial structure of the world capitalist system, it was the very development of industry in Britain, as we observed earlier, which generated the underdevelopment and de-industrialisation of India. There, the artisans and peasants whose former sources of livelihood were being destroyed by capitalist development (even if painfully for them and their children as in England) were not, and could not be, reabsorbed in a concomitant process of industrial development. In India, the elimination of the previously highly developed village artisanry only displaced this work force into village agriculture at precisely the time when, also as a result of the same capitalist development in the metropolis, this agriculture was obliged to undergo a transformation of its own that made it even less able to carry this new burden than it would otherwise have been. Thus, it could not be, as Marx had erroneously foreseen, that British industrialisation showed India the mirror of its future.

This same process of underdevelopment was further significantly reinforced by the de-industrialization and de-urbanization in India's industrial economy. Dutt (114) reports:

> Between 1815 and 1832 the value of Indian cotton goods exported fell from £1.3 million to below £100,000, or a loss of twelve-thirteenths of the trade in sixteen years. In the same period the value of English cotton goods imported into India rose from £26,000 to £400,000, or an increase of sixteen times. By 1850 India, which had for centuries exported cotton goods to the whole world, was importing one-fourth of all British cotton exports . . . 'The population of Dacca (the Manchester of India) has fallen from 150,000 to 30,000 or 40,000,' declared Sir Charles Trevelyan to the parliamentary inquiry in 1840, 'and the jungle and malaria are fast encroaching upon the town' . . .

Not only India's textile industry, but its iron and steel industry were similarly destroyed. How? The British industrial 'free traders' who now ruled India, began by imposing duties on Indian imports into Britain that were five to twenty times higher than the duties they permitted – in the spirit of free trade – on imports from Britain into India and they ended by destroying Indian industry physically where necessary.

The 'Permanent Settlement' in 1793 of the land question from Bengal towards the north began under the rule of the East India Company already (Mukerjee). Here British capitalism took advantage of a pre-existing institution, the *zamindari latifundia*, and transformed its previous essential function into the quite different one of tax collector for the development of capitalism in Britain. The additional introduction of many layers of renters, usurers and tax-collectors substantially transformed the social structure in the villages into one dependent on capitalism, which still exists today, while the old landlords were converted into agents of world capitalism. The later introduction of a system of *ryotwari* smallholders towards the South of Bengal, though formally different, extended the essential function of extracting the economic surplus from the countryside in that direction. The growing need for raw materials and foodstuffs then converted the South of the Indian subcontinent into a plantation economy not dissimilar to the Latin American ones. Dutt (119) reports that the exports of raw cotton rose from 9 million lb. in 1813 to 32 million lb. in 1833, 88 million lb. in 1844 and then to 963 million lb. in 1914. Among foodstuffs, not only tea, but also exports of food-grains, principally rice and wheat, rose from £858,000 in 1849 to £19,300,000 in 1914. As Thorner notes, this production for export increased at the expense of production of basic foodstuffs for local consumption and contributed manifestly to the terrible increase in the frequency and depth of famines, as reported by Dutt and Bhatia, which caused an estimated 1,400,000 deaths in the half-century 1800–50 and 15,000,000 deaths in the quarter-century 1875–1900 (Dutt, 119). But this is getting ahead of our story, and we may return to the transformation and underdevelopment of India below in Chapter 6.

It was most particularly this transformed British India that would play a crucial kingpin role in the international system of multilateral trade imbalances and settlements, which came to characterise metropolitan accumulation and investment and colonial de-accumulation during the imperialist period, as we will see in Chapter 7.

The reasons for the limited internal market and other economic development in India and elsewhere in Asia, and in Africa and Latin America in general, are examined in Chapter 5 through the 'theoretical' analysis of the relations between the 'internal' relations of production and the 'external' relations of exchange, particularly during the (second) stage of industrial capitalism but beginning already during the (first) mercantilist and continuing as well through the (third) imperialist stage and the contemporary neo-imperialist periods (fourth stage ?).

5 That the Extent of the Internal Market is Limited by the International Division of Labour and the Relations of Production

This chapter examines a number of theoretical problems posed in classical and neo-classical analysis and in modern bourgeois attempts to find more progressive solutions to them. These problems are posed on the one hand by the classical and neo-classical theses derived from Smith and Ricardo, which advocate an international division of labour and extension of the market through free trade and comparative advantage, leading to some countries' specialisation in the production and export of staple raw materials for the external market in exchange for manufactures produced in other countries. On the other hand, we may distinguish the theses associated with Friedrich List, Gunnar Myrdal, Raúl Prebisch and lately Arghiri Emmanuel, who seek to challenge the classical thesis by invoking declining secular trends in the terms of trade and/or chronic unequal exchange that disfavour the low-wage raw materials producers, and who recommend an alternative policy of infant industry protection and import substitution intended to develop the internal market.

The present author, though rejecting the former and critical of the latter positions, has in earlier writings and even in previous drafts of the present book shared some of the suppositions of the latter position. Though these issues appear and reappear throughout the historical and cyclical process of capital accumulation on a world scale, the discussion of these issues during the analysis of that process would interfere with the continuity of the analysis and indeed sidetrack it. That is why these issues are treated separately in this chapter. On the other hand, it is precisely the abstract treatment of the problems of the division of labour and the extent of the market in isolation from the concrete reality of the historical process of world capital accumulation – as is traditional with neo-classical and Keynesian as distinct from Marxist economists – which necessarily prevents their satisfactory solution. Similarly, the voluntaristic development policies associated with such abstractions instead of the dictates of objective reality are also destined to failure. These limitations will be evident in the discussion of these issues in this chapter. For our attempts to overcome these and other limitations the reader must be referred to the analysis of the historical and cyclical process of capital accumulation in the remaining text of this book and – for the mercantilist period – to *World Accumulation 1492–1789*.

1. On Trade

A. On Classicals and Reformers

The principal architects of classical economics, Smith and Ricardo, built their theoretical constructs alongside – or rather within – the edifice simultaneously erected by the industrial revolution and in accord with the worldwide interests of the nascent industrial bourgeoisie of Britain. Smith argued that 'especially the industrial division of labour is limited by the extent of the market' at home and particularly in the population dedicated to inefficient agriculture. This limit could be extended by taking advantage of Britain's already existing absolute advantage in manufacturing and export-ing industrial products in exchange for raw materials without mercantilist restrictions to trade. Forty years later, decades after Britain's 1780 take-off into the industrial revolution but in the post-Napoleonic War crisis of limited demand for manufactures and high inflated wage goods food prices, Ricardo extended Smith's thesis in his *Principles of Political Economy and Taxation* published in 1817, and gave paternity to the doctrine of comparative advantage and free trade that has ruled bourgeois economics and has theoretically – or ideologically – justified metropolitan trade and development policy to this day. Ricardo did not believe that the limitations to the division of labour, industrial development and the decline in the rate of profit could be removed or attenuated by export to foreign markets *per se*. Instead, he argued that diminishing returns in agricultural production, and therefore high costs of food or wage goods and consequently low industrial profits could be attenuated by recourse to agriculture with higher yields abroad, whose products should be exchanged for Britain's manufactures to the mutual benefit of all concerned. Accordingly, Ricardo sought the abolition of the Corn Laws, which protected high-cost British agriculture, permitted landlords to receive unearned rent on their land, and kept unnecessarily high the wage costs and undesirably low the profits of industrialists, thus limiting industrial investment and economic development. Relying on their growing economic strength, the industrial interests inflicted successive political defeats on the landed and commercial interests until Britain abolished the Corn Laws in 1847 and repealed the remnants of the commercial monopoly Navigation Acts in 1849. The Free Trade Doctrine was enshrined in Britain and, as List noted, became its principal export product to the rest of the world.

Yet opposition emerged abroad to the British free trade doctrine and also to Britain's trade policy among the representatives of the bourgeois interests that were adversely affected by them.

B. On Comparative Advantage and Free Trade

This is not the occasion to review the 150 years of modification and critique that the doctrine of comparative costs or advantage has undergone, or to formulate our own critique in theoretical terms. (In a never finished or published analysis of the theoretical foundations of the 'law' or doctrine of comparative costs, we identified over thirty underlying assumptions each of which is historically and empirically quite unfounded and several of which are mutually contradictory, thus rendering the 'law' of comparative advantage both empirically and logically untenable.) The most severe critique of comparative advantage and the most serious attempt to formulate an alternative theory so far is that of A. Emmanuel in his *Unequal Exchange*, part of whose argument is critically examined below.

It may none the less be useful to take note of some objections and resistance that the British Free Trade Doctrine and the associated trade policy encountered among adversely affected bourgeois interests and their spokesmen elsewhere in the world. To begin with, the international division of labour associated with the 'law' of comparative advantage has never been 'natural' but was man-made by the very British industrial interests and their overseas allies who then enshrined this division as a supposed natural law. Secondly, free trade has never been only the *laissez faire et laissez aller* of 'free' market forces – though market forces have undeniably been at work – but has been imposed by the substantial exercise of political and military force, reliance on forced labour, and in general through the forceful transformation of modes of production, as reviewed elsewhere in this study. Those who suffered from this 'law' naturally objected, and – where possible – resisted.

Indeed, the celebrated example of the exchange of Portuguese wine for British textiles, with which Ricardo illustrated his law, is in fact an example of how forcefully this division of labour was imposed on Portugal to its detriment – rather than advantage – during 150 years of mercantilist rather than 'free' trade *before* 1817.

In this connection, already well over a century ago, Friedrich List looked back:

> Among the most remarkable consequences of the Act of Navi-gation, we may place . . . chiefly the conclusion with Portugal in 1703 of the treaty of Methuen. . . . By this treaty, the Dutch and the Germans lost entirely an extensive trade with Portugal and her colonies. Portugal was rendered completely subservient to England, and England was enabled, with the gold and silver drawn from her commerce with that country, to increase im-mensely her trade with the East Indies and China, to establish, at a later period, her vast empire in India, and to expel the Dutch from their principal positions. (List, 115)

Indeed this treaty was only the last of a series, beginning with the Treaty of London in 1654, through which Portugal granted England commercial privileges in return for political protection against Spain. The consequences had already been summarised by the Prime Minister and 'Colbert' of Portugal, the Marquis de Pombal, in 1755:

> The Portuguese Monarchy was at its last gasp. The English had firmly bound the nation in a state of dependence. They had conquered it without the incovenience of a conquest . . . Por-tugal was powerless and without vigour and all her movements were regulated by the desires of England . . . In 1754 Portugal

scarcely produced anything towards her own support. Two thirds of her political necessities were supplied by England . . . England has become mistress of the entire commerce of Portugal; all the trade of the country was carried by her agents. The English were at the same time furnishers and retailers of all the necessities of life that the country required. Having a monopoly of everything, no business was carried on but through their hands . . . The English came to Lisbon to monopolize even the commerce of Brazil . . . (quoted in Manchester, 39).

The same Pombal subsequently tried unsuccessfully to reverse this dependence and deterioration of the Portuguese economy by launching a new industrialisation drive in Portugal and to exploit Brazil for the latter's instead of Britain's benefit. But it was too late. The international division of labour and Portugal's dependence had already progressed too far. Moreover, Pombal's and his successor's policy was cut short by the French invasion (which like the entire Napoleonic policy was essentially a reaction) and adjustment to the changing international division of labour attendant on the process of world capital accumulation.

A recent study investigates Portugal's experience with the 'law' of comparative advantage in detail and summarised:

The Anglo-Portuguese commercial treaties of 1642, 1654, 1661 and finally 1703 (Methuen Treaty) established and codified an international division of labour between the two countries very much according to the principle of comparative advantage later established by Ricardo. Yet, the negative effects of this kind of international division of labour on Portugal's economy contradict Smith's affirmation that the Methuen Treaty was 'evidently advantageous to Portugal' and contradict Ricardo's tenet that foreign trade based on the doctrine of comparative advantage was beneficial for all trading partners . . . Such an unfavourable effect for the Portuguese economy was mainly the result of the 'type' of international division of labour ('wrought' = primary vs. 'unwrought' = manufactured goods) which was forced on a Portugal that at the end of the 17th century, really produced both wine and cloth, because of her political and military weakness plus her colonial ambitions. The Anglo-Portuguese relationship which emerged from this economic arrangement was one of strong dependence by Portugal on England, although it reinforced the Barganza House and the landed interests, thus the aristocracy and the Church . . . By guaranteeing the supremacy of Portugal's landed interests the Methuen Treaty established a permanent link between those interests and England, a link which is at the core of Portugal's dependence . . . The large and chronic deficit created by the type of international division of labour in the Portuguese balance of payments caused Brazilian gold (about 1700–1760) to outflow entirely from Portugal and to be directed mostly to England, where, given the different conditions, it contributed to the industrialization of that country much more than it had done in Portugal, whose manufacturing sector had been sacrificed to the production of wine. (Sideri, 4–5, 13)

One of the principal challenges to the theoretical foundation of the free trade doctrine and its rejection as a guide for economic policy came from Friedrich List, the father of the *Zollverein* or customs union, which was designed to further German industrialisation by protecting and expanding the internal market. List wrote in the 1840s: 'The history of England exhibits also the intimate relations existing between politics and political economy.' After reviewing the monopoly benefits derived from centuries of enforcing the Navigation Acts that protected British shipping and industry, List goes on:

England therefore *prohibited* the articles competing with those of her *own factories*, the silk and cotton goods of the East. This prohibition was absolute and under severe penalties, she would not consume a thread from India . . . Did England in so doing act unwisely? Undoubtedly, according to Adam Smith and J. B. Say, and their theory of values . . . We hold a different theory, which we call *the theory of productive power*; a theory which the English ministers obeyed, without fully comprehending, when they determined upon their industrial policy: to buy raw materials, and sell manufactured products . . . Their policy has been attended with the most splendid success. England now produces cotton and silk goods to the value of seventy million pounds; she supplies largely the markets of Europe, and all the world: even India now receives the products of English labor. Her own production is now from fifty to a hundred times greater than her former commerce in the manufactured articles of India.

What would have been her condition, had she purchased for these last hundred years the cheap goods of India? . . . We have shown how England, by her policy, acquired political power; by power, productive force; by productive force, wealth; we are now going to see how, by this policy, she added power to power, and productive force to productive force . . . A country like England, which is far in advance of all its competitors, cannot better maintain and extend its manufacturing and commercial industry than by a trade as free as possible from all restraints. For such a country, the cosmopolitan and the national principles are one and the same thing. This explains the favor with which the most enlightened economists of England regard free trade, and the reluctance of the wise and prudent of other countries to adopt this principle in the actual state of the world . . . If the author had been an Englishman, he would probably never have entertained doubts of the fundamental principle of Adam Smith's theory. It was the condition of his own country which begot him, more than twenty years since, the first doubts of the infallibility of that theory . . . (114, 117–18, 120, 79, 69–70; italics in the original)

List was German, and his country was able to reject free trade, unlike India, for instance, which was politically controlled by England, or unlike Latin America, which had a colonial class structure which inevitably gave its dominant bourgeoisie an economic self-interest in freely exporting raw materials and importing manufactured products.

Another country which was in a position to reject the free trade doctrine even earlier than Germany, indeed even before Ricardo wrote, was the United States (for reasons examined in Chapter 3). Its first Secretary of the Treasury, Alexander Hamilton, wrote in his *Report on Manufactures* in 1891:

Not only the wealth but the independence and security of a country appear to be materially connected with the prosperity of manufactures. Every nation, with a view to those great objects, ought to endeavour to possess within itself, all the essential of national supply . . . The United States cannot exchange with Europe on equal terms; and the want of reciprocity would render them the victim of a system which should induce them to confine their views to Agriculture, and refrain from Manufactures. A constant and increasing necessity, on their part, for the commodities of Europe, and only a partial and occasional demand for their own, in return, could not but expose them to a state of impoverishment, compared to the opulence to which their political and natural advantages authorize them to aspire. (Hamilton, 138).

After more than a half-century of Hamiltonian policy – and (as observed in Chapter 2) a specially privileged participation in the evolving international division of labour – another American states-man, U.S. President Ulysses S. Grant, was able to observe:

> . . . for centuries England has relied on protection, has carried it to extremes, and has obtained satisfactory results from it. There is no doubt that it is to this system that it owes its present strength. After two centuries, England had found it convenient to adopt free trade because it thinks that protection can no longer afford anything. Very well, then, Gentlemen, my knowledge of my country leads me to believe that within two hundred years, when America has gotten all it can out of protection, it too will adopt free trade. (Quoted in Spanish in Pedro Santos M., 125, and retranslated by us into English. Mr Grant's only error was one of timing.)

The free trade doctrine and policy also encountered significant opposition in the nineteenth century from adversely affected interests in the now underdeveloped world. Bipan Chandra summarises in his *The Rise and Growth of Economic Nationalism in India*:

> To the early Indian national leaders India's major economic problem was the condition of its industry: and the explanation of India's poverty most commonly advanced by them was the industrial prostration resulting from the destruction of the indigenous industries and the failure of the modern machine industry to grow rapidly enough to compensate adequately for this destruction. Day after day Indian publicists hammered incessantly at this theme and bemoaned continuously the decline of this or that industry. They pointed out, while tracing the historical process of this decline, that India was once a great manufacturing nation whose industrial products has supplied for centuries the needs of vast Asian and European markets . . .

India, fifty years ago, clothed herself with her own manufactures, and now she is clothed by distant masters . . . This is our condition, and when the whole situation is thus taken in at one view, we feel that we are standing on the edge of a precipice, and the slightest push down will drive us into the abyss below of unmixed and absolute helplessness. (Chandra, 56–7. For a discussion of this process in historical context see Chapters 4 and 6.)

Also 'the Ottoman statesmen were not indifferent to the deterioration of the industry of a nation which had formerly been so flourishing . . . The history of this industrialisation movement has not yet been written. There still has not been sufficient research' (Sarc, 52, 55).

Similarly, in various countries of Latin America the accelerating invasion of British manufactures encountered political and ideological resistance (Frank 1972, Chapter 4).

But all of these efforts were doomed to failure by the development of the international division of labour in the nineteenth century and by the class interests of the groups who directly benefited from this division of labour in the colonies, such as India, and the apparently independent states, such as the Latin American ones. Since the development of this class interest and policy in Asia, Africa, the Middle East and Latin America is analysed in Chapters 4 and 6 we may here simply summarise it by reference to a single country, Chile.

The mining exporters of the north of the country were free traders. This policy was not fundamentally due to reasons of doctrine – though they also had these – but rather to the simple reason that these gentlemen were blessed with common sense. They exported copper, silver, nitrates and other minerals of lesser importance to Europe and the United States, where they were paid in pounds sterling or dollars. With the money they bought equipment, machinery, manufactures, or high-quality consumer goods at very low prices. It is hard to conceive of an altruism or a far-sighted or prophetic vision which would lead these exporters to pay export and import duties with a view to the possible industrialisation of the country . . . The agricultural and livestock exporters of the South were also emphatically free traders. They sent their wheat and flour to Europe, California and

Australia [after the gold rushes there] . . . For these hacendados, who were paid in pounds sterling, the idea of taxing the export of wheat or of imposing protective duties on imports was simply insanity . . . The big import houses of Valparaiso and Santiago also were free traders. Could anyone imagine an import firm (let alone a metropolitan-owned one as was common) supporting the establishment of high import duties to protect national industry? Here, then, is the powerful coalition of strong interests, which dominated the economic policy of Chile during the past century and part of the present century. (Veliz, 237–42)

C. On Deteriorated Terms of Trade

The technological progress and increase in labour productivity in the metropolis during the nineteenth century should have occasioned an increase in wages in the metropolis, according to the theory of marginal productivity, and an extension of the benefits of progress to the rest of the world through lower prices or better terms of trade, according to the theory of comparative advantage. But in fact wages in the metropolis did not rise until well into the second half of the nineteenth century; and the terms of trade declined for Britain and improved for others during the first part of this period and rose for Britain and declined for the raw materials producers after the 1870s.

None the less, the international division of labour and international trade for the whole of the nineteenth century strongly changed to the detriment of, and largely at the expense of, the now underdeveloped countries; and this was so both when their terms of trade improved and when they declined again. This happened for several reasons. In the the first place, as Schlote (46–7) points out, while Britain's terms of trade declined during the first part of the period, her exports increased more rapidly than her imports in order to pay for the latter, and the volume of trade as a whole increased sufficiently more than the terms of trade declined to leave Britain on balance with an increase in total returns from trade even if the returns are valued at market prices. In so far as exchange was unequal even at the lowest terms of trade for Britain, her real gain and the now underdeveloped countries' real loss from international trade during these years was correspondingly greater. Yet the greatest gain for the metropolis and loss for the colonialised countries from this international division of labour were not reaped during these years themselves, but later when the terms of trade shifted against the colonialised raw materials exporters. Indeed, the earlier decline and later improvement of metropolitan terms of trade were not independent of each other, as Schlote, Saul and others seem to assume. On the contrary, these changes were intimately related cause and effect: Britain's terms of trade declined and her exports increased during the first part of the period when Britain was conquering overseas markets for her industrial, especially cotton textile, exports through low prices and was destroying manufactures and even industry in Latin America, Africa and Asia, and most notably in India (see Chapters 4 and 5). When this process had successfully forestalled industrial development in these areas (even if some of them were later able to increase textile production again), Britain increasingly relied on the export of technologically more complex metal goods and machinery; and her terms of trade began to improve at the end of the nineteenth century even though it was only then that, excepting for cotton, Britain first became really dependent on raw materials and particularly food imports for her continued development (Saul, 12, 29). That is, the international division of labour and the world market operated as though the metropolitan Britain 'intentionally' lowered her prices in order to destroy local manufacturing competition during the expansion of free trade, and then again raised her prices once this competition was effectively eliminated in the colonialised countries. Then, at the end of the century, metropolitan imperialist monopoly capitalism increasingly replaced free trade and the industrially crippled colonialised countries were increasingly exploited through declining terms of trade. These countries were and have been powerless to combat this decline successfully, despite the increasing dependence of the metropolis on their raw materials (which one might suppose would increase the raw materials suppliers' bargaining power) and even though the colonialised countries again began themselves to produce industrial products. But they always remained one or two technological stages behind the metropolis so that the technological gap, which moreover grew despite industrial production in the colonies, always helped the metropolis maintain and increase its price and other domination over the now underdeveloped countries.

The challenge to the free trade policy and to the law of comparative advantage, which stresses the secular deterioration of the terms of trade of the primary products exporting underdeveloped countries and which is associated with Prebisch, Singer and Myrdal, thus suffers from important limitations. The limitation is not so much an empirical problem, as the bourgeois critics from the right argue, who claim that the statistics do not show an undisputable deterioration of the primary producers' terms of trade during the past century (Kindleberger, Meier). Nor is it a theoretical – or ideological – matter of trying, as Meier does, to save the classical doctrine and policy by denying this change in the terms of trade. The nineteenth-century international division of labour contributed to the development of underdevelopment in most of the world both when the terms of trade went in one direction and when they went in the other. Moreover, as we have noted elsewhere, twentieth-century industrial growth accelerated in most 'Third World' countries precisely when, during the depression, their terms of trade deteriorated most seriously and when, during the war, favourable terms of trade were not immediately significant because the import use of foreign exchange so earned was blocked by that war (Frank 1967, 1969, 1972). That is, the terms of trade, like the other considerations discussed here, only take on significance in the context of the process of capital accumulation, division of labour and transformation of modes of production, which the terms of trade primarily reflect and only secondarily help to reinforce.

D. On Unequal Exchange

Beyond the measure of comparative advantage through *changes* in the terms of trade, it is necessary to consider the terms of trade or of exchange themselves. Are they equal or are they unequal, and why? It is sometimes supposed that exchange between raw materials and manufactures is *per se* unequal and unfavourable to the producers of the former. But Emmanuel and Amin deny that raw materials production *per se* accounts for low wages and unequal exchange, and Emmanuel offers substantial persuasive evidence to support his denial. Emmanuel argues that in the USA, the British Dominions and South Africa high wages have automatically induced entrepreneurs into capital-intensive investment and production in order to keep costs down (Emmanuel, 161–2). Presumably, this happened significantly less in the now underdeveloped countries, where wages were not only low but their level was related to a different kind of monoexport mode of production based on super-exploitation of labour. Furthermore, Emmanuel (174–8) argues that beyond the organic composition of capital, underdevelopment is linked to what he calls the 'organic composition of labor' or the structure of the economy with respect to sectors or products with low-skill/low-wage as distinct from high-skill/high-wage productive processes. Specialisation in the former impedes development, since it implies not only producing low-price products, but producing them at low wages. To overcome this obstacle, Emmanuel suggests, there are only two theoretical possibilities, more autarchy, which impedes the resultant transfer of value through unequal exchange, or diversification into high-skill/high-wage capital-intensive sectors. Emmanuel regards the former as a surer, but the latter as an easier policy for underdeveloped countries (185, 292). (The former in effect requires socialist revolution and a Soviet/Chinese-style foreign trade policy, while the latter can be begun through capitalist reform.)

Emmanuel supplies many illustrations throughout his book. Wood and petroleum are both raw materials, and the production of the latter requires more capital and advanced technology than that of the former. Yet petroleum-producing countries receive little for their product (before 1973 and less than statistics at first sight suggest, Emmanuel argues), while wood is relatively high-priced (except for the scarcest most exotic tropical woods): petroleum is produced by low-wage countries, and wood (excepting tropical varieties) by Scandinavian and North American high-wage countries (201–3). England converted India and Australia into her suppliers of cotton and wool respectively for the British textile industry, but in one country this raw materials export production led to underdevelopment and in the other to development (293). Now that the underdeveloped countries increasingly produce textiles and certain other manufactures, Britain switches to other products; and textile export becomes a low-price export because it is now a low-wage product.

There is no determinant connection between raw materials export and underdevelopment or relative poverty and between industry and development: the raw materials exporting British Dominions and Denmark are rich; while Spain, Italy and Japan are relatively poor (290). Indeed, Emmanuel discards diversification as a practical solution as well. Especially if underdeveloped countries diversify into high-price goods (first textiles, now steel and import-substituted manufactures) these become low-price goods, *because* low-wage underdeveloped countries produce them and the high-wage developed countries switch their production to new more sophisticated (and even old hand-crafted) high-price goods. It is not the product that defines the producer, but the producer that defines the product, Emmanuel argues; and 'dirty' underdeveloped producers immediately 'dirty' whatever they touch. The particular international division of labour changes, but the principle remains the same (Emmanuel, 183–9). In theory then, the solution for underdeveloped countries would seem to be simply to raise their wages. But Emmanuel recognises explictly that, except within very narrow limits, this is no solution either, because 'this formulation is no more than a simple theoretical scheme . . . without any consideration of the practical possibilities of application . . . on the capitalist road . . .' (Emmanuel, 170).

The first serious and pathbreaking analysis of unequal exchange in the third stage of world capital accumulation, which advances an alternative to, rather than merely criticises, the 150-year-old Ricardian theory of comparative advantage, is that of Emmanuel:

We have inverted the fundamental hypothesis of the Ricardian theorem of international trade. Instead of equal wages and unequal rates of profit, we have adopted the hypothesis of unequal wages and of profits that are subject to standardization and tend towards equality. These premises have led us to take the opposite line to the official theory of international trade on all points. . . . In rejecting its fundamental hypothesis – the immobility of capital – . . . it is not the comparative costs that determine the equilibrium prices in international trade but the absolute costs . . . We are conscious of the fact that our definition contains a matter of principle. It treats wages as the independent variable of the system. . . . Wages differ by geographical regions and independently of the fluctuations in the merchandize exchanges. . . . While wages differed from one country to another by a factor of 1 to 2 or even of 1 to 3 or 1 to 4, it was perhaps legitimate to suppose that the fluctuations of the commodities market could be the cause of these differences. But once wages differ by factors of 1 to 20 or 1 to 30 and when they differ only in space but are on the contrary very rigid over time over which only a slow and linear trend is visible . . . then they do indeed constitute the independent variables of the system. (291, 286, 111, 113, 118)

Emmanuel argues that these enormous difference in wage levels between some countries and others (essentially the metropolitan ones and the colonies or neo-colonies of Asia, Africa and Latin America) are not associated with similar differences in labour productivity and that these are of an entirely different order or magnitude and much smaller. Therefore, according to Emmanuel, international exchange between the former and the latter at world market prices necessarily results in 'unequal exchange' which benefits the metropolis at the expense of the colonies. Moreover, once unequal exchange begins, its consequences are cumulative: it transfers investible surplus from the poor, who thus cannot invest it, to the rich who do so. This widens the wage gap and increases unequal exchange still more and furthermore it affects the structures and modes of production in the thus underdeveloping and developing countries (Emmanuel, 167 and elsewhere). Moreover, since it has scarcely received notice, especially by holier-than-thou 'self'-made men in countries like Germany, Sweden and Australia (or more recently in some socialist countries), it may be well to make a special mention of third countries that appear to have derived little or no benefit from any exploitative relation with the colonial world. Yet Adam Smith already observed two centuries ago, in his chapter 'Of the Advantages which Europe has Derived . . .': 'The discovery and colonization of America, it will readily be allowed, have contributed to augment the industry, first, of all the countries which trade to it directly . . . and, secondly, of all those which, without trading to it directly, send through the medium of other countries, goods of their own produce; such as Austrian Flanders, and some provinces of Germany . . . But, that those great events should likewise have contributed to encourage the industry of countries, such as Hungary and Poland [elsewhere Smith also names Sweden in this context], which may never, perhaps, have sent a single commodity of their own produce to America, is not perhaps altogether so evident. That those events have done so, however, cannot be doubted. . . . By being carried thither they create a new and more extensive market for that surplus produce [of Hungary and Poland]. They raise its value and thereby contribute to encourage its increase. Though no part of it may ever have been carried to America . . . it may find a market by means of the circulation of that trade which was originally put into motion by the surplus produce of America (Smith, 557–8). What according to Smith 'cannot be doubted', those who have since spoken in his name

have totally neglected or denied; and only recently has a writer in
the Marxist tradition (though Bettelheim denies him even that),
Emmanuel, analysed and emphasised this complex relationship of
the internal relations of production, even in third countries, with the
relations of unequal exchange on the capitalist world market –
although Che Guevara (whom Bettelheim compares to Emmanuel
in precisely this connection, and to whom he perhaps also denies the
Marxist label) in his speech to the 1964 Afro-Asian Economic
Seminar in Algiers already emphasised the monopoly portion of
unequal exchange that socialist countries derive from trade with
capitalist underdeveloped countries at capitalist monopoly 'world'
market prices (whose determination in part by capitalist productive
relations and in part by monopoly had been previously analysed
under the title 'Comercio exterior, intercambio desigual, desarrollo
economico' in an internal mimeographed document prepared in
Guevara's Ministry of Industry in Cuba by Carlos Romeo).

Samir Amin has made some estimates of the amounts of capital
transferred from the underdeveloped countries to the developed
ones in recent times through this kind of unequal exchange. Total
exports from the underdeveloped countries in 1966 were valued
(by the 'world market') at about US$35,000 million. Of these
the 'ultra-modern' petroleum, mining, plantation and other
export sectors accounted for about 75 per cent or US$ 26,000
million. Had the same products been produced by the developed
countries with the same techniques and thus the same productivity
(at 15 per cent profit on invested capital, seven-year depreciation, a
capital coefficient of 3.5, and a 100 per cent rate of surplus value) the
value price of these products would have been US$ 8000 million
more. The underdeveloped countries' remaining exports, which are
valued at $ 9000 million (the difference between the total of $35
billion and the $ 26 billion from the 'modern' sector), would – by his
estimate of the difference between the wage gap of about 20 to 1 and
a productivity gap of at most 2 to 1 if metropolitan techniques were
(or could be) used – be valued at US$ 23,000 million, or
US$14,000 more than the 'world market' assigns to them. The two
underpayments the underdeveloped countries receive for the value
they produce added together amount to US$ 22,000 million (8 plus
14), which would make the total payment that they would receive,
if prices and wages corresponded to productivity, US$ 57,000
million instead of the US$ 35,000 they did receive. The estimated
US$ 22,000 million difference transferred to the developed count-

ries through this unequal exchange mechanism represents only about 1.5 per cent of their net domestic product, but it amounts to about 15 per cent of the net domestic product of the underdeveloped countries (Amin, 1/23–5). Beyond the fact that this is about equal to the underdeveloped countries' total gross investment (and therefore much more than their net investment), the economic and political significance of this transfer cannot be adequately seen until it is established to what extent the 1.5 per cent transfer to the developed countries accrues not to their people but to a small number of their monopolies and their owners (as Magdoff, argues for the U.S.), and to what extent even the 15 per cent of the underdeveloped countries' product also accrues to these or other metropolitan monopolies who own the means of production that produces these products in the underdeveloped countries or control their merchandising (as Baran 1957 argues).

Emmanuel's work has given rise to a serious debate among those (including himself) who agree that this unequal exchange exists but disagree about its causes in relation to the mode(s) of production and its consequences on development, underdevelopment and the political forces and strategies or possibilities in the (neo-) colonial and metropolitan countries. It would be beyond our scope to take explicit part in this debate, though parts of our analysis necessarily have implications for several of the issues under debate.

Though Emmanuel devotes his own analysis primarily to the relation between the wage level and unequal exchange, he recognises that the wage level is intimately related to, and even determined by, the mode and even the kind of production. Emmanuel writes:

> It becomes evident that the institutional factors that determine the equilibrium wage in the first place are not accidents that are exogenous to human society. . . . The wage level acts *directly* . . . on the economic factors *in that it determines the necessity of an intensification of the organic composition of capital and in that it induces investments through the widening of the market.* . . . The choice of a branch that has many possibilities to absorb fixed capital with a view to reserving the future [and] the choice of a branch that permits and even trains the employment of a higher proportion of qualified workers also help determine the wage level and the equality or not of international exchange as well as the develop-

ment of productive forces. (Emmanuel, 161–3, emphasis in the original)

And

> It is this variation of the 'organic composition' of labor from one branch to another which, we believe, explains at least in the greatest measure the differences in the development of the various regions in the interior of a state. (177)

Amin emphasises the relations between these and other factors in Chapter II of his *Accumulation on a World Scale*, and it would be impossible to summarise these here. We may, however, briefly quote the opinions of Bettelheim and of Palloix in this regard. Bettelheim writes in his introductory 'Theoretical Remarks' on Emmanuel:

> 'Unequal exchange' cannot be explained only by the 'rates of factor remuneration' because these are – and this is an essential point – an *objective base*. . . . Imperialist exploitation is linked at the same time to the important fact of the 'penetration' of the capitalist mode of production in the dominated countries and to the structural changes that the *capital movements provoke* in the heart of the world capitalist economy. . . . It is the nature and the specific combination of the productive forces and of the relations of production of the poor countries within the world capitalist relations that constitute the *objective base* of the 'poverty' of certain dominated countries, and which explain the low wages and the 'unequal exchange' that may derive therefrom. In order definitively to escape from 'unequal exchange' there is no other way than to transform this *objective base* and, thus, to eliminate the relations of production that 'block the development of the productive forces . . . (Bettelheim in Emmanuel 318, 327, 314)

In his comment on the debate – not reproduced here – between Bettelheim and Emmanuel, Palloix concludes:

> In fact, it is characteristic of the capitalist mode of production to affect the different branches of production with a different rate of accumulation from branch to branch at the level of the whole process: the law of uneven development becomes a fact of this

process. It is only through the law of unequal development of capitalist production – which itself depends on the process of labor value – that the price of production, which accentuates the inegality of the development of different branches, manifests itself. Emmanuel's price of production appears as a form in itself, although it is the product of the contradictions of the C.M.P. [capitalist mode of production]. Unequal exchange then ceases to be an end, which the author [Emmanuel] confers on it, and becomes *only a means* of the accentuation of the development gaps. . . . Unequal exchange is indeed the result of a wage inequality, *but the latter is itself determined by differences in the level of productive forces*. . . . There cannot be equality of exchanges in a world characterised by inequality of development. (Palloix, n. d., 132, 135, 136, emphasis in original)

We agree; and we draw on these opinions here only to clarify some elements of our own analysis, and not to reproduce the entire argument among the debators, to whom we could not do justice here.

2.   On Markets

Another aspect of the discussion centres more on the production – or really only the marketing – of raw materials in which some areas supposedly have a comparative advantage and which engenders a dependence on an 'external' rather than on an 'internal' market as the supposed motor of industrial and economic development. In this connection, we may note in turn some aspects of the discussion of dualism and enclave economies, the staple theory of economic growth, backward and forward linkages, the internal market, infant industry and import substitution.

E.   On Dualism

Very influential in bourgeois analysis and policy, sometimes explicitly and often implicitly, has been the supposed existence of 'dualism' – social, economic and technological – within the under-developed countries (Boeke, Lewis, Fei and Ranis, etc.) and between these countries and the metropolis (Singer). Their thesis is that development occurs or may be generated in the leading of the dual sectors to the virtual exclusion of the lagging one, to which development is and must be diffused from the leading sector. We have already argued elsewhere (Frank 1967, 1969) that, apart from the policy supposedly derived from dualism, the very thesis that dualism exists is theoretically quite untenable. Additionally, the discussion of the New World in Chapter 3 and the review of the historical experience of Asia and Africa in Chapters 4 and 6 suggest that the expansion of the mercantile and industrial capitalist system excluded dual societies or economies as envisaged by these bourgeois theorists. Moreover, as this entire book and any serious analysis of the process of world capital accumulation and of the related transformation of modes of production throughout the world suggests, the international division of labour and its theoretical analysis has long since been incompatible with the dual economy or society thesis.

One kind of policy – the most reactionary – associated with the dual society thesis is summarised by such common expressions as Kipling's 'East is East and West is West, and never the twain shall meet' or that part of Indonesia is 'Tropical Holland' or that 'Britain chooses to grow its (sugar, etc.) in such and such a place'. This dualist thesis is that metropolitan and other development is confined to a few areas, including some metropolitan 'enclaves' overseas, and that this is enough and all to the good – as Boeke for instance, argued.

The other kind of policy, premised on the same dualist supposition, is that development must be diffused from the 'advanced' 'capitalist' sector to the 'backward' 'traditional' one, and that the latter is being or must progressively be 'modernised' and 'integrated' into the leading sector of the world society and economy. This conception and policy underlies virtually all 'progressive' and reformist bourgeois ideology, theory and policy, internationally between the industrialised countries and the 'Third World' and nationally within the latter's 'dual' societies (as well as between the national and 'marginal' populations of the imperialist countries as expressed by U.S. President Johnson's domestic 'War on Poverty' and 'Great Society' programmes). We have also already criticised this approach previously (Frank 1969, Chapter 2), arguing that it is theoretically unfounded, empirically untrue and policy-wise ineffective. A variant of this approach is the 'staple theory of growth', which recommends the production and export of staple raw materials as an engine of growth, which will or can spill over into other – industrial – sectors and generate the later development of, or the basis of, an internal market.

F. On Staple Theory

The staple theory of growth was developed by Harold Innis and his followers on the basis of Canadian experience and is summarised by Melvin Watkins:

> The fundamental assumption of the staple theory is that staple exports are the leading sector of the economy and set the pace for economic growth. The limited – at first possibly non-existent – domestic market, and the factor proportions – an abundance of land relative to labour and capital – create a comparative advantage in resource-intensive exports, or staples. Economic development will be a process of diversification around an export base. The central concept of a staple theory, therefore, is the spread effects of the export sector, that is the impact of export activity on domestic economy and society. To construct a staple theory, then, it is necessary to classify these spread effects and indicate their determinants . . . By classifying these income flows, we can state a staple theory in the form of a disaggregated multiplier-accelerator mechanism. In Hirschman's terms, the inducement to domestic investment resulting from the increased activity of the export sector can be broken down into three linkage effects: backward linkage, forward linkage, and what we shall call final demand linkage. The staple theory then becomes a theory of capital formation . . . emphasize the importance of capital intensive agriculture in supplying linkage to domestic agricultural machine production. Theory and history suggest that the most important example of backward linkage is the building of transport systems for collection of the staple, for that can have further and powerful spread effects. Forward linkage is a measure of the inducement to invest in industries using the output of the export industry as an input. The most obvious, and typically most important, example is . . . further processing [of the raw material] . . . Final demand linkage is a measure of the inducement to invest in domestic industries producing consumer goods for factors in the export sector. Its prime determinant is the size of the domestic market, which is in turn dependent on the

level of income-aggregate and average – and its distribution. (Watkins 53–5)

Elsewhere following Kindleberger, Watkins refers to 'a capacity to transform' by staple production and the ability to avoid getting 'caught in a "staple trap"'; and Watkins insists 'we have taken pains throughout to emphasize the special character of the staple theory' (Watkins, 60, 63, 64).

Evidently, the production and export of staple raw materials after one to four centuries has not yet had 'a capacity to transform' most of Asia, Africa and Latin America into industrial capitalist producers of producer and consumer goods and has drawn them, if not universally, into a 'staple trap', at least into a 'low-level (dis)equilibrium trap', from which they are less and less able to escape through capitalist development. What then are some of the circumstances that made the Canadian and similar experience as well as the staple theory itself so 'special'?

G. On Linkages

Leaving aside the problem of the non-investment in domestic accumulation of part of the surplus because of its transfer abroad (discussed in Section 1 of this chapter), we may ask why in the underdeveloped world generally backward and forward linkages have not – or have only tardily – generated development based on a domestic producer goods sector.

In fact, the production of mining and plantation raw materials for export during the first stage of world capital accumulation *did* provide some backward linkages to the production of the means of production – mining, smelting and sugar-processing installations and equipment – and transport of these raw materials. Although some of these were undoubtedly produced in and imported from the European metropolis (and the North American neo-metropolis), many of them were also produced on the spot, if only because transportation of these capital goods was impossible or too costly and their local production by low-wage labour was competitive with their importation. Perhaps these backward linkages did not have many or important further spread effects because they involved technologically simple labour instead of technologically advanced capital-intensive production of capital goods. But at that stage of capitalist development, production of these colonial capital goods in the metropolis itself could not have involved qualitatively very different technological complexity or labor-/capital-intensiveness. It is not entirely clear, therefore, why the metropolis should have had or obtained a competitive – and still less a development-generating – advantage over its colonies in this regard. There are perhaps two important exceptions, one negative and one positive: in the sugar islands, lack of resources (minerals and timber, inasmuch as the latter was used for fuel) and a shortage of labour probably made many such backward linkages relatively uncompetitive relative to sugar production in the islands and production of the means of production in Europe and North America (which had, as we observed, a special competitive advantage). On the other hand, England and New England probably had an advantage (albeit in part reinforced if not created by the Navigation Acts) in shipbuilding; and this particular backward linkage into the means of production had very widespread effects, not so much through other productive activities as through the commercial monopoly power to exploit the production of others through shipping. On the other hand, simple appeal to metropolitan mercantilist monopoly regulations to explain the different development paths is, on reflection, less convincing. For in principle, all mercantilist metropolises had recourse to the same regulations; though as Smith observed, in practice they were rather different. These same regulations also forbade, but did not prevent, the local production of a variety of manufactured consumer goods for the narrow home market and even for export, especially in the Spanish mining colonies (and in the eighteenth century in the Brazilian mining and ex-mining regions of Minas Gerais). Indeed, this manufacturing development for the consumer market and also some capital goods production in the Spanish colonies also represented some forward linkage into the processing of local raw materials, such as cotton(which was not even grown for export). As we observed in Chapter 4, this development created the economic, social and political nucleus of incipient national capitalist development in parts of post-Independence Latin America. The same was all the more so the case in India, albeit part of its development of textile manufacturing was (perhaps ironically) export-induced in the eighteenth century and stimulated by the very East India Company that plundered India.

In the nineteenth century, various internal and external dimensions of our problem changed increasingly. British industrialisation,

through forward linkage into production by and for the pro-
letarianised peasant and through backward linkage from textile
production to the production of textile machinery and from there to
machine building, iron, steel and railroads, altered the length,
strength and direction of linkages in all the colonial parts of the
increasingly integrated world economy. The scale of production of
textiles, and presumably of textile and then other machinery, in
Britain required, as we observed, the deliberate and forced de-
industrialisation of India and its rupture of both backward and
forward linkages there or the transfer of these linkages to the
metropolitan economy. If it was possible for the British economy to
absorb (at considerable social cost) its labour force in industry (and
raw material, coalmining), it was at least in part because Indian
agriculture was obliged – not through the competitive market but
through discriminatory tariffs and brute force – to absorb the labour
force previously engaged in manufacturing and handicrafts. This
separation of agriculture and manufacturing in India could not,
however – à la Lenin or Hirschman – forge forward linkages into
further processing or backward linkages into machine building and
the production of producers' goods, except in Britain. In Latin
America, during the first half of the nineteenth century, the process
of de-industrialisation and de-linking was less drastic, but then there
was less necessity for Britain and France to do so. At the same time,
the metropolitan merchant penetration of Latin American wholesale and retail trade afforded more and more opportunities to sever
existing linkages with Latin American manufacturing or to redirect
them into the importation of metropolitan machinery, which was
becoming increasingly competitive, for use by the little Latin
American industry that survived. The same was not possible in the
United States, where Northern capital was increasingly able to take
advantage of potential forward and backward linkages in both the
North and the South to accumulate capital and to invest it in
development-generating industry – in the North – and cotton production in the South.

This brings us back to the problem of raw materials production.
Why did the rapid expansion of raw materials production – first
cotton in the U.S. South, India, Indonesia and Egypt, vegetable oils
in West Africa, sugar (and cotton) in the Caribbean, beverages
(coffee, cocoa, tea) in all three continents, food-grains in South and
South-east Asia, the Americas and Oceania, wool and meat in the
last-named, and finally in the last part of the nineteenth century

(but barring minor exceptions not before) minerals, other than precious metals, and other raw materials for metropolitan development – not permit or generate a take-off into a self-sustaining domestic production of backward-linked producers or forward-linked processed goods in Asia, Africa, and Latin America, but only in the white British Dominions and the United States itself?

In this part of the inquiry, we shall still try to reserve the external exchange effects on and through the capital drain *per se* for later examination. But it will be impossible to isolate the 'external' relations from the 'internal' mode of production, since our problem resides precisely in establishing the modalities of this relation in the varieties of productive processes and modes in the underdeveloping parts of the world capitalist system. On the other hand, we shall not examine these varieties here, since they are treated in our discussion of the transformations of the modes of production in Asia, Africa and Latin America in the third stage of world capital accumulation during the last part of the nineteenth century (in Chapter 6). Here we shall merely abstract out some aspects of the particularities of raw materials production and capital accumulation (or to generalise from some of them where we are unable to abstract from them).

We may begin by asking whether the large-scale production of raw materials does not in itself constitute the production of means of production for productive consumption in Lenin's sense? We would venture an answer in the affirmative, in so far as these raw materials are not consumed in their raw state and constitute an input in an intermediate stage of the capitalist productive process. Though this is more evidently the case for industrial raw materials (minerals and some organic ones such as rubber toward the end of the century and cotton already since the beginning), to some extent it is also true even in the production of 'dessert crops' such as sugar and coffee, and all the more so of food-grains and meat, which are imported to free other resources for use elsewhere in the productive process. Moreover, like 'orthodox' industrial capital goods industries, raw materials production in the colonies (whose production is no less 'traditional' or 'normal' than that of industrial capital goods) has since the nineteenth century been increasingly capital-intensive, technologically innovative, and in part skilled labour using. (Though large-scale mining and agriculture may use much un-skilled labour, it also requires considerable skilled personnel; and mass textile or assembly line industrial production is not especially characterised by skilled labour inputs.)

Amin suggests that today about 75 per cent of the under-developed countries' raw materials exports come not from 'traditional' low-productivity, but from 'modern' high-productivity productive processes and sectors, as in mining, plantation agriculture, to say nothing of, in our day, petroleum (Amin, Introduction, 44–5, Chapter I, 23–5). In this sense, the production of raw producers' goods need not *per se* be so different from that of industrial producers' goods. Moreover, the industrialising countries such as Britain and the United States also produced important amounts of raw materials and exported them – the former coal and the latter cotton and wheat – in the course of their development.

But in so far as the domestic production of raw materials – and the more so of a single dominant raw material rather than several of them simultaneously – is predominantly for export abroad, the long-term secular linkages and the short-term cyclical accelerator are also predominantly extended or transferred abroad. This would seem to be so largely irrespective of whether the major means of production in the export sector are domestically owned or not and whether their commercialisation is (as has predominantly been the case) controlled by foreigners or not. In so far as any domestic multiplier can be said to exist in these economies at all, which Amin denies, the accrual of income to foreigners from their control of merchandising – and additionally where it exists from their ownership of the means of producing – these raw materials of course transfer much of the derived expansive multiplier abroad. (In case of a contraction, however, the multiplier effects largely stay at home. Thus, nineteenth-century and even earlier specialisation in the production of raw materials for export and their exchange for imported manufactures severely handicapped capital accumulation and productive consumption among the producers of primary compared to those of manufactured products, even disregarding the capital drain from the former to the latter through unequal exchange. Only very few non-metropolitan raw materials producers were able to overcome this handicap, and each – Australia, Canada, etc. – did so under quite 'special' circumstances, which were not sufficiently general to permit even Argentina or Uruguay, let alone all of Latin America, Africa and Asia, to do the same.

The forward linkages of this raw materials production were relatively few in the colonialised countries and their spread effects were limited, as the processing of their raw materials was still a major business of the metropolitan countries that imported them. These forward linkages into textile, food processing and other consumer goods industries (for either the home or the foreign market) did not become 'available' to the raw materials producing countries until the metropolitan economies had developed to a stage in which – in the international division of labour – they had passed on to more advanced productive processes and could increasingly leave the relatively simple processing operations (or processes) to the underdeveloped countries. Even then, this process of 'import substitution' in the latter countries usually only accelerated during metropolitan crises – the two world wars and the intervening depression – that prevented the metropolis from supplying these processed consumer goods (though during the last fifteen years this process has been induced in the underdeveloped countries by metropolitan foreign investment itself).

By the time the underdeveloping countries were able to link their raw materials forward into processing them or backward to produce the necessary equipment, this linkage was no longer so domestically development-generating and/or internationally competitive as to generate internal capital accumulation or to avoid external capital drain (except, as we will see below, under the 'special' circumstances of isolation from the world market).

In the meantime, during the nineteenth and part of the twentieth centuries, the forward linkages in Asia, Africa and Latin America were few or their spread effects limited, for several reasons. Foreign control of the commercialisation of the raw materials, and even more so foreign ownership of the principal means of producing them, (1) limited the potential spread effects of available forward linkages by transferring processing to the metropolis (or in some cases to other dependent economies); (2) they limited domestic processing expansion if the line of processing conflicted with the metropolitan economic, financial or political interest; (3) they diverted capital investment and the provision of infrastructure into export productive directions other than those of the possibly available forward linkages; and (4) they induced the importation of goods that competed with forward-linked domestic production through prices that were competitive or even privileged through tariffs and/or exchange rates. Where some raw materials processing occurred locally anyway, it was usually financially or commercially controlled or its installations owned outright by metropolitans, who then imposed similar limitations on potential domestic spread effects of this processing. Market competition of imported foreign products or (in Africa) domestic production was, and still is, wherever necessary, supplemented or even supplanted by foreign (or settler) political power in the colonial or neo-colonial countries. The most extreme cases perhaps were the discriminatory tariff and physical destruction of Indian industry, the privileged treaty ports of China, and the sixteenth-century-style colonialist methods employed in the Middle East, North and Black Africa (examined in Chapters 4 and 6). But the special privileges that foreigners received from sovereign Latin American states were also useful in breaking or diverting forward linkages. The source of these privileges then and now must be sought not only in the economic, political and ideological alliance of private domestic export interests with foreign ones, but also in the great dependence on the metropolitan powers of the supposedly independent states. In this regard state dependence on raw materials export and import duty for fiscal revenue and financial subjugation by the metropolis, not only through direct foreign loans but through metropolitan management of the world capitalist monetary institutions and mechanisms, deserve special mention.

Forward (though also backward) linkages are also inhibited by a demand structure of the export economy and by its state bureaucracy, which have engendered the rapid and overblown development of a tertiary service sector that is both domestic productive processing and import 'substituting' in effect. The metropolitan economies also experienced an expansion of the tertiary sector. But it grew not only slower relative to income levels and productive capacity but in some cases even absolutely later than in the underdeveloped countries. Cordoba (VIII, 41) compares 33 per cent of Germany's labour force in the tertiary sector in 1950 with 45.9 per cent of Venezuela's in 1936!. Additionally, the growth of the developed countries' tertiary sector has been largely labour-saving and more capital-intensive. In the underdeveloped countries with a large and elastic labour supply the growth of the tertiary sector has been mostly labour – and very unskilled labour – intensive and has pre-empted potentially productive linkages. (Herein the relatively early growth of the tertiary sector in the white settler export economies has been very different in that it was even more labour saving and capital-using than in the older metropolitan economies precisely because of the settler countries' relatively great labour shortage and high wages.)

Turning to the question of backward linkages to inputs for the leading raw materials sector, we may recall that Watkins observed that most important ones were in transportation and other infrastructure for the export sector. This kind of backward linkage undoubtedly did occur in the raw materials export economies during the last part of the nineteenth century, but they did not usually have enough spread effects to permit them to take off out of their staple traps and to achieve productive consumption capable of transforming and developing their economies then or since. In most of these export economies, the domestic transport system, to say nothing of the port facilities and foreign shipping lines, only facilitated the extraction of the raw materials to, and the introduction of manufactured and other products from, the metropolis. Thus, the spread effects of the backward linkages, both in the direct production of rails, railway rolling stock and in some cases even of the fuel used by the railways and other installations, as well as in the indirect production of further backward-linked metal-mechanical products and the equipment used to operate the export economy and the consumer goods that were pumped through the ship-port-rail link, all spread into the metropolitan economy, despite – indeed because – of the physical location in the colonies of the productive consumption from which the metropolis derived this part of its productive demand. (Much of this often European-financed railroad construction took place in the United States and the British Dominions, more so than in the now underdeveloped countries.) But in the United States this backward linkage did not simply spread back to Europe but fed the process of capital accumulation and productive industrial investment within the American economy itself. For a time, this linkage also occurred less in Canada and Australia, both of which seem to have suffered an important lull in their development during the last two decades of the nineteenth century. (For Canada see Bertram in Easterbrook and Watkins, eds.; for Australia see Wheelwright, ed.)

Japan was able to develop consumer and producer goods industries in the early stages of her development, which were not competitive with those of the world market, because of her isolation from competition by that world market. Not until Japan had achieved a certain stage of development did it try to develop industries that were competitive and even in technological leadership. But without the earlier protection from this competition *in producer goods industries*, Japan would hardly have been able to generate the productive (albeit not world market competitive) consumption that later served as the basis of its take-off. Soviet isolation under socialism achieved the same result with a considerable technological lag; or to put it differently, isolation permitted development with or despite this lag. This development path is definitely not available to any now underdeveloped country that is tied to the world capitalist market through national capitalism, even though it be state capitalism. It still remains to be seen whether the economies of Eastern Europe can achieve take-off and sustained growth with this lag, and the evidence is rapidly accumulating against them.

The question remains why Canada and Australia were able to achieve capitalist development, not only without isolation from the world market but with raw materials export to it. Though it is by no means a full answer, it may be suggested that part of the reason is that both were able to take advantage of a home market crisis created by world wars after having already achieved productive power within a special mode of production that permitted them to utilise this crisis-created opportunity (which they shared to some extent with some now underdeveloped countries) for kinds of capital accumulation and sustained development that were not available to the now underdeveloped countries. It may even be that for this reason foreign investment in Australia and Canada – and then Western Europe as well – has been attracted into, and has provided capital and technology for, technologically advanced development-generating sectors (for both the home and the export market) into which they cannot and will not flow in the underdeveloped countries.

H. On Developing the Internal Market

The observation that specialisation in staple raw materials production and export has not in fact generated economic development in most of the world has engendered the development of a thesis which is rather the opposite of the staple theory of growth. This thesis is associated with the United Nations Economic Commission for Latin America (ECLA), but it is also indentifiable in some North American interpretations of the historical development of the United States. According to this thesis, staple production for export induces underdevelopment rather than development; and economic, and especially industrial, development is instead dependent on the growth of an internal market. This view is summarised by Ferrer and was quoted with approval by the present author in previous works:

> There can hardly be any doubt that, aside from the restriction which the authorities imposed on colonial activities competing with those of the metropolis, the structure of the export sector, as well as the concentration of wealth, were the basic obstacles to the diversification of the internal productive structure and, therefore, to the consequent elevation of the technical and cultural levels of the population, the development of social groups connected with the evolution of the internal market, and the search for new lines of exportation free from the metropolitan authority. This narrow horizon of economic and social development explains for the most part the experience of the colonial American world and, notoriously, of the Spanish-Portuguese possessions. (Ferrer 31–2, as quoted in Frank 1967, 26, Frank 1969, 376, and Frank 1972, 38)

Though I still cannot accept the opposite bourgeois thesis, I have since come to find increasingly serious limitations to this thesis as summarised by Ferrer and can no longer agree that 'there can hardly be any doubt [about] that'.

In the first manuscript draft (1969) of the present book I still wrote:

> What then are the common factors among these modes of production, the class structure to which they give rise, and the underdevelopment policy they generate? Production is generally concentrated in a single export product which dominates the economy and society. Ownership of the principal means of production is very concentrated in a few hands, and other means of production are monopolized by these same and/or related other people, thus denying large masses of the population access to means of production and sources of livelihood that are not in, or directly related to, the export production industry in which they accordingly are obliged to work at very low wages if not in outright slavery. This monopoly concentration of ownership creates an extremely unequal distribution of income, which in turn impedes the development of a substantial internal market. A

substantial share of the economic surplus produced in the colonial economy is appropriated by the metropolis. This is especially so if the fundamental means of production, mines, equipment, plantations, etc. are owned by metropolitans or other foreigners, who consume or invest their incomes abroad or who return or retire to the metropolis after making their fortune in the colony. Through unequal exchange, monopolistic control of the commercialization of the export product in the colony's metropolis and other mechanisms, a substantial part of the surplus produced in the colonial economy is also remitted to the metropolis, especially if the principal means of production are substantially or even entirely owned by non-nationals or economic non-residents of the colonial economy. This colonial economic structure (with some relatively minor exceptions to be noted later) gives the colonial bourgeoisie, irrespective of whether it is metropolitan or local, the following economic and class interests: refrain from developing substantial local manufacturing production for the internal market, whose size does not warrant it because of the unequal distribution of income; devote all suitable natural and human resources to the production of the export goods, even at the price of restraining the diversification of agricultural production; import manufactured goods and even basic foodstuffs from abroad to sustain the working population; import luxury consumer goods for their own elite consumption or consume them abroad on extended trips or foreign residence; devote the maximum investible surplus or capital – beyond that which is remitted abroad – to the expansion of the same export good productive apparatus that generates this surplus, especially in boom times; import a substantial part of the productive equipment that may be necessary for the export industry from abroad; produce the maximum of the remainder and generate all working capital out of the super-exploitation of low-wage labor at home; in short, expand the monoproduction export economy at the expense of creating a productive structure that is capable of generating self-sustained economic development. (Frank, first draft of this book, 1969)

A similar interpretation is found among some students of North American economic history, which contrasts the underdevelopment of the South with the development of the North. Thus Eugene Genovese writes in *The Political Economy of Slavery:*

The South found itself in a dilemma similar to that facing many underdeveloped countries today. On the one hand, it provided a market for outside industry. On the other hand, that very market was too small to sustain industry on a scale large enough to compete with outsiders who could draw on wider markets . . . The root of insufficient demand must be sought in the poverty of the rural majority composed of slaves, subsistence farmers, and poor whites . . . Slavery led to the rapid concentration of land and wealth and prevented the expansion of a southern home market . . . Instead of providing a basis for industrial growth, the Southern countryside economically dominated by a few large estates, provided only a limited market for industry . . . For the present let us focus on another factor, which in itself provides an adequate explanation of the South's inability to industrialize the retardation of the home market for both industrial and agricultural commodities. (165, 162, 24, 158)

The development of the North of the United States has often been attributed to the supposed existence of a wide internal market already at the beginning of development. In his important study of *The Economic Growth of the United States 1790–1860*, Douglass North writes:

The timing, pace, and character of American manufacturing development before the Civil War resulted from the following factors: (1) By all odds, the most important influence was the growth in the size of the domestic market . . . The markets for textiles, clothing, boots and shoes, and other consumer goods were national in scope, reflecting the decline of self-sufficiency and the growth of specialization and division of labor. Derived demand for machinery and products of iron expanded in response to the consumer goods industries . . . (2) concentration of manufacturing in the Northeast stemmed from a number of factors . . . The most important underlying reason was the development in the years before 1815, particularly during the French and Nepoleonic Wars, when the groundwork was laid. The growth of large urban centres, the development of a capital market – first around foreign trade and then for the cotton trade, social overhead investment in transportation facilities, and the growing supply of labor – first from agriculture and then from immigrants . . . The development of the New England textile industry was implemented by the shift of capital from shipping into textiles . . . The Irish (immigrants) were destitute, and formed a reservoir of unskilled labor in the Northeast . . . (166–70)

In the South, the situation was altogether different. North notes, 'expansion in the Northeast and in the South stand in marked contrast to each other . . . The rapid spread of cotton culture throughout [the South] . . . The notable fact about cotton is that the income of the South flowed directly out in the form of: (1) services and transport to implement that trade; (2) import of foodstuffs to feed slaves and planters; (3) import of manufactured goods . . . The South provided neither the services to market its own exports nor the consumer goods and services to supply its own needs, and a very high propensity to import' (52, 57).

Elsewhere North (128–30) goes on:

The salient features of the South's economic structure were these: (1) There was concentrated production for the market (outside the region) of a few staple commodities, with cotton by far the most important. (2) Large-scale . . . plantation system in cotton, sugar and rice . . . large amounts of labor and land for lowest unit cost. (3) The supply of labor for the plantation system was, of course, in slaves. . . . (4) The availability of land to the [South-west] for extensive expansion of cotton culture and the rich quality of this land . . . took place in surges that clearly reflected the pull of increased profitability of cotton production on western lands. The price of cotton was the most decisive factor in this regard . . . (5) . . . A rise in cotton prices precipitated another move into new lands of the Southwest by planters and their slaves . . . (6) Those members of the southern white population who possessed slaves and engaged in the production of southern staples were in the minority . . . A large percentage of the population made very little cash income . . . (7) A notable lack of urbanization characterized the area. Aside from the growth of a few ports to implement the cotton trade . . . (8) It is not surprising that locally oriented industries and services were conspicuously fewer in the South, on a per capita basis, than elsewhere . . . (10) Investment in human capital in the South was conspicuously lower than in the other two regions . . . Illiteracy . . .

The same emphasis of the distribution of property and income determination and explaining the growth or stagnation of an internal market appear in some attempts to account for the differences in development between Argentina and Australia.

> The reasons for these differences arose from factors fundamental to the economic structure of the countries concerned . . . The Australian economy was never geared so completely to the export trade as was that of Argentina after 1900. More emphasis was placed on stimulating industrial output. Despite the long period of investment, British imports from Australia increased more slowly than those from Argentina between the early 80's and the turn of the century. After 1900 this divergence became most marked: Argentine exports increased twice as much as Australia's until 1913. (Saul, 84–5).

The resource base of Australia, to say nothing of Canada, was more diversified than that of Argentina. This obliged the latter to devote foreign exchange to importing coal, while it permitted the former to put its earnings from the wheat boom of the 1880s to better use (Geller, 18, 21). Already at the beginning of the 1880s the income level of Australia was higher (Geller, 18) and more equally distributed (Saul, 81, and Geller) than in Argentina. Saul observes:

> Possibly a smaller proportion of loans to Australia was used directly to purchase goods from abroad, with the result that the secondary (linkage) effects of investment would be greater than in Argentina. It might also be argued that changes in the composition of imports would depend upon how far the mass of the population benefited from foreign investment by a rise in their real incomes. The maldistribution of income in Argentina certainly led to a sharp rise of imports of luxuries . . . A wider distribution of income in Australia resulted in a growth of imports of a less exotic character. (81).

The reasons for these differences have perhaps not yet been entirely clarified. One reason certainly is the difference in the distribution of land ownership or occupancy. The relatively higher degree of *prior* monopolisation of land – and of political power – that emerged from Argentina's colonial past, which Australia did not share, certainly led to differences in the distribution of income and the structure of the home market, as Geller (8) and others have observed. It also resulted in important differences in the policy and pattern of immigration. As a result, immigration in Argentina was much more concentrated in the cities and perhaps stimulated an earlier and greater growth of a labour-intensive tertiary sector than in Australia. Moreover, different immigration and land settlement policies, which in Argentina favoured the large landholders more than in Australia, where squatting, if not always family-size landownership, was very much more permitted and practised. Another factor (emphasised and called to my attention in an unpublished paper by my former student David Seymour) reinforced these divergent tendencies: the discovery and production of gold in Australia in the 1860s attracted a rush of immigration and helped to form a labour force and a labour movement with enough self-interest and political power to pressure the Australian government into adopting tariff and other policies to protect their relatively high wage level and – simultaneously though perhaps less intentionally – to protect the internal market. The result of this political action was to protect Australia's internal market in time to channel the foreign exchange earnings from the worldwide wheat boom after 1880 into more productive uses in Australia than in Argentina. Moreover, the gold permitted Australia to pay for some of its imports with bullion and to free other resources for productive investment at home. (The production of gold and silver was of similar benefit to the development of the United States, which used this bullion as foreign exchange to pay its debts to Britain – which in turn sent it on to India. Gold production in the Brazilian Minas Gerais region in the eighteenth century also stimulated the growth of some local manufacturing, which was then destroyed again through Imperial order and British competition, at least in part because of the wider distribution of income associated with gold placer, compared with deep silver, mining. Further study is needed to determine why bullion mining facilitated, rather than hindered the development of other productive forces in these particular times and places and not in some others.)

In the meantime, at precisely this crucial stage in their respective histories, Argentina experienced the opposite political develpment: the provincial 'developmentist' forces were substantially defeated by 1860, when the 'European' party took over the government of Buenos Aires under Mitre, and they were totally defeated by 1880, when the outward-looking and export-promoting hegemony of

Buenos Aires was definitely established over all of Argentina by the governments of Rocca and Pelegrini.

Our discussion of the development of the internal market so far has been in terms of the stimulation of industrial development through what Watkins calls final demand linkage.

In this discussion the existence of the internal market has largely been viewed as given or determined independently of the development itself, though some writers, including the present one, have also made an effort to trace the existence or lack of an internal market to the mode of production, international exchange relationships and the international division of labour. In fact, the pre-existence of such an internal market is questionable not only for some of the cases reviewed in the previous pages but even (as is suggested in Chapter 4) in the case of the metropolitan economies such as Britain.

This thesis has been severely questioned by Marx and Lenin on *theoretical grounds* that are examined below. But whatever the limitations of the internal market and final consumer demand thesis of the autonomous existence or development of the internal market, these limitations would appear to be still greater with regard to the extension of the same analysis to induced market formation through infant industry protection, import substitution or most recently export substitution.

I. On Infant Industry and Import Substitution

The infant industry argument is as old as industrial and even as mercantile capitalism: much mercantilist policy was intended to protect and develop infant industry, and this policy and analysis found renewed application in the nineteenth century where economic and political circumstances permitted. But in the face of the historical evidence, it is difficult to sustain the proposition that such infant industrial development stimulated or even accompanied a greater equality or equalisation of the distribution of income of property – as was supposedly the case in the 'autonomous' internal market development discussed above or as is explicitly recommended by post-1950 proponents of import-substituting industrialisation, such as that proposed by Prebisch for ECLA and many others (see below). Instead, the distribution of property and income became rather more unequal.

Moreover, without negating the marginal importance that

induced infant industry development or import substitution may have had, any such development policy or analysis has certainly always, and especially since industrial capitalism's nineteenth-century development of the international division of labour and transformation of modes of production, been essentially limited by these objective conditions. Chapter 4 suggests that England, New England, Germany and Japan were able to promote infant industry development successfully under various circumstances, because in each case the objective conditions were ripe and not simply because their people were more enterprising, wilful or wise. Similarly, Pombal's Portugal, Mohammed Ali's Egypt, and the Lopez's Paraguay were unsuccessful in their 'Bismarckian' industrial development policies (reviewed above and in Chapter 4), because the process of world capital accumulation, capitalist development, and division of labour, not to mention military power, did not permit such development at those times and places. (Of course, this does not mean that in the absence of such development efforts which were condemned by Britain then and are still unacceptable to imperialist orthodoxy today, these countries would necessarily have fared better in world history.)

During the two decades past, import substitution – and in the last few years export substitution as well – have been welcomed and heralded well nigh as a panacea for underdevelopment by bourgeois governments and spokesmen all over Asia, Africa and Latin America. The real or imagined substitution of imports by home production of industrial commodities for the domestic market became the official strategy of the United Nations Economic Commission for Latin America and most of its member governments, though in practice it started earlier and went farther in India. Through UNCTAD, the underdeveloped member governments have lately sought to extend their 'industrialisation' still further by exporting manufactures to the industrialised countries and asking them to grant them duty-free entry.

As a development policy, import substitution has turned out to be a failure; and as an analysis of the development process it has left the principal factors, imperialism and the class structure, out of consideration. Even ECLA has been obliged to recognise the 'decline' of import substitution through the publication of an important article by its staff member, Maria de Concepcão Tavares, in ECLA's *Economic Bulletin for Latin America*. It has become clear that import substitution has not been the enlightened policy of progressive industrialists and governments, but rather the reaction of the bourgeoisie – including the part of it previously dependent on raw materials exports – to their inability to continue producing, investing, and profiting during the war and depression crisis of international capitalism.

In recent years this same bourgeoisie has become an enthusiastic junior partner of the multinational monopolies in the newly emerging international division of labour, which the latter, like the conquerors, pirates and planters of old, are propagating throughout the world. This development of the international division of labour requires the underdeveloped countries to substitute one kind of imports for another, consonant with the metropolitan economies' replacement of consumer goods exports by producer goods and technology exports. Thus, some peripheral countries now produce certain industrial commodities at home, first for the domestic market, than for export to neighbouring markets and finally for export to the metropolis itself when they can no longer be so profitably produced there. It may be predicted that the current increase in metropolitan resistance to textile and related imports from Asia is no more than a temporary cyclical measure. Far from decreasing the underdeveloped countries' dependence on the metropolitan ones, this process only intensifies dependence and fails to resolve the central problem of internal market development in most underdeveloped countries.

J. On the Division of Labour and Technological Gaps

The problem of internal market development and import substitution in the underdeveloped countries is further complicated, and rendered insoluble within the confines of world capitalism, by the development of technology and the increased cost of investment, which are known as the 'technological gap'. In the eighteenth century, before the industrial revolution, manufacturing and agricultural technology in Europe and many other parts of the world were not radically different. In many respects, India and China had long been technologically more advanced than Europe. The industrial revolution changed all that (as is discussed in Chapter 4). The revolution (or evolution as some writers contend) in industrial and transport technology revolutionised the economic, social and political structure throughout the world. It destroyed traditional manufacturing and artisanry all over the world and replaced them by domestic or foreign industry. In the now developed countries, traditional manufacturing was replaced by domestic industry. (In some regions of recent settlement, new industry developed in the absence of the old.) In the now underdeveloped countries traditional manufacturing and its economic and social ties with other sectors of the economy were also destroyed; but instead of being replaced by the domestic growth of industry as in Europe, it was replaced or displaced by that same European, especially British, industry. This industry gained access to consumers abroad through technologically and economically, as well as politically, generated cost and price reductions of the industrial revolution, through elimination of natural protection by drastic declines in transportation costs, and through the imposition or acceptance of 'free trade' in accord with the export bourgeoisies' economic and political interests (see above and Chapter 4).

The industrial revolution typically began first in consumer goods industries, especially textiles and food processing, and then spread to capital goods through the metal-mechanical industries (Hoffmann). In Britain the industrial revolution began in cotton textiles followed by the metallurgical industries and machine-building for transportation and textile production. At the mid-nineteenth century some European countries and the United States began to follow suit, while most of the rest of the world turned to free trade and specialised in food and raw materials production to feed European industry and its workers. Significantly, the countries or industrial centres that embarked on industrialisation at that stage of world capitalist development, even though they lagged behind Britain, relied substantially on domestic production of the necessary means of production like textile machinery. That is, they used British models but local technology for the manufacture of their machinery (Hoffman, 42–57; Bairoch, Chapter 8, Section B 3; Hinkelammert 90–1). Saul (141–4) on the other hand emphasises British exports of textile and other machinery to other European countries, which did not however depend on such imports to the exclusion of local manufacture. Indeed, the shift from consumer goods to capital goods production, which Hoffmann observed in all the economies he studied, appears to have occurred increasingly rapidly in these later starters – so much so that by the end of the nineteenth century Britain had lost its commanding lead (Hoffmann, Chapter 7).

Since the turn of the twentieth century – during the fourth period of industrialisation according to Hoffmann, or since the post-1896 cyclical up-swing – the technological and industrial revolution and the international division of labour appear to have undergone a further radical and qualitative change. Since then, with Britain having lost its lead to new leading and dynamic industries elsewhere, capital producers' goods, have no longer been produced by traditional manufacturing technology or methods, but rather by industry itself – machines built by machines. Consumer goods and other industries have since then been established (or, as in India, re-established) in a number of other countries. But they have been technologically and economically obliged for the most part to import, rather than to produce domestically, the producer goods necessary to sustain their 'import substitute' consumer goods production. In Asia, Africa and Latin America only one country, Japan, has avoided this fate. Exceptional circumstances isolated Japan from competition in the world market long enough, while its consumer and producer goods were qualitatively inferior and excessively priced relative to those of the world market, to be able to start its own producer goods industries and to develop some technologically advanced and economically competitive industry. The Soviet Union later proceeded similarly. Elsewhere in the capitalist world industrial, import substituting or other measures have not eliminated underdevelopment, except in some settler regions.

During the 1930s and 1940s the economic and political crisis in the imperialist metropolis rendered industrial growth for the national market profitable in such countries as India, Brazil and Argentina, which initially relied on greater utilisation of already installed excess industrial capacity. These countries, and more recently others like Mexico and Egypt have even advanced to the production of durable consumer and capital goods for the national market. In some countries, such as, under differing circumstances, Brazil and South Africa, industrial growth is now even directed to foreign, including metropolitan, markets. But this industrial growth without economic development is essentially part and parcel of the newly emerging international division of labour in which the most dynamic and research-intensive industries like electronic cybernetics and petrochemicals are centred in the United States. Other less dynamic industries are developed in Western Europe and Japan, while the socialist economies and some capitalist under-developed ones increasingly take over the production of no longer leading or highly profitable capital goods and certain consumer goods. (The socialist countries increasingly import advanced technology from the industrial capitalist countries and export consumer goods and low-technology producer goods to the under-developed countries, some of which in turn export light consumer goods to the industrial capitalist countries.) But many under-developed countries continue to specialize (sometimes even more so) in raw materials that are increasingly essential for industrial development in the imperialist metropolis. (For evidence about this emerging division of labour, and especially the participation of some socialist countries, see for instance numbers of the *Far Eastern Economic Review* for 1971–72 and the more hypothetical discussion in Amin [108] and Palloix [II, 174–6 and I, 111–15]. A theoretical treatment of sub-imperialism in this international division of labour can be found in Marini.)

Thus, industrial production for the internal market, even of some capital goods, no longer guarantees to economic development, and, except in the industrially already advanced economies, it is no longer possible within the capitalist division of labour without increasing dependence on producers' goods and technology produced elsewhere. Some underdeveloped countries now produce their consumer goods with some locally produced producer goods that were technologically advanced at an earlier stage of world capitalist development. Now, however, these countries are none the less obliged to import many additional producer goods and technology (or 'raw materials' and semi-manufactures embodying the latter) which are now essential for the local production of other consumer and producer goods. Local production of these tech-nologically advanced producer goods or inputs, to say nothing of national production of the underlying technological research, has become prohibitively expensive for these underdeveloped countries; and it has become economically and politically impossible within the framework of world and national capitalism as long as investment in other sectors is substantially more profitable.

The analysis of this problem requires closer examination of the class and sectoral structure of 'internal' and 'external' markets in the underdeveloped countries in the age of imperialism.

3. On Production and Accumulation

K. On Economic Sectors and Classes

The problem may be introduced by noting, a disjunction between Adam Smith and Marx or Lenin. We may recall that in Smith's *Inquiry into the Nature and Causes of the Wealth of Nations,* 'the division of labour is limited by the extent of the market.' Marx, on the other hand, entitled the first volume of his *Capital,* 'The Productive Process of Capital' and Lenin, following him, subtitled his *The Development of Capitalism in Russia,* 'The Process of the Formation of a Home Market for Large-Scale Industry'. In his theoretical first chapter, Lenin writers:

The basic process of the formation of a home market (i.e. of the development of commodity production and of capitalism) is the social division of labour . . . The 'home market' for capitalism is created by developing capitalism itself, which deepens the social division of labour and resolves the direct producers into capitalists and workers. The degree of the development of the home market is the degree of development of capitalism in the country. To raise the question of the limits of the home market separately from that of the development of capitalism (as the Narodnik economists do) is wrong . . . On the problem of interest to us, that of the home market, the main conclusion from Marx's theory of realisation is the following: capitalist production, and, consequently, the home market, grow not so much on account of articles of consumption as on account of means of production. In other words, the increase in the means of production outstrips the increase in articles of consumption . . . For capitalism, therefore, the growth of the home market is to a certain extent 'independent' of the growth of personal consumption, and takes place mostly on account of productive consumption. . . . [In his concluding chapter, Lenin continues] In chapter I we pointed to the erroneous chapter of the theory that links the problem of a foreign market for capitalism with that of the realisation of the product (pp. 64–65 and foll.). Capitalism's need of a foreign market is by no means to be explained by the impossibility of realising the product on the home market, but by the circumstance that capitalism is in no position to go on repeating the same processes of production on the former scale, under changing conditions (as was the case under pre-capitalist regimes), and that it inevitably leads to an unlimited growth of production which overflows the old, narrow limits of earlier economic units. With the unevenness of development inherent in capitalism, one branch of production outstrips the others and strives to transcend the bounds of the old field of economic relations. (Lenin, 67, 69, 54, 590. This problem is analysed and related to the theory of Rosa Luxemburg by Palloix, 1970.)

In dwelling on the internal market, Lenin – who, it must be remembered, also wrote a book on imperialism – did not deny the existence or importance of the external market in capitalist development. He only denied the lack of effective demand, as expounded by non-Marxist underconsumptionists, and the realisation problem as envisaged by Rosa Luxemburg. Lenin denied that this (non-existent) problem need or could be resolved by relying on a pre-existing demand prior to capitalist development or on a pre-capitalist market 'external' to capitalism.

Lenin's chief purpose in his *The Development of Capitalism in Russia* was to criticise the populist Narodnik claim that capitalism could not develop in Russia for lack of an 'internal' market. Lenin argued that the development of an internal or external market does not depend on or require demand from a pre- or non-capitalist sector. (Therefore, Lenin would also have rejected the thesis we discussed above, according to which the development of the United States and the underdevelopment of Latin America were the result of their respective distributions of income and pre-industrial internal markets.) Like Marx before him, Lenin argued that capitalist development and the development of both the internal and the external market are associated with the progressive nationally and international division of labour, the increasing preponderance of producer relative to consumer goods, the transformation of various kinds of pre-capitalist modes of production by their incorporation in the world capitalist system (which renders the distribution of income and property – especially of the means of production – less and not more equal), and the associated unequal development of the national and international economy, which spurs the leading sectors on to export part of their output. This capitalist development manifests itself in stages, one of which Lenin examined in his later work on 'Imperialism, the Highest Stage of Capitalism'.

But this process and particularly the production of producer goods did not take place equally in the now developed and underdeveloped countries. Why not? To reverse the perceived decline in profits and to ward off the feared 'stationary state' Ricardo, as we may recall, sought to extend the exchange of British manufactures for overseas foodstuffs. (We leave aside the theoretical questions whether the stationary state really threatened, whether the rate of profit necessarily falls and whether there is a realisation problem or not. Here we examine only what did happen irrespective of whether theoretically it had to or not.) Ricardo sought to sustain the rate of profit by cheapening British wage goods, increasing the rate of surplus value by reducing variable capital. Ricardo's policy permitted a higher rate of profit in Britain without a concomitant increase – and later with a decrease – in the exploitation of labour, by increasing the productivity of agriculture both in Britain and overseas *and* by increasing the rate of exploitation of agricultural labour overseas.

Marx observed that the British trade policy and practice also supported the rate of profits by lowering the cost of producer goods made with imported raw materials and counteracted the increase in the organic composition of capital (due to the increase in the physical capital/labour ratio) by reducing the value of capital, some of whose components were imported at low cost. These raw materials were produced overseas through increases in labour productivity *and* labour exploitation. The export of British manufactures, first of consumer goods and then also of producer goods, was the link or exchange which made this process possible, irrespective of whether these exports were necessary for 'realisation' through external demand as distinct from the colonies' participation in the metropolitan process of production.

Profitable development of producer goods for the 'internal' market in the metropolitan and new settler countries was not based especially on external demand and still less on any demand generated by the switch from subsistence production to the market. But this development did require the super-exploitation of labour, expecially in the colonies and neo-colonies in which the relations of production were being forcibly transformed, and the transfer of this value to the metropolis through unequal exchange. (The transformation is examined in Chapter 6 and the exchange in Chapter 7.) The increase in super-exploitation and labour productivity in the colonies and the transfer of the value so produced to the metropolis through unequal exchange therefore contributed significantly to the 'internal' and external market for metropolitan manufactures and to the solution of the 'realisation problem'. Thus, the now underdeveloped countries provided many of the 'counteracting influences' on the tendency for the rate of profit to fall, which Marx noted in his Book III, Chapter XIV. The underdeveloped countries contributed to the profitable production of all manufactures in the metropolis through their supply of cheap wage goods and to the metropolitan production of producer goods through their supply of cheap raw materials. This metropolitan production was realised through consumer and producer ('productive consumption') demand in the metropolis and the periphery, except when excessive expansion of metropolitan industrial and colonial raw materials production and capacity brought on periodic crises, against which the periphery also acted as a partial shock-absorber.

In the periphery, the production of raw materials for export supplied a small sector of the population, and through the mediation of the state sometimes sectors of the growing middle classes, with an income that they spent on imported consumer goods and luxuries. The vast bulk of the population, in the meantime, consumed the few local products that their low income permitted them to purchase and/or sub-consumed at levels below subsistence. Since the market for colonial production was overseas, their purchasing power was not necessary for the realisation of colonial production. And from the point of view of international and national capital as a whole their wages did not represent a purchasing power to be increased, but only a labour cost to be reduced; and it was.

The essentials of this situation have remained the same in the twentieth century in many underdeveloped countries. When some regions of Africa were reinserted in the international division of labour the same relationships came to prevail there as well (see Chapter 6). In some countries of Latin America, import substitution at first seemed to lend wages an importance as a source of internal demand as well. But subsequently it became clear that this modification was more apparent than real. We observed above that import substitution took off during the imperialist economic crisis, which hindered the exchange of raw materials produced by low-wage labour for manufactures destined for the high-income market. This dilemma led some countries to produce consumer goods for this high-income market locally instead of importing them. That is, import substitution was initially for an already existing 'internal' market of the kind held to be impossible by the Narodnik populists and unnecessary by their antagonist Lenin in Russia. Lenin argued that capitalist development creates its own internal market. But this import *substitute* development did *not* create its own internal market. At most, import substitution created an 'internal' market for external producer goods and foreign investment from abroad. Rather than leading to a rise in wages – to expand internal market purchasing power as it had in the metropolis and the new settler countries – this dependent capitalist development only raised wages marginally and temporarily and then began to lower them again. When balance of payments crises hindered the importation of the foreign capital equipment necessary to keep domestic industry operating, these dependent capitalist economies launched another drive to increase exports – first of raw materials produced by increasingly super-exploited agricultural and mine workers and then also of manufactures produced by super-exploited industrial workers. The market in which this peripheral production is realised again turns out to be abroad in the metropolis, and the peripheral wages, now for industrial as well as primary production, again turn out to be not a source of purchasing power that is to be increased but a cost factor that must be reduced; and it is, through repression if necessary. Domestic realisation on the 'internal' market is still through the final consumer demand of the upper and upper-middle classes and through productive consumption. But both of these in turn are ultimately dependent on earnings from the external sector and increasingly on their distribution through the mediation of the state. Thus, dependent capitalist development (or underdevelopment) of the 'internal' market depends increasingly on the production and export of raw materials and more recently also of industrial products, whose production in turn depends on the super-exploitation of wage labour drawn from a growing industrial reserve army of 'marginal' workers, who, far from constituting a source of effective demand on the internal market, are essential for profitable production, realisation and capital accumulation through the reduction of wage costs. (For further analysis, see Marini.)

In the imperialist metropolis – or in the imperialist system as a whole – the counterpart of this continued development of underdevelopment under 'modernised' conditions is the continued development of the international division of labour and the accumulation of capital. The recent development of technology and that of the multinational corporation in some industries, including agro-industries and synthetic substitutes for some raw materials or economic processing of low-grade ores in the metropolitan countries, assign changing tasks, though not so changing roles, to the underdeveloped countries in the international division of labour and the process of capital accumulation. (These developments are discussed in my collection of essays published in 1977 in Spanish under the title *Reflexions on the Economic Crisis* and are the object of further analysis in my *The Contemporary World Crisis*, in preparation.) Today as in the past, both in fact and in theory (or analysis), the problems posed by the international division of labour and the extension of the internal or external market are not resolved or resolvable in abstract unhistorical comparative terms of advantage or otherwise. Nor are they subject to voluntaristic manipulation beyond the limits of objective material and political reality. It is not to counsel fatalism but to aspire to freedom, to recognize that in the present as in the past history is still determinant and that, as Marx and Lenin observed, freedom is to achieve the necessary within the possible.

6 Imperialism and the Transformation of Modes of Production in Asia, Africa and Latin America, 1870–1930

Our analysis of the three stages of world capital accumulation and the development of underdevelopment in Asia, Africa and Latin America has sought to contribute to the clarification of the relations between the world historical process of uneven capitalist development, the exchange relations and mechanisms that drain capital from the colonialised countries to the metropolis, and the transformations in the modes of production in the latter, which permit this drain but at the same time develop their own structural underdevelopment. Often, more than supplying answers, we have been obliged to raise questions about this process. And we shall have to do the same in our examination below of the transformation of the modes of production in Asia, the Middle East, Africa and Latin America during the third –imperialist – stage of world capital accumulation and capitalist development.

The transformation of the modes of production and the development of underdevelopment in Asia, Africa, and Latin America during the third stage of world capitalist accumulation and capitalist development have been the object of only little historical (or contemporary) examination and scarcely any theoretical analysis (prior to 1970). Metropolitan economists have forgotten Adam Smith's observation and warning about misery in the colonies and have almost universally assumed a 'white man's burden' attitude that increased contact, closer integration, diffusion of capital, technology, institutions, etc., could only result in the development of these regions (for critiques see Aguilar and

Coatsworth). Anthropologists – who 'specialise' in the study of 'natives' abroad – have, for their part, assumed instead that the societies they study have been 'traditionally' at rest as they find them and unchanging: on reading Radcliffe-Brown's and his followers' studies on Africa, for instance, one would never suspect that his countrymen Cecil Rhodes and Lord Lugard had lived at all or that imperialism ever existed (for critiques, see Gough, 'Anthropology: Child of Imperialism', and Frank 1968). Many intellectuals in the colonialised and neo-colonial countries themselves have been so culturally colonialised and brainwashed by the metropolis as to study their own societies only in the metropolitan image- civilization or barbary, in the words of Sarmineto referring to Argentina in the 1860s. (Only during the last decade have Africans begun to [re]write their own history.)

Marxists have done only a little better. Marx himself did not live to witness the transformation of the colonial world in the third stage of world capital accumulation. Lenin gave the matter attention but mostly in connection only with problems of immediate political strategy. Since his time, and until recently, the scholars of the Soviet Union have also devoted their attention to problems of immediate concern, as have most Marxists in the developed capitalist countries. Thus, only recently (and at the time of writing in 1970 often in still unpublished works) have students of, and often – like Amin – from, the underdeveloped countries begun to dedicate empirical research and theoretical analysis to the transformation of the mode of production in the underdeveloped world during the last century. There has been only one outstanding exception to this pattern, Rosa Luxemburg, who dedicated considerable attention to the problem and attempted a theoretical synthesis over half a century ago. (The fact that she was led to do so by her concern with the theoretical problem of the realisation of surplus value and the continuation of metropolitan capitalist development, and that her theoretical argument in this regard has been rejected as unfounded by virtually all Marxists since Lenin, does not belittle the importance and usefulness of her resulting analysis of the colonial transformation – particularly since no better analysis was undertaken in the subsequent fifty years.)

1. Rosa Luxemburg on Imperialist Struggle against Natural and Peasant Economy

We may therefore summarise the theoretical synthesis by Luxemburg on the nineteenth-century development of underdevelopment in the Middle East and North Africa, and to some extent in Black Africa, made at the beginning of the twentieth century:

> In detail, capital in its struggle against societies with a natural economy pursues the following ends: (1) To gain immediate possession of important sources of productive forces such as land, game in primeval forests, minerals, precious stones and ores, products of exotic flora such as rubber, etc. (2) To 'liberate' labour power and to coerce it into service. (3) To introduce a commodity economy. (4) To separate trade and agriculture . . . Since the primitive associations of the natives are the strongest protection for their social organizations and for their material bases of existence, capital must begin by planning for the systematic destruction and annihilation of all non-capitalist social units which obstruct its development . . . Each new colonial expansion is accompained, as a matter of course, by a relentless battle of capital against the social and economic ties of the natives, who are forcibly robbed of their means of production and labour power.
>
> Any hope of restricting the accumulation of capital exclusively to peaceful competition, i.e. to regular commodity exchange such as takes place between capitalist producer countries, rests on the pious belief that capital can accumulate without mediation of productive forces and without the demand of the more primitive organisations, and that it can rely upon the slow internal process of a disintegrating economy . . . Force is the only solution open to capital; the accumulation of capital, seen as a historical process, employs force as a permanent weapon, not only at its genesis, but further on down to the present day. From the point of view of the primitive societies involved, it is a matter of life or death; for them there can be no other attitude than opposition and fight to the finish – complete exhaustion and extinction. Hence permanent occupation of the colonies by the military, native risings and punitive expeditions are the order of the day for the colonial regime . . . In spite of the ups and downs of internal French politics, French colonial policy persevered for fifty years

in its systematic and deliberate efforts to destroy and disrupt communal property. It served two distinct purposes: the break-up of communal property was primarily intended to smash the social power of the Arab family associations and to quell their stubborn resistance against the French yoke . . . Secondly, communal property had to be disrupted in order to gain the economic assets of the conquered country; the Arabs, that is to say, had to be deprived of the land they had owned for thousands of years, so that French capitalists could get it . . . This is the double significance of the decree of the Senate dated April 22, 1864. General Allard declared in the Senate: 'The government does not lose sight of the fact that the general aim of its policy is to weaken the influence of the tribal chieftains and to dissolve the family associations. By this means, it will sweep away the last remnants of feudalism [*sic*!] defended by the opponents of the government bill . . . The surest method of accelerating the process of dissolving the family associations will be to institute private property and to settle European colonists among Arab families'. . . . The second condition of importance for acquiring means of production and raising the surplus value is that commodity exchange and commodity economy should be introduced in societies based on natural economy as soon as their independence has been abrogated or rather in the course of this disruptive process . . . In districts where natural economy formerly prevailed the introduction of means of transport – railways, navigation, canals – is vital for the spreading of commodity economy . . . An important final phase in the campaign against natural economy is to separate industry from agriculture, to eradicate rural industries altogether from peasant economy . . . Capital must get the peasants to buy its commodities and will therefore begin by restricting peasant economy to a single sphere – that of agriculture . . .

To all outward appearance, this process is quite peaceful . . . In reality, however, the process of separating agriculture and industry is determined by factors such as oppressive taxation, war or squandering and monopolisation of the nation's land, and thus belongs to the spheres of political power and criminal law no less than with economics . . . The imperialist phase of capitalist accumulation implies . . . lending abroad, railroad constructions, revolutions, and wars . . . At present the achievement of capitalist autonomy in the *hinterland* and backward colonies is attained amidst wars and revolutions. Revolution is an essential for the process of capitalist emancipation. The backward communities must shed their obsolete political organisations, relics of natural and simple commodity economy, and create a modern state machinery adapted to the purposes of capitalist production. The revolutions in Turkey, Russia and China fall under this heading . . . The forward-thrusts of capital are approximately reflected in the development of the railway network . . . Between the thirties and the sixties of the nineteenth century, railway building and the loans necessary for it mainly served to oust natural economy, to spread commodity economy – as in the case of the Russian railway loans in the sixties, or in that of the American railways which were built with European capital. Railway construction in Africa and Asia during the last twenty years, on the other hand, almost exclusively served the purposes of imperialist policy, of economic monopolisation and economic subjugation of backward communities . . . Foreign loans . . . are yet the surest ties by which the old capitalist states maintain their influence, exercise financial control and exert pressure on customs, foreign and commercial policy of the young capitalist states . . . In the first place, there was an element of usury in every loan, anything between one-fifth and one-third of the money ostensibly lent sticking to the fingers of European bankers. Ultimately, the exorbitant interest had to be paid somehow, but how – where were the means to come from? Egypt herself was to supply them; their source was the Egyptian fellah-peasant economy providing in the final analysis all the most important elements of large-scale capitalist enterprise. He provided the land . . . As forced labour, he also proved the labour power and, what is more, he was exploited without payment and even had to provide his own means of subsistence while he was at work . . . But not alone that it supplied the land and labour power, peasant economy also provided the money. Under the influence of capitalist economy, the screws were put on the fellaheen by taxation . . . The greater the debt to European capital became, the more had to be extracted from the peasants. . .

It should now be clear that the transactions between European loan capital and European industrial capital are based on relations which are extremely rational and 'sound' for the accumulation of capital, although they appear absurd to the casual observer . . . Stripped of all obscuring links, these relations consist in the simple fact that European capital has largely swallowed up the Egyptian peasant economy. Enormous tracts of land, labour, and labour products without number, accruing to the state in taxes, have ultimately been converted into European capital and have been accumulated . . . As against the fantastic increase of capital on the one hand, the other economic result is the ruin of peasant economy together with the growth of commodity exchange which is rooted in the supreme exertion of the country's productive forces . . . Thus, the economic metabolism between the peasants of Asia Minor, Syria and Mesopotamia on the one hand and German capital on the other proceeds in the following way: in the *vilayets* Konya, Baghdad, Bazra, etc., the grain comes into being as a simple use-product of primitive peasant economy. It immediately falls to the tithe-farmer as a state levy. Only then, in the hands of this latter, does it become a commodity and, as such, money which falls to the state. This money is nothing but converted peasant grain; it is not even produced as a commodity. But now, as a state guarantee, it serves towards paying for the construction and operation of railways, i.e. to realise both the value of the means of production and the surplus value extorted from the Asiatic peasants and proletariat in the building and running of the railways. In this process further means of production of German origin are used, and so the peasant grain of Asia, converted into money, also serves to turn into cash the surplus value that has been extorted from the German workers . . . This is the coarse and straightforward metabolism between European capital and Asiatic peasant economy, with the Turkish state reduced to its real role, that of a political machinery for exploiting peasant economy for capitalist purposes – the real function, this, of all Oriental states in the period of capitalist imperialism.' (Luxemburg, 369–71, 380–2, 386, 395–6, 419–21, 434–8, 444–5)

Though writing about the nineteenth-century imperialist phase of, capitalist development and distilling her analysis primarily from the experience of the Middle East, Rosa Luxemburg finds some of the same fundamental processes of world capitalist development and colonial capitalist development of underdevelopment as we already encountered in Latin America and the Caribbean since the sixteenth century: the expansion of the world capitalist system; its colonial structure; the transformation and determination of the mode of production and economic structure in the colonies by their colonial relationship with the metropolis and in the interest of the development of the latter; the intentional and unintentional transformation of the class structure and social organisation adapting some institutional forms to function as agents of the colonial relationship and the new productive necessities and destroying those institutions – first and foremost communal property and its socio-cultural manifestations and supports – that turn out to be unadaptable or which serve the local population as sources of strength to resist this process; the incorporation – or where necessary the creation – of a local class and its subordinate agents whose economic and political interests are tied to the metropolis, and whose pursuit of economic and political policies in their own self-interest will also serve the interests of the metropolis, though it will generate the development of underdevelopment for their country and people.

We may examine the development of underdevelopment in these 'Luxemburgian' terms during the nineteenth century in turn in Asia, the Middle East and North Africa, Black Africa, and again in Latin America, where the 'free trade' and imperialist phases of world capitalist development again transformed the modes of production, class structure and underdevelopment policy in the interests of metropolitan development.

2. Imperialism in Asia

The degree of underdevelopment in Asia today is very substantially proportional to its degree of colonisation in the nineteenth century. The most underdeveloped – and most miserable – populations today are India and much of South East Asia, which were subject to the most brutal colonial capitalist exploitation. China, which was only a semi-colonial country, suffered less and somewhat differently; and, of course, since its liberation from capitalism since 1949 this country has made literally incomparable progress. The other major area of Asia, Japan managed to achieve considerable industrial development under capitalism since 1868; and, the fact that this development was possible must be attributed to Japan's independent non-colonial status and even to the absence of foreign investment in its development effort.

The most serious case of the development of underdevelopment is undoubtedly that of India. Since we have already examined the Indian experience in Chapter 4, section 5 above, and since the continuity between the second and third stages of world capital accumulation was perhaps greater – or the third stage began earlier – in India than in other colonial and neo-colonial countries, we may limit our further examination of India's experience here to only a few observations. But it is perhaps worth emphasising that both the Indian experience reviewed above in Chapter 4 and that examined immediately below appear to conform remarkably closely to the essentials of the transformation of the mode of production that Rosa Luxemburg synthesised in her analysis, primarily of the Middle Eastern experience.

With the development of imperialism, all British policy in India reinforced the development of underdevelopment in a million ways. Two of the principal instruments the British used to drain India of its capital were the railroads and the debt. The railroads were not only the physical instruments used to restructure the economy in order to be able to suck raw materials out and pump manufactured commodities in along the right of way. The Indians were also obliged to pay themselves for the installation of this exploitative mechanism on their soil. And the 'Indian debt' to which all imaginable and unimaginable items of British colonial administration of India were charged became in the particular circumstances of India one of the principal fiscal instruments – functionally equivalent to a host of other instruments elsewhere – for extracting the economic surplus from the colony to the metropolis.

The transformation of the economic structure and the class and political character of this transformation were noted by no less of an authorised and non-Marxist observer as Jawaharlal Nehru in his *The Discovery of India*:

> The techniques of British rule, which had already been well established, were now [after 1857] clarified and confirmed and deliberately acted upon. Essentially these were: the creation and protection of vested interests bound up with British rule; and a policy of balancing and counterpoising of different elements, and the encouragement of fissiparous tendencies and divisions among them. The princes and the big landlords were the basic vested interests thus created and encouraged. But now a new class, even more tied up with British rule, grew in importance. This consisted of the Indian members of the services, usually in subordinate

positions . . . Indians so employed were so dependent on the British administration and rule that they could be relied upon and treated as agents of that rule . . . Thus began the process of the indianization of the administrative machine in its subordinate ranks, all real power and initiative again, however, concentrated in the hands of the English personnel . . . By giving greater importance to the Indian states than they had ever had before, by encouraging reactionary elements and looking to them for support, by promoting divisions and encouraging one group against another, by encouraging fissiparous tendencies due to religion or province, and by organizing Quisling classes which were afraid of a change which might engulf them. All this was a natural and understandable policy for a foreign imperialist power to pursue, and it is a little naive to be surprised at it, harmful from the Indian nationalist point of view though it was . . . But the fact that it was so must be remembered if we are to understand subsequent developments . . . [this natural alliance of British power with the reactionaries in India – including we might add the political development and behaviour of Gandhi and Nehru themselves, who however seemingly 'nationalist' they may have been none the less did not fail to represent these 'reactionary elements'] . . . Nearly all our major problems today have grown up during British rule and as a direct result of British policy: the princes; the minority problem; various vested interests, foreign and Indian; the lack of industry and the neglect of agriculture; the extreme backwardness in the social services; and, above all, the tragic poverty of the people . . . A significant fact which stands out is that those parts of India which have been longest under British rule are the poorest today. Indeed some kind of chart might be drawn up to indicate the close connection between length of British rule and progressive growth of poverty . . . there can be no doubt that the poorest parts of India are Bengal, Bihar, Orissa and parts of Madras presidency; the mass level and standards of living are highest in Punjab. (Nehru, 240–4, 221, 208)

Thus, the most classic case history of the development of under-development, India, exemplified all of the major structural factors in the capitalist development of underdevelopment that we also encountered in Latin America and elsewhere: the development of an export economy with an excessively unequal distribution of income, the drain of economic surplus to the metropolis, the transformation of the national and local economic and class structure as a function of world capitalist development and metropolitan developmental needs, the natural alliance between the metropolitan colonial power and the local reactionary interests and their underdevelopment policy, the close connection between the length and intensity of capitalist colonialisation and ultra-underdevelopment, which we have observed regionally in the New World and domestically in India, and which further examination of Asia will demonstrate internationally there as well.

In many parts of South East Asia as well developed agricultural and handicrafts systems were destroyed by their incorporation into world capitalist development, particularly in the nineteenth century. Traditional trade relations with China were broken and replaced by capitalist trade relations with the European metropolis, through which South East Asia also was forced into an unequal exchange of its raw materials for European manufactured goods. In some parts of South East Asia, notably in the Malay peninsula and Java, the forced development of export crops for metropolitan development replaced the production of foodstuffs for local or regional consumption even more than in the south of India. As in India as well as in Latin America and the Caribbean, the development of world capitalism also determined the growth of a class in South East Asia whose interests were tied to the development of the metropolis and to the underdevelopment of their own economies. Buchanon (80) writes: 'Most disastrous of all, the impact of capitalism created a new class – the colonial middle class; this was largely administrative and commercial in its functions and actively collaborated with the colonial power in the government and economic exploitation of the dependent territory . . . it was little interested in economic progress but was largely a parasitic group.'

Geertz summarises the process of development of underdevelopment in South East Asia:

East Indian colonial history was marked by a series of political-economic devices (the East Indian Company, the Culture System, the Corporate Plantation system) by means of which the European 'merchant capitalism' side of the dual economy was to be more efficiently organized for the production and marketing of export crops, and the Indonesian 'peasant household' side was to be better protected against the disruptive effects of this large-scale commercial agriculture. Driven on by ever-increasing capital requirements, the Dutch moved from the institutional contrivances of adventurous capitalism in the eighteenth century, to those of state capitalism in the nineteenth, and to those of bureaucratic capitalism in the twentieth. But as each contrivance or device, building upon the ruins of its predecessor, entailed a yet deeper penetration of the rural economy by Western enterprise, it actually made it more difficult to isolate native life from the economic forces with which such enterprise deals . . . As Reinsma has well argued . . . 'so far as capital supply is concerned, private enterprise in the motherland played a much less powerful role in supporting the successor of the Culture System than has commonly been suggested in the literature.' . . . The capital-intensive side of the Indonesian dual economy was not merely imported from Holland . . . but was a direct product of the workings of the Colonial System after about 1830 . . . From the developmental point of view, therefore, the Culture System represented an attempt to raise an estate economy by a peasantry's bootstraps; and in this it was remarkably successful. . . . Peasant agriculture became a functioning element in the Indies' export economy rather than merely its backstop; peasant agriculture was developed, at least in part, into a business proposition rather than becoming frozen into a kind of outdoor relief. . . . There was just that admittedly highly autonomous branch of the Dutch economy which was situated in the Indies, 'tropical Holland', as it was sometimes called; and, cheek-by-jowl, the autonomous Indonesian economy also situated there. And though, indeed, the two interacted continuously in ways which fundamentally shaped their separate courses, they steadily diverged, largely as a result of this interaction, to the point where the structural contrasts between them became overwhelming. What Boeke (father of the 'dual society thesis') regarded as an intrinsic and permanent characteristic of Indonesian (or 'Eastern') economic life, 'a primarily spiritual phenomenon,' was really a historically created condition: it grew not from the immutable essence of the Eastern soul as it encountered the incarnate spirit of Western dynamism, but from the in no way predestined shape of colonial policy as it impressed itself upon the traditional pattern of Indonesian Agriculture. . . . The difference in 'economic mentality' between Dutch and Javanese which

Boeke took to be the cause of dualism was in fact in great part its result. The Javanese did not become impoverished because they were 'static'; they became 'static' because they were impoverished . . .

The sugar-lease system and, to a lesser extent, the similar practices connected with other crops, did not isolate the disequilibrating forces of commercial capitalism from village life; they introduced them, following the path the Company and the Culture System had blazed, into the very heart of it . . . The Javanese cane worker remained a peasant at the same time that he became a coolie. One comes to the same conclusion as the Dutch agronomist Tergast: . . . 'Around 1900 the amount of annual per capita quantity available was about 110 Kg. of rice, 30 Kg. of tubers, and 3 Kg. of pulses. Around 1940 this had changed to 85 Kg. of rice, 40 Kg. of maize, 180 Kg. tubers, and about 10 Kg. pulses. This change has locally reduced, often seriously, the quality of the diet . . . In fact, it seems likely that there was actually a decline in caloric intake between 1900 and 1940 . . . The real tragedy of colonial history in Java after 1830 is not that the peasantry suffered . . . The tragedy is that it suffered for nothing . . . But what makes this development tragic rather than merely decadent is that around 1830 the Javanese (and, thus, the Indonesian) economy could have made the transition to modernism, never a painless experience, with more ease than it can today.'

'The true measure of van den Bosch's greatness,' Furnivall has justly written, 'is the renascence of the Netherlands.' The true measure of van den Bosch's malignancy, however, is the stultification of Indonesia. (Geertz 50, 65–6, 60–2, 89, 96, 143, 82, 69)

What clearer mark of the development of underdevelopment could there be than that Indonesia could have proceeded to develop more easily before a century and a half of capitalist development than after it? – not because capitalist development has left a supposedly traditional part of a supposedly dual economy untouched, but because on the contrary capitalism has penetrated into the very heart of village life. And this has been the cause of underdevelopment not only in Indonesia, but throughout Asia, Africa and Latin America.

China never became a colony and was never colonialised to the degree that India and parts of South East Asia were. The forces of world capitalist development therefore never penetrated quite so deeply into the heart of village life as they did elsewhere and where they did so penetrate it was in South China, as analysed by Ch'en, which was most integrated into the world capitalist system. None the less, the development of capitalism did not spare China from the development of underdevelopment, and the metropolitan powers and the Chinese comprador bourgeoisie which came to be at their service invented new instruments appropriate to their needs and China's special circumstances in the world: the opium trade; the treaty ports and courts; and the treaties themselves, which extended special privileges to foreigners but not to Chinese nationals; the 'most favoured nation' clause and finally the 'open door' policy.

Barrington Moore summarises:

Let us now try to understand what the coming of the modern world did to the peasant, the base of this structure. During the nineteenth century there appeared scattered but unmistakeable signs of a decline in the peasant's economic situation: abandonment of tillage, deterioration of irrigation systems, increasing agricultural unemployment . . . Peasant handicrafts, an important supplement to the peasants' meager resources and a way of using surplus labor power during the black times of the agricultural cycle, suffered severe blows at the hands of cheap Western textiles . . . In the meantime near the coastal cities and along large rivers, the local village market gave way to the large urban market, while the effects of a market economy penetrated more and more deeply into rural areas . . . As the market evolved toward a more efficient and centrally organized institution, the peasant was left behind and his bargaining power deteriorated. Without reserves and operating close to the margin of subsistence, the peasant often had to sell immediately after the harvest when prices were falling . . . The peasant's plight favored the dealer and speculator, generally in league with the landlord . . . As the peasants fell into debt, they had to borrow, often at very high rates. When they could not repay, they had to transfer title to the land to the landlord, remaining on the soil to work it more or less indefinitely . . . In the light of the connection between property and social cohesion, perhaps the most important aspect of the changes under discussion was the growth of a mass of marginal peasants at the bottom of the social hierarchy in the village. Local modern studies indicate that they amounted to about half or more of the inhabitants. How much of an increase, if any, this may represent over the nineteenth century, we have no way of knowing as yet . . . All these processes had their heaviest impact in the coastal provinces . . . (Moore, 218–19)

The only major area in Asia, and indeed in Africa and Latin America, that did not suffer the development of underdevelopment in the nineteenth century or before and was instead able to undertake capitalist development on its own was Japan. Baran summarises:

What was the historical constellation that left room for a bourgeois revolution in Japan which in turn led to the establishment of a bourgeoisie-dominated regime serving from its very inception as a vigorous and relentless engine of Japanese capitalism? The answer to this question is extraordinarily complex and at the same time extraordinarily simple. It is simple because, reduced to its core, it comes down to the fact that Japan is the only country in Asia (and in Africa and Latin America) that escaped being turned into a colony or dependency of Western European or American capitalism; that had a change of independent national development. It is complex because it was only a felicitous confluence of a large number of more or less independent factors that gave Japan its lucky break. Basic among them . . . was the backwardness and poverty of the Japanese people and the paucity of their country's natural resources. 'Japan had very little to offer either as a market for foreign manufactures or as a granary of raw materials for Western industry.' Consequently the lure of Japan to Western European capitalists and governments came nowhere near the irresistible attraction exercised by the gold of Latin America, the flora, fauna, and minerals of Africa, the fabulous riches of the Indies, or the supposedly bottomless markets of China. (Baran, 158–9. For essentially the same argument in further detail see Smith, Lockwood and especially Norman.)

In this most fundamental of circumstances, Japan resembled North America and Oceania, which as we argued above, were similarly spared colonisation for the same reasons. Thus, the case of Japan also confirms the apparently inexorable law of world capitalist development that riches, through the exploitation they invite, generate the development of underdevelopment; and pre-capitalist poverty permits economic development because it makes the same colonialist exploitation impossible. The Japanese looked across the sea and saw how world capitalism, now entering its stage of imperialist development, was underdeveloping China; and the Japanese ruling class became intent on avoiding this same fate for Japan. That it was able to do so, apart from certain domestic factors such as the existence of a relatively strong feudal regime, was due both to its poverty, which first made it unattractive to world capitalism, and then to intra-imperialist rivalry at the end of the nineteenth century, which prevented any one imperialist power from asserting control over Japan. Notably, not only did Japan thus avoid becoming colonialised, but her national capitalist class also avoided the underdevelopment-generating consequences of foreign investment in productive resources, which imperialist development in the metropolis expanded and intensified elsewhere in Asia, Africa and Latin America, as we may observe below.

3. Imperialism and the Arab World

The Islamic peoples of the Middle East and North Africa, who during the Middle Ages had not only achieved a high degree of civilisation and development and had – along with China – made essential technological and cultural contributions to Western Europe's ability to achieve subsequent development under capitalism, were not spared the development of underdevelopment as an essential result of this same historical process. As Sarç notes, first Ottoman industry and then her village handicrafts were destroyed by British manufactures after the latter country's victory over Napoleon in 1815. And as Luxemburg notes, this de-industrialisation was but the first step in harnessing the peasant economy and in subordinating the Turkish state to the needs of world capitalist development.

The most spectacular process of incorporating a Middle Eastern economy in the process of world capitalist development – and along with the Indian one of the classic case histories of the development of underdevelopment – occurred in Egypt. There Mohammed Ali had tried to incorporate his country in this historical process in the second quarter of the nineteenth century, while maintaining national control and stimulating national, including industrial, development. But all he succeeded in doing was effectively to pave the way for Egypt's incorporation in the process of world capitalist development under foreign control. His industrialisation policy failed in part because of Egypt's lack of sufficient political autonomy within the Turkish empire, which made the necessary tariff protection impossible. This circumstance also rendered Ali's other – that is cotton – development effort fruitless – and in fact turned it into an underdevelopment policy – because his major effort consisted in creating the productive and social structure necessary to produce cotton for export to Europe. Under his rule, Egyptian cotton exports rose from about £1.5 million in 1823 to £5 million in 1850. Then, as European control became effective in Egypt after Ali's rule, the export of cotton grew much more rapidly to £22 million by 1880 and to £60 million in 1913, though the real value grew much more still than these monopolistically priced official values (Issawi, 8). In the meantime, as the British Consul-General, Lord Cromer, who governed Egypt between 1883 and 1907, announced: 'The policy of the government may be summed up thus: (1) export of cotton to Europe subject to 1 per cent export duty; (2) imports of textile products manufactured abroad subject to 8 per cent import duty; nothing else enters into the government's intentions, nor will it protect the Egyptian cotton industry, because of the danger and evils that arise from such measures . . . Since Egypt is by her nature an agricultural country, it follows logically that industrial training could lead only to neglect of agriculture while diverting the Egyptians from the land, and both these things would be disasters for the nation.' Twenty-five years later, Lord Cromer looked back and summarised what his policy had achieved: 'The difference is apparent to any man whose recollections go back some ten or fifteen years. Some quarters [of Cairo] that formerly used to be veritable centres of varied industries – spinning, weaving, ribbonmaking, dyeing, tent-making, embroidery, shoemaking, jewellery making, spice grinding, cooper work, the manufacture of bottles out of animal skins, saddlery, sieve making, locksmithing in wood and metal, etc. – have shrunk considerably or vanished. Now there are coffee houses and European novelty shops where once there were prosperous work-shops' (quoted in Abdel-Malek, 7–8). The parallel consequences in the countryside are reviewed by Issawi, Luxemburg, Riad and others.

Abdel-Malek (8) goes on to note:

> The wretchedness of city and country was countered by the enrichment of the large landed proprietors, who had finally found a regular customer in the occupying power. It was able to guarantee them incessantly growing wealth, since Egypt had become from end to end a gigantic cotton plantation for the factories of Lancashire. Thus was born the political alliance between Great Britain and the large landowners, headed by the royal family, which was to dominate Egyptian political life for three-quarters of a century.

Thus, the same process of the development of underdevelopment – colonial transformation of the economic and class structure and the consequent underdevelopment policy of the colonial ruling class, be it foreign or 'national' – was imposed by world capitalist development on Egypt as well.

Essentially the same process of capitalist underdevelopment befell the Arabs of the Maghreb, and especially of Algeria, which after 1830 was not only colonised but even more colonialised by French capitalism. For the Maghreb as a whole, the process is reviewed by Amin; and the development of underdevelopment in Algeria is analysed by Lacoste *et al.* as indicated by their subtitles:

> The decline of the urban economy. It begins by the destruction of the towns and the definitive decadence of the traditional urban society . . . The decline of the rural economy . . . of the agricultural and pastrol activities . . . The demographic decline is no less important . . . Social regression and re-enforcement of feudalism . . . The inequality of the regimes is not only maintained but aggravated . . . The destruction of the economic equilibrium to the advantage of colonization. Traditional social structures broken up . . . The Agricultural crisis and the famine (1866–1870) . . . Private speculation with the tribal lands . . . The new structures of agrarian colonization: absenteeism and concentration . . . The triumph of big colonization (1881–1900) and the conquest of the Sahara . . . The vineyard boom . . . The consequences of the crisis in wine-growing: land concentration and political predominance of big colonization . . . The other side of the colonial ledger: the pauperization of the Algerian peasantry. The peasantry excluded from the forest . . . The

Moslem peasantry forced to sell its land . . . The extension of speculative colonization . . . The degradation of the peasant condition and of Moslem agriculture. The proletarianization . . . The stagnation of [agricultural] techniques and the degradation of the soil . . . A policy favorable to the [European] colon and to the disadvantage of the [Algerian] fellah . . . The appearance of the underdevelopment of Algeria . . . (Lacoste, 315–444)

Thus, the same pattern and process of underdevelopment also repeat themselves in Algeria and the Maghreb in general.

4. Imperialism and Africa

As we observed above (Chapter 4), the African slave trade was not abolished simply out of humanitarian motives but also in response to the changing economic interests that world capitalist development had occasioned in the metropolis, and particularly in Britain (if the latter was for a long time unable to impose its 'abolition' of the trade, it was primarily because in this same process of world capitalist development others, and particularly the French, had not yet acquired the same 'humanitarian' interest – and this despite the French Revolution which did induce Napoleon to give up trying to reimpose French control over Haiti, for instance). Moreover, the abolition of the African slave trade could not restore the *status quo ante* of two centuries earlier in Africa. The fundamentals of the economic and class structure of the single-product export economy necessarily survived abolition, and they were now employed in many parts of West Africa to replace the same by the palm oil trade, as Dike and Sik among others have shown. Although this mid-nineteenth century development did not affect all of the former slave trade areas equally, by the end of the nineteenth century much of West Africa was well on the way to substantial reconversion to mono-crop export economies of peanuts and other oil seeds, copra, cocoa, etc. Mining only played a relatively minor role because mines were scarce.

This export agriculture was organised through a plantation system to the greatest extent by the Belgians in the Congo, less so by the French in Equatorial Africa and still less in West Africa, and least of all by the British in West Africa.

None the less, many of the underdevelopment-generating factors of other export economies also appeared where plantations were relatively unimportant. Wholesale trade in the export economies was quickly monopolised by the major European trading companies, such as United Africa (Unilever) and Compagnie Française de l'Afrique Occidentale, which also controlled the merchandising of imported goods at the wholesale and often much of the retail level. Their principal powers provided an efficient mechanism for the extraction of economic surplus from the African areas under their control. When their control of the export products was later supplemented or replaced by that of the marketing boards, which were formally in the hands of the colonial and then of the independent governments, this element of monopsony power was not diminished, and it was used to the benefit of the metropolitan power no less than before, as when the marketing boards paid the growers substantially less than the 'world market' price and held the difference as sterling balances in London, which were – and are – then made available for metropolitan development. Domestically, the production, financing, and commercialisation of export crops increasingly polarised the rural economy and society. Despite the common claim that the West African rural economy is based on smallholders, the expansion of export agriculture has generated a rural bourgeoisie and what amounts to a rural proletariat, as we may surmise from two types of evidence among others. As Polly Hill has shown, no more than 20 per cent of Ghanaian cocoa farmers actually do their own work, while 80 per cent employ the labour of others. Secondly and relatedly, the development of production for export has given rise to massive inter-tribal and international movements of migratory labour in West Africa, which perhaps has not received the attention it deserves, because it appears only moderate besides the even more massive migrations in the mining regions of Central-South Africa, which we will examine below. It is true that this development of a rural bourgeois or at least kulak class has also laid the socio-economic basis for the development of a class of Africans – emerging as Amin has pointed out, from the countryside rather than, as is usual elsewhere, from the cities – which could direct *potential* capitalist development in Africa. But as in other parts of the colonial and neo-colonial world, and as Fanon, Arrighi and Amin have also shown in Africa even more than elsewhere, this potential is in turn limited by the preponderant interests of the metropolitan powers or, in settler Africa, by their local descendents. Indeed, as Amin and Arrighi show, such African capitalist development as did occur around the turn of the century, was – once it competed with their new interests – later deliberately underdeveloped by the metropolis and/or by the white settlers.

The institutional instruments which the metropolitan powers used to facilitate the further transformation of African society in the interests of metropolitan development varied in accordance with local possibilities. Under the 'dual mandate' and following Lord Lugard's policy, the British instituted their 'indirect rule' of Africans through Africans, wherever possible. This implied the preservation, and sometimes even extension, of the power of the African tribal chiefs and the use of the 'legitimacy' of their rule for new ends. The functional significance of chiefly rule, of course, changed considerably as the chiefs increasingly converted the tribal property they previously administered into private property, which they devoted to production of export crops for their own profit. And this functional transformation of African institutions, which for the value of their 'legitimacy' were preserved in form, increased all the more so as the privatisation of other lands also grew apace. Herein, the British only reinvented in nineteenth- and twentieth-century Africa, what the Spaniards – equally obliged by circumstances – had already invented and put into practice in sixteenth-century Mexico and Peru. And where circumstances differed, as Benoit points out that they largely did in the areas of West Africa that came into French possession, the metropolitan power and its representatives in Africa had recourse to other institutional policies, including the building up of a 'traditional' and 'African' chieftancy system where it hardly existed before. As the British 'indianised' the civil service in the sub-continent, the French 'assimilated' Africans, both in the colonial administration and in the comprador bourgeoisie of the port cities such as Dakar and Abidjan, as is analysed by Suret-Canale.

In the mining and white settler areas of East, Central and South Africa, the major sources of African economic surplus for metropolitan development has been generated through mining and large-scale commercial agriculture run by Europeans and their descendants. Unlike those that went to Australia and New Zealand, the European settlers that went to Africa did not exterminate the indigenous population. Nor would this have been readily possible in Africa unless the Europeans had been prepared to eliminate a relatively much greater and denser population than in Oceania and to remain without an available labour supply to work the mines and farms, or to bring in much more white or Asian labour. Thus, the Europeans not only colonised this part of Africa, as they did Canada, Australia and New Zealand, but they also colonialised this part of the world as they did others in Asia and Latin America. For this reason, also, the indigenous population in East-Central-South Africa also suffered markedly more severe development of under-development than parts of West Africa did (though not so much more than the indigenous inhabitants of North America and Oceania suffered).

The first problem the Euopeans faced in trying to build an export economy – or any kind of economy – in this part of Africa was to assure themselves of a supply of labour and to eliminate or control rival indigenous sources of employment and of competitive agricul-tural produce. The principal solution the Europeans adopted from East to South Africa was in essence the same as the one the Spaniards had already relied on in Latin America in the sixteenth century and that their descendants had only just employed again in mid- and late nineteenth-century Latin America: deprive the indigenous population of their land. By denying Africans control over the principal means of production in their indigenous economy, the metropolis and the settlers naturally forced a total change in the mode of production and the social organisation of indigenous society and obliged its members to participate in the development of a new mode of production in which the settlers and the metropolis would be the principal beneficiaries. Woddis (7–9) explains:

> *Only a very small proportion of the land reserved for Europeans has, in fact, been used by them.* What is the reason for this apparent mys-tery? . . . The reason for this, and for the wholesale taking of land in so much of Africa, was two-fold: to prevent the African peasant from becoming a competitor to the European farmer or plan-tation owner; and to impoverish the African peasantry to such an extent that the majorty of adult males would be compelled to work for Europeans, in the mines or on the farms . . . *To put it in a nutshell, a major aim of European land policy in Africa is to ensure cheap labour for European mines and farms* . . . *Thus not only the enrichment of the Europeans but the deliberate impoverishment of the Africans became a cornerstone of official policy.* (italics in the original)

Though this would also be the natural result of colonial capitalist development, *if* it had a chance to start to develop, countless official documents leave no doubt that the metropolis and settlers consciously and deliberatedly used – and still use – coercive political instruments, such as more recently the pass laws, to ensure first the initiation and then the acceleration and maintenance of this process of development of underdevelopment. Two other instruments, noted by Rosa Luxemburg in her theoretical synthesis and reported by countless students of Africa, such as Woddis, Padmore, Schapera, and the various Royal Commissions themselves, were also used not only in their own right but to reinforce the first one where appropriate: taxes and other means to monetise the economy. The hut or poll tax, which was payable only in money – or in default thereof in forced labour – could only be earned by working for the Europeans as wage labourers. And the introduction of European-produced commodities gave the resulting trend an additional impulse.

These measures have been mutually reinforcing, all the more so inasmuch as the Europeans systematically took the best lands and herded the Africans in large numbers on to poor lands that were unable to support the population and were soon eroded through over-cropping. The inevitable result was the accelerated development of underdevelopment through the intervention of a number of additional factors, principal among which has been migratory labour in proportions that were unheard of in other times and places, the slave trade itself perhaps excepted, but including even the *repartimiento* forced labour migrations to the Mexican and Peruvian mines in the sixteenth to eighteenth centuries. The Keiskammahock Rural Survey reports:

> The people of this district are . . . seen to be dependent upon the earnings of emigrants for their very existence, and it is poverty which forces them out to work. But this very exodus is itself a potent cause of the perpetuation of the poverty at home, for the absence of so many in the prime of life inhibits economic progress and certainly accounts in no small measure for the low agricultural productivity of the district. In many cases land is not ploughed for the simple reason that there is no one to do the plowing . . . Cursory analysis of economic conditions in the remaining twenty-five districts . . . suggests that the picture which has emerged from this economic survey of Keiskam-

mahock, a picture of overpopulation, overstocking, poverty, mass emigration, inefficient farming and destruction of pasture and the soil is, with only minor modifications, true of a vast area . . . . (quoted in Woddis, 26–8)

A United Nations Report summarises the general process: 'where migrant labour has been drawn from the indigenous agricultural economies in high proportions, this has often had a deleterious effect on output and on farming practices, giving rise to a vicious circle in which the outflow of labour reduces productivity, and falling productivity increases still further the pressure on workers to seek wage employment' (quoted in Woddis, 24). A principal 'primary product' export from Mozambique, and an important source of foreign exchange for Portugal, is still that of half a million migrant labourers annually to the Republic of South Africa. In drawing his conclusions, Basil Davidson (85) can hardly be accused of overstatement: 'This many-sided movement, repeated year by year, has had profound social consequences and none of them can be said to have been good.'

This accelerated development of underdevelopment did not, of course, affect all regions equally. None the less, it is certainly a credit to Africans in East or Central Africa who were able to resist this 'development'. However, where they did resist and succeed, it was also to their own undoing; since their very success in responding to the pressures the Europeans had imposed on them challenged the Europeans to use still additional power to force the Africans into underdevelopment. For instance, in the *Seventh Annual Report of the Chamber of Mines of Rhodesia*, the President observed in 1902: 'With this cheap form of [family] labour at his command, coupled with the fact that, provided he lives on Native Reserves, he has no rent to pay, and that his taxation is reduced to a minimum, the native is enabled year after year to produce a large amount of grain, which is in due course purchased from him by the trader, and eventually at an enhanced price by the mine owner, and in fact he continues year by year to become more affluent, less inclined to do any work himself, and to enter most successfully into competition with the white man in that most important of articles, namely, grain. I would suggest that a remedy can be found in two ways, namely, by taxation and the adoption of a cooperative system of farming by the mine owner (quoted in Arrighi, 45). After noting that Africans in the Union were also threatening to compete successfully with

Europeans not only as farmers but also as skilled workers, Frankel (26) concludes: 'In other words, if European income standards continued to be threatened, the European workers, given sufficient political power, would insist on artificial measures to maintain them, even if, by doing so, they might retard the rate of growth of national income. And this is precisely what happened . . .' Similarly, Arrighi (30) reports that in response to the challenge of African producers in Rhodesia, 'throughout the period under consideration, the Government continued to play an important role in undermining the African peasantry's ability to participate in the produce market . . .' As a result,

> while the sale of produce had accounted for some 70 per cent of total cash earnings of the indigenous African population at the beginning of the present century, it accounted for less than 20 per cent of such earnings in 1932 . . . As the African peasantry began to be affected by a shortage of land, the production of a marketable surplus on their part tended to become 'impossible', not just 'uneconomic', and a return to the *status quo ante* in relative produce prices would not restore their previous ability to participate in the money economy through the sale of produce. It is mainly for this reason that the enhanced importance of cash earnings after the 1920's must be considered as largely 'irreversible' rather than 'cyclical' . . . We are now in a position to explain why, after the early 1920's African responsiveness to wage-employment opportunities increased continuously, irrespective of whether real wages were rising, falling or remaining constant. Our analysis has shown that this tendency must be traced to the increasingly 'necessary' character of African participation in the money economy and to the steady increase in the relative effort-price of participation in the produce market which was in return the result of the development of capitalist agriculture and of the pattern of surplus absorption in the peasant sector. (Arrighi, 30, 26–7, 32).

Metropolitan depression, which caused declines in African mining employment, of course, forced many Africans into unemployment and into dependence of the land again. But by then the lack of productive resources in agriculture, and often the transformation of the social structure of indigenous rural society, no longer permitted the productive absorption of this labour or the production of an adequate level of living. Thus his analysis of the development of underdevelopment in Africa forces Arrighi (33) to the same conclusion that we reached with respect to colonial Latin America and that Geertz reached in his analysis of Indonesia. 'An analysis of the supply of African labour in historical perspective has thus invalidated . . . [the dualistic] . . . interpretation of the development of the African wage-labour force in Rhodesia. For one thing, dualism in Rhodesia (i.e. the technological, economic and political distance between the two races) was less an "original state" progressively reduced by market force, than it was the outcome of the development of capitalism itself.' And Arrighi also goes on to emphasise another conclusion that is consistent with Luxemburg's and our analysis of other people's experience of the development of underdevelopment: 'Market forces did not *ab initio* favour capitalist development. Real wages remained at a level which promoted capitalist accumulation not because of the forces of supply and demand, but because of political-economic mechanisms that ensured *the "desired" supply at the "desired" wage rate*. Before the determination of wage rates and rates of accumulation could be "safely" left to market forces, the Rhodesian capitalist system had to undergo the process of "primary accumulation" . . .' (Arrighi, 33). Thus, the fundamental factors of world capitalist development of underdevelopment, which we have found in Latin America, Asia and the Middle East, were equally at work in Africa in the nineteenth and twentieth centuries.

5. Imperialism in Latin America

What is distinctive in Latin America in this period, compared to most of Asia and Africa, is that Latin Americans had only recently won, rather than lost, their formal independence and that they maintained it throughout the third stage of world capital accumulation and capitalist development and underdevelopment. And what is remarkable, despite these and other important differences from the other continents – or within Latin America itself for that matter – is how fundamentally similar the formation of the mode of production and the development of underdevelopment in Latin America was to these processes in Asia and Africa. It is instructive, therefore, in our review of the Latin American experience to devote special attention to the great and growing economic, political and ideological dependence on the metropolis of the Latin American bourgeoisies and their 'independent' states. In our review of the second stage of world capital accumulation, we already observed how the Latin American bourgeoisies – after defeating their enemies within their own and other classes – voluntarily and enthusiastically adopted the free trade doctrine and policy, which elsewhere the metropolitan powers often had to impose by force. Another instance of this kind of Latin American bourgeois collaboration in the process of world capital accumulation and capitalist development was the political measures of social change – and of far-reaching economic consequence – which were initiated inside many of the national societies after the middle of the nineteenth century: the liberal reforms.

The liberal reforms in mid-nineteenth-century Latin America are generally interpreted – by the liberals and their ideological descendants themselves – as a major transformation of domestic society, which was stimulated by a wave of ideological enlightenment coming from the metropolis. The metropolitan influence is undeniable, but it was not simply ideological or cultural. And Latin American acceptance of this ideology, like that of free trade somewhat earlier, was not due simply to the logic or innate attractiveness of liberal ideas. On the contrary, the liberal reforms were still another important instance of transformation of the Latin American economic, political, social and cultural structure and of a change in political policy in response to changes in the colonial capitalist relationship with the metropolis. It can be no accident that the liberal reforms occurred in Latin America while new metropolitan needs sharply accelerated the production and export of Latin American foodstuffs and raw materials to the metropolis, and not when liberal ideas had some time earlier first arrived from overseas. The liberal reforms were not directed simply at the conservative influence of the Catholic Church and its most devout adherents. The liberal reforms took over the lands of the Church and of the Indian communities as well. Sanctified by the supposed superiority of private property over the corporate property of the Church and the communal property of the Indian communities, both were deprived of their lands to a degree far greater than in Spanish colonial times; and the land was rapidly concentrated into a few private and soon foreign and domestic 'private' corporation hands. The massive loss of their lands – as in white settler Africa soon thereafter – forced the indigenous population to work as peons in the rapidly expanding agricultural and mining export enterprises.

The liberal reform took place at different times in different countries. We may hazard the perhaps somewhat oversimplified hypothesis that the liberal reform of the capture of state power by the liberals and the implementation of their liberal political-economic policies in any particular country did not occur simply when liberal ideas had arrived there, but when the new mono-export product of coffee, sugar, meat, wheat, cotton, tin, etc. had expanded sufficiently to account for say, over 50 per cent of total national exports. Although some people may have wanted the liberal reform for a long time for ideological reasons, it is this metropolitan-stimulated expansion of Latin American export production that in each country gave certain sectors of the bourgeoisie the economic and political reason and power to undertake the liberal reform. And now the liberals converted the word 'feudalism' into a red flag with which to combat their conservative opponents. To my knowledge this hypothesis has not been tested because it has not been previously advanced. But examination of the historical experience in Central America would seem to provisionally confirm it.

In Guatemala, for instance, coffee production began in 1856; by 1875 coffee was already the principal export product; and liberal revolution ocurred in 1871–3. In El Salvador coffee became the principal export product in 1880, and the liberal revolution occurred in 1885. Yet in Costa Rica, where coffee had already become the principal export product before 1860, the liberal dictatorship began in 1858 and lasted until 1868. In contrast, Honduras never became an important coffee exporter; and there the attempted liberal revolution failed altogether, and when liberal reforms were introduced in 1876 it was on a very limited scale. And in Nicaragua, which never became a major exporter but at end-century offered the most likely route for the inter-ocean canal (before it was finally built in Panama), the liberal revolution occurred in 1892. Export and land prices had already begun to rise in 1851 in Mexico before the most famous liberal reform of all began there is 1857 (Torres, 21–50).

In each of these cases, of course, the liberal reform served to accelerate the very economic process that had given it birth. Once in power, the erstwhile liberals associated themselves ever more with the trade and foreign capital of the developing imperialist metropolis, which was and is its natural ally. If this colonial alliance and domestic policy created grave economic problems of underdevelopment which generated political tensions at home, and which required domination through dictatorial political repression, it was the liberals themselves – who only shortly before had fought the conservatives in the name of liberty – who now were the first to have recourse to this repression to serve their own interests, as was most notoriously the case in the Mexico of Porfirio Diaz and in the coffee, sugar and banana republics of Central America and the Caribbean. (For more detail see Frank 1972, Chapter 5.)

The new metropolitan demand for and Latin American profitability of raw materials production and export attracted public Latin American capital into expanding the infrastructure necessary for this export production. In Brazil, Argentina, Paraguay, Chile, Guatemala, and Mexico (to the author's knowledge, but probably in other countries as well), domestic or national capital built the first railroad in each of these countries. In Chile, it opened up the nitrate and copper mines that were to become the world's principal supplier of commercial fertiliser and red metal, in Brazil the coffee plantations that supplied nearly all the world's tables, and similarly elsewhere. Only after this proved to be a booming business – and after Britain had to find outlets for its steel – did foreign capital enter into these sectors and also take over ownership and management of these initially Latin American enterprises by buying out – often with Latin American capital – the concessions of these natives.

In Latin America, this same imperialist trade and finance did more than increase the amount of production, trade and profit by accumulating about US$10,000 million of investment capital there. The imperialist metropolis used its foreign trade and finance to penetrate the Latin American economy far more completely and to use the latter's productive potential far more efficiently and exhaustively for metropolitan development than the colonial metropolis had ever been able to do. As Rosa Luxemburg noted of a similar process in the Middle East 'stripped of all obscuring connecting links, these relations consist of the simple fact that European capital has largely swallowed up the Egyptian peasant economy. Enormous tracts of land, labour, and labour products without number, accruing to the state as taxes, have ultimately been converted into European capital and have been accumulated' (Luxemburg, 438).

Indeed, in Latin America imperialism went further. It not only availed itself of the state to invade agriculture; it took over nearly all economic and political institutions to incorporate the entire economy into the imperialist system. The latifundia grew at a pace and to proportions unknown in all previous history, especially in Argentina, Uruguay, Cuba, Mexico and Central America. With the aid of the Latin American governments, foreigners came to own – usually for next to nothing – immense tracts of land. And where they did not get the land, they got its products anyway, because the metropolis also took over and monopolised the merchandising of agricultural and most other products. The metropolis took over Latin American mines and expanded their output, sometimes exhausting irreplaceable resources in a few years. To get these raw materials out of Latin America and to get its equipment and goods in, the metropolis stimulated the construction of ports, or railroads, and had to service all this system of public utilities. The railway network and electric grid, far from being net- or grid-like, was ray-like and connected the hinterland of each country and sometimes of several countries with the port of entry and exit, which was in turn connected to the metropolis. Today, four score years later, much of this export-import pattern still remains, in part because the railroad right of way is still laid out that way, and more importantly, because the metropolitan-oriented urban, economic and political development which nineteenth-century imperialism generated in Latin America formed vested class interests who tried, and with metropolitan support managed, to maintain and expand this development of Latin American underdevelopment during the twentieth century.

The dependence and growing weakness of the Latin American bourgeoisie in relation to the metropolis during this period has been noted by many observers, though they may emphasise different aspects of the same. For instances, Marini (6) writes, 'the Latin American export economy booms like never before. This growth, nonetheless, is marked by an accentuation of its dependence on the industrialized countries.' Cordoba (VIII, 32) argues, 'the national capitalist class has its origins in the traditional commercial bourgeoisie, in some groups of enriched landowners and in the stratum of high level public official known as the "bureaucratic bourgeoisie," which used the advantages of political power as a means of accumulation . . . When the commercial bourgeoisie becomes fundamentally an import bourgeoisie, it becomes the domestic right arm of world monopoly capitalism, which permits it to participate as a junior partner in the distribution of the profits . . .' Halperin (280, 282) notes, 'In 1880 – give or take a few years – the advance in almost all of Spanish America of a primary and export economy spells the finally consummated replacement of the colonial pact that had been imposed by the Iberian metropolises by a new colonial pact . . . the neo-colonial order . . . [brings on] a more general tenency: the weakening of the high landowner classes, despite their support in the local political, commercial, and financial structure, in the face of the emissaries of the metropolitan economies.' In his book devoted to the national state – one of the very few works on this important neglected topic – Kaplan emphasises:

> One of the factors that explain the predominant role of the state in Latin America is precisely the need to adjust, reciprocally order and maintain in precarious equilibrium the heterogeneous and divergent elements that make up the unequal and combined development . . . [None the less] the state acts upon the orientation, structure and functioning of economic activity and the social system to permit and assure the successful operation of the model of dependent development . . . The primary productive-export sector . . . is kept under control . . . The availability of the productive resources for the agricultural-mining export sector is maintained and expanded . . . property is inviolable . . . The state takes on the task of extending the internal frontiers . . . of open spaces . . . or inhabited by indigenous tribes . . . One of the most important assignments of the state in this stage is precisely to impede the access of indigenous, *criollo* and immigrant workers to means of production of their own . . . The state aids in domestic capital accumulation (for certain purposes) and attracts foreign funds . . . The state constructs and operates public works and services . . . or grants concessions, guarantees, subsidies and other incentives to foreign companies which thereby are assured high profits . . . The benefits of this state intervention flow to the landowners, merchants, investors, speculators, middlemen, and the lawyers of the big companies . . . (Kaplan, 174, 197–201)

Ceceña (79–80) observes that in Mexico 'during the government of General Porfirio Diaz (1876–1911) foreign capital deeply penetrated the Mexican economy . . . It did not promote the development of an independent Mexican bourgeoisie . . . High officials of the government, including ministers of General Diaz's cabinet, had close ties with foreign investors . . . Quite a few state governors, members of Congress and representatives of the bourgeoisie . . . participated in foreign firms and also had investments in banking, industry, mining, merchandising, etc., and at the same time were large landowners.' Not only modern research but contemporary testimony testifies to the same: the President of Mexico, General Porfirio Diaz, himself said, 'since I am responsible for the investment of hundreds of millions of dollars of foreign capital in my country, I think I should remain in office until I can guarantee a competent successor' (quoted in Cosio Villegas, VII, 1183). A generation later the Treasury Minister of Argentina, Federico Pinedo, declared frankly: 'If it is being a fatherland sell-out (*vendepatria*) to have been lawyer of the railroads, streetcars, banks, electricity companies, shipping and insurance companies, grain merchants, and of the big industrial and financial consortia that were established in this country by Argentinians and foreigners, then fatherland sell-outs would also have been those prominent Argentinians who in the previous generation were, in merit of their professional capabilities, called upon to serve these firms, and some of whom now have monuments built in memory of their eminent services to the country. Almost all the firms that I have had at one time or another the honor to participate in or serve as a professional, were at some time clients of the law firm of my father, who was a partner of the Argentine Presidents, Doctors Pellegrini and Saenz Peña . . .' (the former of whom, we observed above, 'served' his country so well in the 1890s by promoting a policy so different from that of Australia). (Quoted in Parera Dennis, 14.)

Although this evidence testifies to the ever deeper dependence of the Latin American bourgeoisies on, and ever greater submission to, the metropolis and the process of world capital accumulation in its third stage, it is also important to note the differences between one country and another. As Cardoso and Faletto have emphasised, the countries – mostly mining and tropical agriculture, although in some cases coffee growing as well – in which the major means of productions of the export sector fell into foreign ownership suffered (with the exception, perhaps, of Chile) a much greater weakening of their bourgeoisies, a lower level of domestic capital accumulation and diversification of the productive structure and a more polarised society than did those, like Argentina, Uruguay, and Brazil, in which at least the production, though not the merchandising, of the primary export product remained under national ownership (or partially returned to it by revolution as in Mexico). The relatively greater amount of investible surplus available and the greater national control over its use possible in these latter countries permitted a greater growth of national income and/or more diversification, and afforded the bourgeoisies of these countries much greater possibilities to take advantage of the war and depression-created opportunities for the expansion of import-substituting industry in the first half of the twentieth century. None the less – though this is beyond the time-scope of the present book – it is now evident that not even these countries were able to achieve take-off into self-sustained national capitalist economic development, despite these relatively favourable circumstances. The other countries in Latin America – and in colonialised Asia and Africa – were, of course, still less able to achieve such development.

The reason for this failure of even the least handicapped of these countries to achieve national capitalist development, or to escape from ever-accelerated development of underdevelopment irrespective of their rates of economic growth, lies in the transformation of the entire world capitalist economy and of the modes of production in all of Asia, Africa and Latin America (with the significant exception of Japan) during the third stage of world capital accumulation and capitalist development, which finally and definitely foreclosed all future possibilities for these economies to achieve quantitatively and qualitatively cumulative capital accumulation and condemned as hopeless all political aspirations of their 'national' bourgeoisies – if they exist at all – to promote economic development within the now *narrow* confines of the national (and even state) capitalist mode of production in the era of neo-imperialism.

To complement the above analysis of the development of underdevelopment in Asia, the Middle East, Africa and Latin America through their dependent 'internal' modes of production during the classical imperialist period, we examine import aspects of these continents' 'external' relations of exchange and especially their significant excess of merchandise as exports over imports – as an essential factor of world capitalist uneven development – and these continents' underdevelopment as the basis for accumulation elsewhere – during this same (third) imperialist stage of capitalist development. This structure and process of imperialism is examined in Chapter 7, which follows.

7 Multilateral Merchandise Trade Imbalances and Uneven Economic Development

Contrary to orthodox international trade and national development theory, the uneven development of world capitalism was not accompanied by balanced trade (or growth) but rested in fact on a fundamental imbalance of international trade between the developing metropolis and the underdeveloping, colonialised, countries. Except for the years of worst depression in the metropolis, the latter had a constant but growing trade deficit and the underdeveloped countries a trade surplus during the classical imperialist period of world capitalist development at the end of the nineteenth and the beginning of the twentieth centuries. The almost exclusive theoretical and empirical interest in the *balance of payments*, and obsession with the mechanisms that make it balance, has cast a 'veil of money' over the underlying merchandise *imbalance of trade* whose role, which we believe is fundamental in the process of uneven capitalist development and underdevelopment, has remained all but unperceived. (For this reason also the following discussion can be no more than the preliminary formulation of research hypotheses that demand empirical investigation and theoretical reformulation.)

To summarise the discussion that follows, the secular excess of the underdeveloped countries' exports over imports has throughout this period made a fundamental contribution to the accumulation of capital, technological progress and economic development of the now developed countries; and the generation of this exports surplus from the now underdeveloped countries has there developed the mode of production which underdeveloped Asia, Africa and Latin America.

The importance of these trade imbalances in exchange in no way

denies the importance of the internal mode of production, and its
relationship with exchange in developing underdevelopment. Nor
does the imbalance of trade belittle the importance of unequal
exchange, or vice versa. On the contrary, each significantly rein-
forces and aggravates the other. If the underdeveloped countries
have a persistent export surplus when their exports are measured, as
in the sources mentioned above, in world market prices, then they
have a much greater real export surplus if their exports are
measured in terms of the real value, of more than their market
prices, as suggested by Emmanuel's and Amin's analysis of unequal
exchange. Similarly, if the underdeveloped countries suffer from
unequal exchange even if their merchandise trade balances (as
orthodox theory assumes), then their exchange is all the more
unequal and their loss greater if, as is the case, they persistently
export more goods than they import at market prices.

1. Patterns of World Trade Imbalances

The development of the imbalance of merchandise trade and the
associated system of multilateral settlements on a world scale has
been the subject of only one serious study: and that was undertaken
by the League of Nations (1942) when and because, as its director
Folke Hilgerdt himself pointed out (League, p. 84), 'its functioning
was upset by disturbances in trade during the thirties'. Until then,
he wrote, 'this system hardly attracted any interest', and since the
post-war development of neo-imperialism, we may add, the
metropolis and its representatives seem again to have lost all
interest. Hilgerdt (1943, 400, 394) summarised his survey as follows:

> The particular world-wide system just described is not very
> old. It arose during the last few decades of the nineteenth century
> and was from the beginning linked up with the transfer of the
> yield of British investments . . . (397). The development of the
> system of multilateral trade, accomplished over a period of a few
> decades, was similar to the unfolding of a fan: more and more
> countries became involved, and their insertion took place in a
> given order, each country being farther away from the United
> Kingdom on the transfer routes to that country from its debtors.
> This development was undoubtedly as important to the growth of
> modern economy as it was neglected by economists. It is not by

chance that we usually think of this economy as beginning to develop around 1870 – the time when, as we have seen, the system of multilateral trade came into being [phrase between dashes is Hilgerdt's: AGF] – or that it agrees with our notions that international economy had reached a stage of maturity in the early years of our century, when the multilateral system had assumed the shape, if not the quantitative growth, that it retained until the early thirties . . . The outline of this system became clear when it was found that almost all countries could be arranged in the order of the direction of their balances of trade, so that each country had an import balance from practically all countries that preceded it in the list and an export balance to practically all countries that succeeded it. At beginning of this list we find the tropical debtor countries with export balances in almost all directions, and at the end of it the European creditor countries with import balances from almost all countries, the United Kingdom being the most typical case. But between these two extremes the countries arrange themselves. . . .

Hilgerdt's study of the pattern of trade between 173 countries, 96 minor groups and 17 major groups of countries is summarized by Condliffe (283):

The trading areas of the world are finally grouped into six broad categories. These are arranged . . . in a neat circular diagram which is not just a theoretical design, but a summation of the actually recorded values of world trade. The tropical countries exported more to the United States than they imported from it; the United States sent more to the British Dominions and non-tropical Latin America (comprising Argentina, Uruguay, Paraguay and Falkland Islands) than it received from these areas; they in turn exported more to continental Europe; continental Europe exported more to Britain, and the circle was closed by Britain exporting [very little] more to the tropics than it imported from them.

A sixth 'area', 'Rest of the World' (including China and continental Asia, but not India, Japan and North Africa) accounted for about 10 per cent of world trade but did not fit well into the arrangement (see below).

We shall describe shortly Hilgerdt's calculation of the trade imbalances (for 1928), and our own recomputation of some of them to highlight better the place of the now underdeveloped countries in the system, and our own interpretation of the significance of the same for the development of underdevelopment in the latter countries and their contribution to the development of the other countries. But this will be clearer if we precede it with a brief review of some of Hilgerdt's own observations about the functioning of this world system and complement them with some recent observations by S. B. Saul of Britain.

By the 1920s – Hilgerdt observed – multilateral, as distinct from bilateral, trade accounted for about 25 per cent of all merchandise transactions (League, 87). But, Hilgerdt (League, 1928) argued, 'the significance of such trade can by no means be gauged by its percentage share in total trade'. Saul (45, 70, 225 and elsewhere) agrees: 'There is hardly any important aspect of modern economy that is not adversely affected by the breakdown of the system of multilateral trade . . . Multilateral settlement on a world-wide basis . . . [is] a factor exercising a determinant influence on international monetary equilibrium, on international finance, on the level of prices formed in the world market [and, through them, in the national markets], and accordingly on production employment, and the course of the business cycle . . . The rapid and general economic progress of the period 1870–1930 would not have been possible had not the system of multilateral trade facilitated the development of production in economically young countries with the aid of foreign capital' (Hilgerdt, 405, 403–4). But, as we will observe below, this 'general economic progress' was not general enough to include Asia, Africa and Latin America, which were the ultimate suppliers of the 'foreign capital' and themselves suffered progressive underdevelopment. Similarly, Saul (88) observes 'the great amount of multilateral settlement that Britain made through India . . . Had not British exports, particularly British cottons, found a wide-open market in India during the last few years before the outbreak of the war, it would have been impossible for her to have indulged so heavily in investment on the American continent and elsewhere . . . Usually, a quarter of Britain's imports from India were subsequently re-exported', which is a matter to which we shall return below.

We may conclude these introductory remarks with two further observations: 'The orientation of balances was determined by the nature of production and of requirements embedded in the economic structure and consumption habits of partaking countries' (Hilgerdt in League 1942, 88). For the underdeveloped countries, this observation is complemented by the insight of Levin (174) in his study of *The Export Economies*: 'One characteristic sign of the presence of foreign factors is a surplus of merchandise exports over merchandise imports . . . the existence of a surplus of exports over imports is a normal effect of foreign factors' operations. Indeed, in most export economies, where invisible earnings are quite small, an export surplus constitutes a necessary condition – barring the use of reserves or the entry of new capital – for the remittance of earnings abroad.' That is, beyond unequal exchange, which Levin does not consider, it is precisely through an excess of merchandise exports from the colonial country that the metropolis realised its investment and other services there. Let us examine this mechanism in operation.

The worldwide system of multilateral trade imbalances and settlements in 1928 may be illustrated – with an important modification to be introduced below – by J. B. Condliffe's following diagram which he adapted from Hilgerdt.

Reading clockwise and beginning with the Tropics or Underdeveloped Regions (for definitions, see the Statistical and Methodological Appendix, p. 199 below), we see that this region sends more exports than it receives to the United States, to the Regions of Recent Settlement or Dominions, and to Continental Europe. The United States, in turn, has an export surplus (= import deficit) with each of the other regions, that is the Dominions, Continental Europe and Britain, though part of the U.S. export surplus to these is 'cancelled out' or made up for by its import surplus from the tropical underdeveloped regions. The Regions of Recent Settlement or Dominions occupy an intermediary position in the trade circuit. On balance, they receive an excess of merchandise from the underdeveloped regions and the United States (which appear in the circuit before them), and they in turn send an excess of exports to Continental Europe and to Britain. Continental Europe receives an excess of imports from the three regions – underdeveloped, United States, and of recent settlement – before it in the circuit; and the Continent in turn sends more to Britain than it receives from it. Finally, Britain receives more from each of the preceding regions, but sends more – albeit very little more – to the underdeveloped countries than it receives from them. This last relation ostensibly

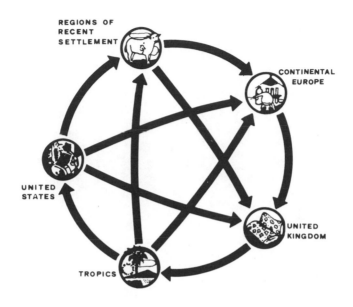

THE CIRCUIT OF PAYMENTS, 1928

Read clockwise, this diagram shows the main streams in the multilateral trading system. The arrows indicate the flows.

The exports of each region exceed the imports with the next region. Thus in 1928 the United States enjoyed export surpluses to every region except the tropical raw-material-producing countries.

The diagram is adapted from the similar one in the League of Nations, *The Network of World Trade*, Geneva, 1942.

From J. E. Condliffe, *The Commerce of Nations*, (New York: W. W. Norton & Co., 1950), p. 285.

'completes' or 'closes' the circle of this circuitous system of trade imbalances.

Alternatively, the same circuit may be observed in terms of the receipt of excess imports, beginning with Britain, which receives an excess from all the regions behind it, Continental Europe which sends more to the Continent but receives more from each of the other regions, and passing through the Dominions, which have an export surplus with two regions and an import surplus with the other two; and going back to the United States, which has an export surplus with all the other regions except the underdeveloped ones,

TABLE I

Merchandise Export Deficits = Import Surpluses (+) and Merchandise Export Surpluses = Import Deficits
(−) among Five Major World Regions in 1928
(in millions of dollars)

Trade of With	Britain	Continental Europe + U.S.S.R. + Japan	Dominions	United States	Under-developed	Totals
	1	2	3	4	5	6
1. Britain	x	− 730	− 110	− 630	+ 40	−1,430
2. Continental Europe + U.S.S.R. + Japan	+ 730	x	− 610	− 720	− 870	−1,470
3. Dominions	+ 110	+ 610	x	− 530	− 50	+ 140
4. United States	+ 630	+ 720	+ 530	x	− 610	+1,270
5. Underdeveloped	− 40	+ 870	+ 50	+ 610	x	+1,490
6. TOTAL	+1,430	+1,470	− 140	−1,270	−1,490	x

Source: See Table 5, pp. 202−3.

Table 1 Column 1 = Table 5 Column 1
,,   1   ,,   2 = ,,   5   ,,   5
,,   1   ,,   3 = ,,   5   ,,   9
,,   1   ,,   4 = ,,   5   ,,   10
,,   1   ,,   5 = ,,   5   ,,   16

from which it enjoys a merchandise import surplus; and ending up with the underdeveloped regions, which have an export surplus and import deficit with all the regions 'in front of' or 'above', them, except for a small import surplus from Britain.

In Table 1, the same multilateral trade imbalances appear in tabular and numerical form, referring to millions of dollars of merchandise export deficits or import surpluses and export surpluses or import deficits in 1928. The export deficits = import surpluses are indicated by + signs, to signify and emphasise the taking of merchandise in excess of the giving of the same; and the export surpluses = import deficits are indicated by − signs, to signify and emphasise the lesser taking than giving of merchandise export, particularly by the underdeveloped countries. Thus reading the columns, beginning with Britain (col. 1), we find that it receives an excess of merchandise from Continental Europe, including the U.S.S.R. and Japan (line 2), the Dominions (line 3) and the United States (line 4) of + $730, + $110, and + $630 million, respectively, while it has a modest export surplus of − $40 million with the underdeveloped countries. Adding the arithmetic sums of these three import surpluses and one small export surplus, Britain is left in line 6 with a total balance of + $1430 million of merchandise imports in excess of exports.

Continental Europe (col. 2), for its part, has an export surplus = import deficit with Britain (line 1) of − $730 million, but it has an import surplus = export deficit in turn with each of the three other regions; and its import surplus = export deficit with the underdeveloped region (col. 2, line 5) of + $870 million is more than enough to cover its own export surplus of − $730 million with Britain. Thus, Continental Europe is left with an overall merchandise import surplus = export deficit of + $1470 million.

The Dominions (col. 3) maintain an excess of exports over imports with both British and Continental Europe (lines 1 and 2), but in turn receive an excess of imports over exports from the United States and the underdeveloped countries (lines 4 and 5). Similarly, the United States – a 'new debtor' country in 1928 – maintains a substantial export surplus with Britain, with Continental Europe and with the Dominions (col. 4, lines 1, 2, 3), but receives a significant import surplus from the underdeveloped countries (line 5) of + $610 million (equivalent to 45 per cent of its own export to Europe or 32 per cent of its total gross export surplus). Thus the United States is left with a net export surplus of − $1410 million.

Finally, the underdeveloped countries (col. 5), though they receive + $40 million more in merchandise from Britain than they send there, export in excess to Continental Europe, the Dominions and the United States, in the sums of − $870, − $50, and − $610 million respectively, for a net export surplus = import deficit of − $1490 million. In its 'bilateral' relations with each of the other regions, therefore, the underdeveloped region pays for more than all of Continental Europe's own export surplus to Britain, one third of the Dominions' net export surplus, and nearly one half of the United States' net export surplus, while receiving a moderate 'recompense' of $40 million from Britain.

Looking at the four major regions, and omitting the economically smaller Dominions for the moment, we may observe that each of the four regions has a total export or import surplus of between $1400 and $1500 million, but that Britain and Continental Europe each imports that amount of merchandise in excess of its exports while the United States and the underdeveloped countries each exports similar sums in excess of its imports. These trade imbalance relations are further summarised in Table 2, where Britain and Continental Europe (including U.S.S.R. and Japan) are added together to form 'All Europe' (col./line 1); the United States and the Dominions are grouped together to form a single 'region' (col./line 2); and the underdeveloped countries are maintained as a single 'region' as in Table 1. We then see that 'All Europe' has a total (col. 1, line 4)

TABLE 2

Merchandise Export Deficits = Import Surpluses (+) and Merchandise Export Surpluses = Import Deficits (−) Regrouped into Three Major World 'Regions' in 1928

(*in millions of dollars*)

Trade of With	All Europe 1	U.S. + Dominions 2	Underdeveloped 3	Total 4
1. All Europe	x	−2,070	− 830	−2,900
2. U.S. + Dominions	+2,070	x	− 660	+1,410
3. Underdeveloped	+ 830	+ 660	x	+1,490
4. TOTAL	+2,900	−1,410	−1,490	x

Source: See Table 1, p. 178, and Table 5, pp. 202–3.
    Column 1: Table 1, columns 1 + 2; or Table 5, column   6
        ,,   2: ,, 1,   ,,   3 + 4; ,,   ,,   5,   ,,   11
        ,,   3: ,, 1,   ,,   5; ,,   5,   ,,   16

merchandise import surplus of + $ 2900 million, which is supplied half (− $ 1410 million) by the U.S.A. and Dominions, and half (− $1490 million) by the underdeveloped countries. The weight – if not the significance, as Hilgerdt pointed out – of these merchandise trade surpluses and deficits may be measured by comparing them with the values of total world and region exports for the same year. Total world exports in 1928 were approximately $32,000 million and imports into Europe, calculated at export values from other regions (see Statistical and Methodological Appendix), were approximately $18,000 million (League 1942, 45). Therefore, the − $ 2900 million excess of European imports represented about 9 per cent of total exports and 16 per cent of total European imports. Of these, the underdeveloped countries supplied over half, or about 5 per cent and 9 per cent respectively. But from the point of view of the underdeveloped countries themselves – which unlike the U.S.A. and Dominions had no one to 'help' them pay for their export surplus – their − $ 1490 million excess of exports over imports represented 18 per cent of their total, including their excess, exports of $ 8330 million (League 1942, 45).

Moreover, if (as in Appendix Table 5, cols 17 and 18) we exclude China and North Africa – which had merchandise import surpluses of + $300 million and + $20 million respectively – from the group of underdeveloped countries, then the remaining ones had a net export surplus = import deficit of − $1810 million, or nearly 6 per cent of total world exports, 10 per cent of European imports and 28 per cent of their own (excluding China and North Africa's) total exports of $6520 million. This then is a measure of the significance of the contribution of the underdeveloped countries' excess of merchandise exports over their 'corresponding' merchandise imports to the imports of the developed regions of the world; and this is so even when these exports are measured at the world market prices, which do not allow for the possibilities of 'unequal' exchange in balanced trade. The importance of these merchandise trade imbalances for Europe, the United States and the Dominions, however, far exceed their simple share in their own imports – which is a problem to be discussed below in the examination of the further implications of the world system of multilateral merchandise trade imbalances.

As to the representativeness of the 1928 data, they are of course quantitatively higher than in the nineteenth century; but the fundamental pattern of trade imbalances they display is not qualitatively different from that which characterised the whole third stage of world capital accumulation and capitalist development. The total of world exports grew from about US $500 million in 1820 to about $5000 million in 1867–8, $20,000 million in 1913, and $34,000 million in 1928 (Woytinsky, 39). But concomitantly, as all students of the problem (such as Schlote, League of Nations, Imlah, Saul) agree, Britain, for instance, had a permanent merchandise export deficit in every year since 1816; and this deficit grew from about £10 million in 1815–20 to £100 million in 1876 and reached about £140 million before World War I after passing a maximum of £188 million in 1903 (Barrat-Browne, 75, and Saul, 53, based on Imlah). The underdeveloped countries' export surplus certainly also grew over this same period.

The partial merchandise import and export data for some countries of Europe and the United States, shown in the Statistical Appendix Table 6 and summarised in the following Table 3, suggest that Britain had a growing merchandise export deficit-import surplus from 1881 to 1905 and a lesser one in 1911–13, while the principal countries of Continental Western Europe taken together began with a lower import surplus than Britain at the beginning of this period and ended up with an import surplus nearly double that of Britain in 1911–13. The principal beneficiary of this growing merchandise import surplus was Germany. The United States, on the other hand, displays a merchandise export surplus = import deficit as early as 1881–5. The same becomes much more marked, however, after the turn of the century, when the United States came to export more manufactures (Table 6, line 1 M) as well as more raw materials (line 1 R) than they imported. Though these data do not refer specifically to the trade balances of the underdeveloped countries, they do permit some inferences about their direction and general order of magnitude. Since in each of these years and perhaps throughout this period the import surpluses of Europe, either Britain or Continental and all the more so of both combined, are far larger than export surpluses of the United States, we may infer that these European import surpluses much correspond to the merchandise export surpluses of some regions other than the United States as well. And since in the earlier part of this period the importance of the Dominions in world trade was still relatively modest, we may infer that the underdeveloped countries must have had a significant export surplus = import deficit by the last decades of the nineteenth century and the first of the twentieth century.

TABLE 3

Excess Exports and Imports Europe and U.S.A., 1881–1913
(in millions of current dollars)

	1881–85	*1891–95*	*1901–05*	*1911–13*
Export Deficits =				
Import Surpluses				
Britain	507	634	850	652
Continental Europe	381	505	522	1,142
Export Surpluses =				
Import Deficits				
U.S.A.	108	91	455	536

Source: Table 6.

Moreover, we may suspect that–as in 1928–the United States paid for part of its surplus exports with the surplus imports it derived in turn from the underdeveloped countries. This suspicion would seem to be confirmed by balance of trade data for the United States alone, which show that in the years 1891–1900, 1901–10, and 1911–15, the United States had an import surplus=export deficit with the underdeveloped countries (Central America, South America, Asia and Africa) which amounted to 43 per cent, 34 per cent, and 40 per cent respectively of its export surplus = import deficit with Europe for these same years (computed from Woytinsky, 78–9). For the year 1928, Hilgerdt's data show an analogous percentage of 45 per cent (Table 1, col. 4, line 5 as percentage of lines 1 and 2).

Other partial estimates, in part confirmatory and in part contradictory, of the historical development of this world system of multilateral trade imbalances for the years 1876–80, 1896–1900, and 1913 are given in the Statistical Appendix Table 7 and summarised in Table 4. (For a discussion of our methods of computation, see Statistical Appendix.) These data permit estimates, albeit rougher and more inaccurate, of the pattern of multilateral trade imbalances for these earlier years that are more analogous to those presented in Tables 1, 2 and 5 for 1928. They include the merchandise trade balances of the underdeveloped countries along with those of Europe and the United States (with Canada), though all balances are still expressed between a particular region and all the others put together rather than with any of the others taken separately. Table 4 (and Table 7) also show

TABLE 4

Excess Merchandise Imports over Exports (+) and Excess Merchandise Exports over Imports (−)

(in millions of current dollars)

	1876–80	*1896–1900*	*1913*
Britain	+367	+540	+374
Continental Europe	−250	+207	+711
U.S. + Canada	−258	−490	−656
Underdeveloped	+133	+ 99	−640

Source: Table 7.
Calculations and Error; see Appendix.

a growing merchandise trade import surplus = export deficit for Britain from 1876–80 to 1896–1900 and a renewed decline to 1913 as well as an analogous import surplus for Continental Europe, which grows to nearly double that of Britain by the latter date. In these tables, however, Continental Europe appears with an export surplus = import deficit and North-western Continental Europe with an export/import balance for the years 1876–80. The United States (with Canada), as always, shows a growing export surplus = import deficit and the underdeveloped countries display an export surplus = import deficit and the underdeveloped countries display an export surplus = import deficit that is equal to that of the United States and Canada in 1913. For the two earlier periods, however, in these data the underdeveloped countries show an import surplus = export deficit. All these data for the earlier years, like those for 1928 in Tables 1, 2 and 5, are in terms of then current world market prices. Thus, in so far as these 'undervalue' the exports of the underdeveloped countries due to 'unequal exchange', the same data also underestimate the 'real' merchandise exports surpluses of the countries. The export deficits of the underdeveloped countries in 1876–80 and 1896–1900, according to Table 4, show the beginning precisely in this period of the so called 'secular' decline in the terms of trade of the primary producing underdeveloped countries (see Chapter 5).

Thus, although our most detailed data for this period are for the year 1928, these partial data suggest that its multilateral trade imbalances had been already developing on substantially the same pattern for several, and at least three or four, decades earlier

Further evidence showing that this was the case is given as part of our discussion of the theoretical implications of this pattern of multilateral world trade imbalances.

As to the stability of the pattern of trade imbalances and Hilgerdt's analogy with an expanding fan, it is true that additional countries were inserted in this system in the course of its development. But this insertion took place primarily within the major regions and not between them, as was the case for instance with Germany, which according to Hilgerdt came to occupy a link in its own right within the European region. Or a particular country may have changed from an export surplus to an export deficit, or vice versa, with respect to another country or region. Thus, perhaps, the 1928 export deficit of Argentina with the United States (Table 5, col. 13, line 10) was of recent origin and may have been an export surplus earlier; and Argentina may have had an export surplus with Britain at some times, since her exports were primarily to the continental European countries and her imports primarily from Britain (Saul, 74–9). But none of these changes alters the fundamental relationships between the major regions.

Before going on to interpret the significance of these three merchandise trade balances and their relationships, we may turn to the matter of transportation and insurance charges on traded goods. According to Hilgerdt, 'two-thirds of the tonnage of all merchant vessels were European, and the European groups . . . were net receivers not only of the freights included in the C.I.F. value of their imports, but also of large amounts earned from the rest of the world on account of transport to or between non-European countries' (League, 78). We may safely assume that most of the other third of world tonnage belonged to the United States and Dominions and that the now underdeveloped countries owned hardly any shipping and derived negligible earnings from transport and insurance services – though they paid considerably for them, as we may now observe.

We can roughly estimate the payments – also in the form of merchandise exports – by the underdeveloped countries for the ocean transport and insurance of both the goods they exported and the goods they imported. (This involves essentially computing the difference between the underdeveloped countries' exports to other regions and other regions' imports from the underdeveloped countries – that is, the transportation costs of the underdeveloped countries' exports, *plus* the difference between the underdeveloped countries' imports from other regions and other regions' exports to the underdeveloped countries, or the transport costs of the underdeveloped countries' imports. For the tropics this amounts to the difference between the export surplus and the import surplus as reported in Hilgerdt's Diagram 6, or the difference between the tropics' balances with other regions and the latter's with the tropics as reported in his Table 44.)

For the Tropics, these transport payments amount to 110 with Britain, 350 with Europe (or 460 with All of Europe), 100 with Recently Settled Regions, and 310 with the United States (or 410 with the last two combined). This amounts to US $870 million for transportation of merchandise from and to the Tropics, and this amount should be compared with the US $1450 merchandise export surplus (column 12), which the Tropics had with these regions and the rest of the world. But to construct the estimate of transportation payments by all the underdeveloped countries we still have to compute and add those of Argentina, China and other Continental Asia, and North Africa in their trade with Britain, Europe, the United States and other areas. For Argentina these transport payments amounted to 253 with All of Europe and 31 with the United States, or over 280 in all. For China and Continental Asia, they were 120 with All of Europe and 57 with the United States, but because of the importance of its intra-Asian trade which was undoubtedly carried on European ships, we have also computed its cost of 70, which adds up to 247 or nearly 250. For North Africa, we only computed transportation costs in its trade with Europe, which was 26. Summarising, this amounts to about 280 for Argentina and 270 for China including Continental Asia plus North Africa, or about 550 for these 'non-tropical' underdeveloped regions. Adding these to the transportation payments of 870 by the tropical regions, we arrive at transportation payments by all underdeveloped countries with other regions (but not including those among underdeveloped countries themselves, except for the China-Asia ones) of US $1320 million other than the US $1490 (or 1810) million export surplus on merchandise account.

The calculations of transport charges also reveal another pattern: typically the transport charges on the goods exported by the underdeveloped countries are much greater than the transport charges of the goods exported by the metropolitan countries and imported by the underdeveloped ones. Thus, for instance, the transport charges on the goods Argentina exported to Europe are

189, while they are 64 on the goods it imports from Europe. No doubt this is largely due to the fact that Argentina exported bulkier products, and more of them, to than it imported from Europe. But China, which had an export *deficit* with Europe and did not export such heavy goods, none the less had to pay 80 for transport charges on its exports compared to 40 on its imports from Europe. So there is considerable reason to believe that the underdeveloped countries were also victims of discriminatory freight rates on their exports.

All of these estimates are no doubt very rough and based on the data for only a single year, 1928 (although below we shall examine additional data, referring to some particular countries, especially Britain and India, for some earlier years). One of the major reasons why these estimates are only very rough for our purposes is that they all refer to relations between geographical regions at their frontiers (or between their frontiers in the case of ocean transportation). Thus these data do not permit us to identify foreign, usually metropolitan, production within the frontiers of these geographical regions, and in particular in the underdeveloped ones. For the same reason, the data do not permit us to discriminate between, or to establish the relationship between, foreign and national production – or trade – in these regions or countries. Hilgerdt makes a partially related observation: 'Within the Tropies . . . there is a complicated network of trade relations. Thus, in 1928 the Netherlands Indies recorded an export balance to India of $44 million, and to British Malaya of $80 million, while the last two mentioned countries had an export balance – largely on account of jute sacks – to a number of tropical countries such as Brazil and Cuba which in turn were net exporters to the United States . . . this all goes to prove that what in Diagram 6 is shown as an export balance from the Tropics to the United States is in part the second (and in part even the third) link in chains of transfer originating in individual tropical countries' (League, 79); and it also proves that much of their production which at first sight may appear to be for each other is really produced for the metropolis – and often by metropolitan horizontally and vertically integrated monopolies that produce and trade between various underdeveloped (and developed) countries to suit their own particular needs. (The underdeveloped countries' export surplus is underestimated both at market prices and in terms of real values because the statistics assign corresponding imports to these countries when they enter these countries and physically, geographically and in many cases even when they are only bought by people identified with these countries. But many imports, particularly in the colonialised underdeveloping countries, only appear to be destined to their economics or people, when in fact they are purchased by metropolitan foreigners who operate on colonialised soil for metropolitan enterprises and purposes. If these apparent imports were deducted from the colonialised countries' import statistics, their imports would be considerably smaller and their export surplus correspondingly still larger. It would not be similarly correct 'analogously' to deduct the export by foreign firms in underdeveloped countries from their total exports, since these exports *are* in fact produced by the labour and indeed the capital of the underdeveloped countries, while the imports by foreign and many domestic firms do not benefit the local economy or people.)

In so far as the development of the system was associated with the growth of British foreign investments and her service earnings from them, as Hilgerdt emphasised, we may observe that British investments rose from about £10 million in 1816, to about £700–1000 million in 1870–4, and then to about £4000 million in 1913 (Saul, 10, 67). But since merchandise exports were in deficit throughout this period, and increasingly so, Saul argues for the earlier part of the period 'that only the rise in shipping earnings and other foreign services made the investment possible' (Saul, 10); and later, 'instead of making use of a surplus of new savings for overseas investment – a surplus earned by exports and invisible services – Britain resorted to simple reinvestment of part of the income from previous loans. This took place most noticeably after 1874, when the excess of imports began to rise sharply, and it was only in unusual years thereafter that new exports of capital exceeded income from interest charges' (Saul, 67). This, then, is the other side of the coin, suggested by Halperin Donghi, that Britain enabled Latin America to absorb increasing quantities of her manufactures even during the earlier part of this period by reinvesting there some of her earnings from merchandising services there, which were even more 'invisible' than those from later investment, although the monopoly control of this merchandising was no less obvious to contemporary Latin Americans or Indians. In a word, however much the fan, as Hilgerdt called it, spread, its structure was remarkably stable – and still is, even though the United States may have changed position in the system since 1928; and the underdeveloped countries have been in the same position in the system for over a century. Only their ability to change their position in the capitalist system has changed – it is even more impossible now than it was then.

2. Colonial and Semi-Colonial Capital Contributions to Metropolitan Accumulation and Overseas Investment

Hilgerdt's and Condliffe's circular flow diagram – graphically useful as it is – and Condliffe's description of this system as a 'circle [that] is closed by Britain exporting more to the tropics than it imported from them' obscure much more than they clarify in at least one important respect: the place and function of the underdeveloped countries in the system. It is true that in 1928 the Tropics (Table 5, col. 12) had an import surplus of $+ \$200$ million from Britain (line 1). But that still left them with an overall export surplus = import deficit of $- \$1450$ million. And if Argentina (col. 13) with its export surplus with Britain (line 1) of $- \$150$ is added to the Tropics (whether or not China and North Africa are added as well) to get the underdeveloped countries (col. 16 and/or 17), then the import surplus dwindles down to $+ \$40$ (or $+ \$50$ with China and North Africa) million from Britain. Thus, the extent to which the circle is really 'closed' is negligible by any measure.

Therefore, rather than a 'circle', the system of trade balances and multilateral settlements may better be compared to a chain or a root as follows:

Region	Export Surplus/ Import Deficit with	Export Deficit/ Import Surplus with
Britain	nobody	Europe, Dominions, U.S., Underdeveloped
Europe	Britain	Dominions, U.S. Underdeveloped
Dominions	Britain, Europe	U.S., Underdeveloped
United States	Britain, Europe, Dominions	Underdeveloped
Underdeveloped	Britain, Europe, Dominions, U.S. (everybody)	nobody
	Or more simply	
All Europe (Britain and Europe)	nobody	U.S. and Dominions, Underdeveloped
U.S. and Dominions	All Europe	Underdeveloped
Underdeveloped	All Europe, U.S. and Dominions, (everybody)	nobody

This means that, in fact, even when measured at world market prices (and even more so if estimated in terms of real value), the underdeveloped part of the world through its excess of merchandise exports over merchandise imports really finances all the rest of the world both directly and indirectly. Specifically, the export surplus of the underdeveloped countries (1) supplied much of the excess merchandise consumption of Europe represented by the latter's merchandise export deficit or import surplus, (2) helped finance the export surplus of the United States and Dominions to Europe, (3) helped domestic investment and development in Europe, and/ or (4) helped Europe finance its foreign investment in the United States and Dominions, whose development was thereby accelerated while the underdeveloped countries also financed much of the 'foreign' investment in themselves, which however accelerated their underdevelopment. We may examine these in greater detail below.

(1) Europe's constant excess of merchandise imports over merchandise exports, as reflected in its net export deficit of +$2900 million in 1928, and therefore its excess consumption, was largely supplied directly and indirectly by the underdeveloped countries, as is reflected in their 1928 merchandise export surplus of − $1490 m. (or − $1810 m.). About the period in general, and with references to earlier years Saul observes: 'The broad outline of the pattern of world trade just before the First World War is clear enough. The rapidly industrializing countries of Europe and North America expanded their purchases of raw materials and food-stuffs from the primary producers, and all, with the significant exception of Britain, ran up heavy deficits in their balance of payments with these countries . . . [Britain] was the greatest creditor nation, and enjoyed a very large income from so-called "invisible" payments' (Saul, 45). During the second stage of world capital accumulation and capitalist development, the principal source of these excess exports of primary products – or excess imports and investible capital for the now underdeveloped countries – was undoubtedly Asia. Hilgerdt writes: 'As a supplier of tropical products, tropical Asia – under which name we include India, Burma, Ceylon and the groups "South-East Asia" – is more important than the tropical regions of Africa and America together' (League, 1942, 57). The same is confirmed by Lockwood (1943, 422) who adds, 'And, incidentally, the export surplus of Southeast Asia played an important role in the world network of payment balances. The

region met its heavy net obligations in Europe and the United Kingdom on account of imports and investment earnings to a large extent by rubber and tin shipments to the United States, which in turn financed American exports across the Atlantic.'

But by far most important of all was India. Several students from or of India (see Dutt, Chandra) have examined and estimated 'the drain' of capital out of India and have observed that India had not only a balance of trade but even a balance of payments surplus for much of the period. In his already cited *Studies in British Overseas Trade 1870–1914*, S. B. Saul (43) says, 'our aim is to carry further the analysis of the pre-1914 pattern of world-trading settlements attempted in the League of Nations study, the *Network of World Trade*' (that is, the study directed by Hilgerdt which is the source of much of our own discussion here). Though, as his title implies, Saul concentrates on Britain and its balance of trade and balance of payments surplus, he seeks to account for the latter by looking for, or at, its most important source: India. After pointing out that 'it is worth noting that never from 1857 to 1913 did India import capital on a scale large enough to give her a surplus of merchandise imports over exports' (204–5), Saul observes:

> The importance of India's trade to the pattern of world trade balances can hardly be exaggerated. On one side lay her heavy consumption of cottons and other exports from Britain as well as invisible services, on the other her diverse export trade in manufactures, raw materials and foodstuffs, giving her easy access to the markets of all the great industrial countries . . . In 1880–1883 India provided Britain with a trade surplus of almost £11 million to help settle her deficits in Europe. In the next fifteen years this balance grew only very slightly in terms of sterling though in rupees it almost doubled, but after the mid-90's it expanded extremely quickly and by the end of the pre-war period had passed £50 million. In addition, it must be remembered that in these last years re-exports of Indian produce from Britain averaged well over £11 million. Assuming that most of these re-exports went to Europe and North America, it would appear that India's true earnings with those countries must have been in the region of £50 million also. But in this kind of analysis we must take account of the very significant service payments and capital movements. Our calculations, given in the appendix to chapter III, put these at between £25 million and

£30 million in 1910 with net disinvestment in that year about £9 million. (203–4)

. . . The overall surplus with India [in 1919] must have been something of the order of £25 million, leaving £65 million to be obtained from invisible income from the rest of the world . . . The position was that Britain settled more than one-third of her deficits with Europe and the United States through India. The South American countries together obviously made the next largest contribution, although Turkey and Japan were, after India, the most important individual deficit countries. We have made no allowance here for the export of capital . . . The net effect on the balance of payments was to increase the deficit with the United States and reduce the credit balances with the South American countries. (56)

. . . re-exports of primary products imported from Ceylon and the Straits Settlements were of considerable importance for Britain's settlement pattern, but perhaps most significant in this respect was the emergence of a vital pattern of trade with the British West African colonies. The exports of these territories had begun to expand markedly during the 1890's . . . The colonies therefore had an export surplus of over £3 million in 1913 with Continental Europe, a significant new source for multilateral settlement which was to grow more important for Britain as time went on. The West Indies too, despite their almost complete neglect by Britain, produced useful surpluses . . . All of these patterns of trade were essentially dynamic; the changes of national economies which had given rise to them were constantly going further and modifying the structure of world trade again. The emergence of a huge deficit with Canada was the most striking development of the pre-war years. (227–8)

. . . The key to Britain's whole payments pattern lay in India, financing as she probably did more than two-fifths of Britain's total deficits. India's trade and bullion returns for the year ending 31 March, 1911, gave her an excess of exports to the rest of the Empire of £15.8 million one of £48.6 million with foreign countries. From Europe alone she earned over £30 million, from China and Hong Kong over £10 million, from Japan and the United States just under £7 million each. But this was by no means all, for it was mainly through India that the British balance of payments found the flexibility essential to a great capital exporting country. During the years 1910–1913 the balance of payments with Argentina, Brazil and Canada moved sharply against Britain. There were a number of offsetting favourable changes . . . but much of the burden fell upon India . . . The balance of payments (with India) must have moved in Britain's favour by at least £12 million. This Indian safety-valve brought immense advantages from other points of view as well. It was through her Indian connections that Britain was able to survive the blows of the tariff barriers. The Indian market was kept open to British goods and Indian exports overcame the tariffs for her . . . Thus it was that although Britain took a smaller proportion of the exports of India than of the exports of any other part of the Empire, it suited the world settlements pattern that this should be so. The value of the multilateral system in general to the British economy was immense. . . . (Saul, 62–3)

(2) The export surplus of the underdeveloped countries also contributed materially, both directly and indirectly, to permit the United States and the Dominions to make their own shipments of excess merchandise exports to Europe, as is already suggested by some of the above considerations. Returning to our Table 5, we may note that even in 1928, when Argentina had an export deficit of – $110 million with the United States, the underdeveloped countries had an export surplus of $610 million with the United States (col. 16, line 10) and a surplus of $50 million with the Dominions (col. 16, line 9) for a total of $660 million with the two put together. This is nearly equal to half the export surplus of the United States and Dominions to Europe. We may thus argue that in a sense the U.S. and Dominions were able to ship their own excess of exports over imports to Europe with less sacrifice to themselves, since they were supplied with almost half the equivalent amount of excess exports by the underdeveloped countries, who thereby so to say were the utlimate suppliers of half of the export surplus of the United States and Dominions. This sacrifice of their own products to finance the U.S. export surplus was, of course, not repaid to the underdeveloped countries by anybody since they unlike the U.S., had an export deficit with, nobody.

Saul supplies a few additional details: 'In the early 1880's the United States . . . [had] a strong excess of exports to Europe, and an excess of imports from almost everywhere else . . . The negative balances of trade with India, Ceylon, Brazil, West Africa and the

Straits Settlements had increased sharply [thereafter. The obverse was that] the United States was settling almost the whole of her trade and service deficits through this one favourable balance' (Saul, 45, 48, 47).

(3) The underdeveloped countries' merchandise export surplus may be related to domestic investment and productive consumption which expanded the home market and generated economic development in Europe or Britain. Mandel and others have associated European capital imports with European and British industrial capital stocks in the eighteenth century, and this is also valid for the nineteenth century. We have already observed that Britain's own investments abroad were largely financed out of foreign earnings rather than with autonomous merchandise exports, inasmuch as Britain had a constant and growing merchandise export deficit or import surplus during the entire nineteenth century. Comparing the growth curve already cited of Britain's merchandise import surplus from £10 million in 1816 to £140 million in 1913 (in Barrat-Browne, 75), it is interesting to observe – though Barrat-Browne himself does not do so – that it almost coincides pound for pound, year by year, with the growth curve of British domestic investment, as measured by total new construction of all kinds (in Table 46 of Cairncross) and this is on trade account only, not on service.

(4) More interesting is the examination of some further aspects of the relation between the underdeveloped countries' export surplus to Europe and Europe's investment in the United States and white settler Dominions. As a claimed rebuttal of Lenin's theory of imperialism, it has often been observed – recently most notably by Fieldhouse – that the largest part of European and British foreign investment during the late nineteenth century was not placed in the colonialised and now underdeveloped countries but rather in the United States and the Dominions, despite the fact that special mention of this had already been made by Lenin himself (*Imperialism*, p. 497, and elsewhere). But in view of the flow of capital through merchandise trade imbalances and multilateral settlements, this observation – far from rendering the colonialised underdeveloped countries relatively irrelevant to this process – really calls for the examination of the intimate relation of the underdeveloped countries and their exports to the European foreign investment that occurred *not* in them but elsewhere. Unfortunately this task is also beyond our scope and our present capacity. Indeed Saul rightly

laments, 'the mechanism of the transfer of this capital raises problems at once obscure and fascinating . . . To a large extent our lack of knowledge about this mechanism can be attributed to the great difficulty . . . The number of special studies on the subject is still very small . . .' (Saul, 68).

Beyond the observations about India's capital contribution to Britain, it may be suggested that through their merchandise export surplus the underdeveloped countries made an important direct capital contribution to British foreign investment abroad. Woytinsky (199) reports:

In this year (1913) the United Kingdom exported merchandises valued at £635 million and had imports totalling £769 million. In addition, it imported gold worth £24 million and thus had an import surplus of £158 million in the movement of merchandise and gold. To offset this deficit, the British had items totalling £129 million (from earnings of the merchant marine £94, earnings of traders' commission £25, other earnings £10 million). The British thus would have had a deficit of £29 million except for interest and dividends from their investments abroad, which amounted to £210 million. Addition of this item to other 'invisible' exports reversed the balance of payments in favour of the United Kingdom, giving it a net surplus of £181 million. Theoretically, the British could take this balance in increased imports of merchandise and still have the balance of payments in equilibrium. Actually they left the whole net balance abroad as new investment. In fact, in 1913 London advanced to colonial and foreign concerns long-term loans for £198 million – almost exactly the amount of the current profits from former investments abroad.

This British re-investment of about £200 million in 1913 may be compared with the merchandise export surplus of the underdeveloped countries. Britain itself had a merchandise (including gold) export deficit = import surplus with the rest of the world of £158 for 1913, according to the same source. But as Hilgerdt's research implies and our tables suggest, the ultimate source of these excess exports ultimately lay in the underdeveloped countries, who virtually 'financed' not only their own but also all the other regions' export surpluses. Total world merchandise exports were about U.S.

$20,000 million in 1913 and about $32,000 million in 1928 (cited above); that is, in 1913 they were about 4/7 of the 1928 total. If we may assume that the underdeveloped countries' merchandise export surplus in 1913 relative to 1928 was proportional to the world export totals for the same years, the $-$ $1490 million export surplus of the underdeveloped countries and the $+$ $1430 million export deficit of Britain for 1928 in our table would be reduced (by a factor of 4/7) to roughly $-$ $852 million and $-$ $816 million respectively for 1913, and the underdeveloped countries' transport payments from 1320 to about 800. Converting these dollar values into pounds by dividing by 5 (£1 equalling $4.80), we would arrive at a merchandise export surplus by the underdeveloped countries in 1913 of about £178 m. and a merchandise import surplus by Britain of about £170 m. (Using the trade balance estimates in Tables 6 and 7, the British import surplus for 1913 would be $652 million or $374 million and the underdeveloped countries' export surplus in Table 7 $640 million.) Given the rough and ready estimation procedure used, the orders of magnitude of the 1913 registered (or reported) import surplus of £158 m. and our estimate of £168 m. for the same year are quite similar. Perhaps, then, we may also be justified in suggesting that the estimated merchandise export surplus by the underdeveloped countries of £178 was sufficiently large to supply – even despite their under-valuation by world market prices – almost all the transfer of real goods necessary to convert Britain's financial re-investment of £200 into real investment.

Irrespective of the adequacy of such estimates of the under-developed countries' direct contribution to European foreign investment, they undoubtedly contributed significantly through the particular place they occupied in the chain of trade surpluses and the system of international settlements. After noting that 'the United States and Argentina held pride of place among foreign borrowers' of Britain in an earlier period, Saul notes that 'from the mid-70's onwards investment in the Empire became more and more important, for reasons we shall discuss later' (Saul, 67). For 1913, Saul (67, following Paish) assigns about £1780 million to British Empire investment and £2000 million to the rest of the world. If we take India out of the former and replace it with the U.S. from the latter group, in order to regroup them into U.S. and Dominions and underdeveloped countries (including 110 million for non-Russian Europe), the totals for the two groups are roughly reversed. But elsewhere Saul (218–9) reports the 'relative stagnation of exports to the Empire, a trend so discomfiting to imperialist sentiments, especially as investment in the Empire was so large after 1900 . . . It is obvious that it was not so much trade with the Empire but rather trade with South America and Far Eastern countries which rose to take the place previously held by the United States'.

By 1928–30 the distribution of British investments had shifted still more. Hilgerdt reports:

> The effect of multilateral trade upon the commercial relations of the United Kingdom may be studied by comparing the geographical distribution of the income on account of 'invisible' current items and that of *merchandise import balance through which this income was transferred* . . . The biggest import balances were with the United States and Europe, where British investments were relatively small, while there were export balances to the Tropics and certain of the British Dominions where investments were large. In Diagram 7 [of Hilgerdt, not shown here, which shows a clear inverse relation between British overseas investments and British import balances] . . . this tendency of trade balances to be distributed in a manner quite opposite to what might have been expected at first sight is strikingly illustrated. The explanation for this phenomenon lies in the fact that merchandise trade depends on each country's commodity needs and the localities where these needs can be met, and not upon their financial claims. British capital has been active in developing primary education in various parts of the world for disposal in the world market and not in the United Kingdom alone; . . . The *export surplus* of these countries, representing largely *the yield of British capital*, thus arose in trade with countries which financed their imports of primary goods by an excess of exports to the United Kingdom. British capital thus gave an impetus to the economic development not only of the countries in which it was invested but also of those through which the yield of this capital was transferred. (League, 82–3, our italics)

We cannot but agree that these multilateral relationships were important, as Hilgerdt showed, but we would have to argue that a more realistic examination of the evidence leads to conclusions that are in fact the opposite of Hilgerdt's. First, the historical source of the 'British' capital that was invested abroad was, as Hilgerdt himself recognised in part elsewhere and as Saul emphasises, primarily in the now underdeveloped countries and not in Britain itself. Secondly, the 'impetus' that the foreign investment of this capital gave to economic development was not, as we now recognise, in the colonialised countries of Asia, Africa and Latin America, which first supplied the capital and then received part of it again as 'foreign' (that is, foreign-owned) investment, for in these countries this investment and the process as a whole gave an impetus to the development of underdevelopment. Thirdly, the impetus to economic development was primarily in the countries 'through which the yield of this capital was transferred', that is the United States and Dominions. And fourthly, to a significant extent it was the production and export surplus of the primary goods by the underdeveloping rather than developing countries which permitted the 'yield of this capital' and the development of the United States and Dominions, to say nothing of Europe itself.

Saul supplies some additional evidence, which supports our argument: 'In fact, Britain found it difficult to expand exports to the United States sufficiently to make direct transfer of capital to her at any time in our period . . . in Argentina, a considerable multilateral transfer was still necessary as we shall see . . . France, with her capital goods industries less developed than those of Britain, was forced to transfer most of her investment indirectly' (Saul, 70). 'The bulk of British investment in Canada, for instance, served to finance imports from the United States, Canada's normal supplier of capital goods. Indirect settlement between Britain, Canada and the United States began to become most pronounced during the late 90's . . . Here, then, was indirect settlement matched only by that between Britain, India and the rest of the world' (Saul, 70, 186). But these two major investment and trade triangles were not unconnected, for since Britain occupied one corner of each of them Britain interlocked these triangles with each other. And at the base of the whole complicated structure was India and part of the 'rest of the world'. Part of 'the explanation clearly lies in the great amount of multilateral settlement Britain made through India' (even if Saul's sentence is here quoted out of its original context on p. 88) and another part, of course, also lies in the fact, which Saul notes at the beginning of the same paragraph (on p. 87), that in some years Britain 'was a net importer of capital from India' and much of the rest of the world. Finally, we may again recall Saul's observation that 'Had not British exports . . . found a wide-open market in

India . . . it would have been impossible for her to have indulged so heavily in investment on the American continent and elsewhere' (Saul, 88). Of course, all parts of the world were interrelated in this capitalist system and development, but only the now underdeveloped countries were *at the bottom of it*. A further multilateral balancing function of the underdeveloped countries in this world system and for the developed ones is that of dampening the oscillations, and particularly of cushioning the slumps of the central economies, in the business cycles treated elsewhere in the author's book, *World Accumulation 1492–1784* and in his *The Contemporary World Crisis* (forthcoming).

3. Statistical and Methodological Appendix

Table 5 summarises the following computations: Hilgerdt's Diagram 6 summarised the export and import balances for 1928 between each of the regions (excluding Region 6, 'Rest of the World') in his Table 44. Condliffe in turn simplified Hilgerdt's diagram by including only the import balances. Hilgerdt (League, 77) stated that the difference between the two kinds of balances was that 'the import balances exceed the export balances chiefly on account of transport between the frontiers of the importing and exporting countries', suggesting that the import balances are larger because they include the transportation cost of the imported goods while the export balances do not include the transportation cost of the exported goods. In using the import balances, Condliffe therefore gave not only the net balances on merchandise account alone but those on transport service account as well. However, Hilgerdt calculated his 'export balances for region A by subtracting the exports by region A to each of the other regions from the imports by region A from other regions' (or vice versa, depending on which is greater). But since these imports also contain a transportation component, Hilgerdt's 'export' balances are not on pure merchandise account either and contain at least the transportation cost of the incoming goods (while the 'import' balances contain the transportation costs of both outgoing and incoming goods).

In order to reflect better the pure merchandise trade balances (and later to compare them with the transportation services the underdeveloped countries also paid to the metropolis), we have therefore recomputed Region A's export balances from Hilgerdt's raw data by subtracting the exports by Region A to Region B from the exports by Region B to Region A (or vice versa, depending on which is greater), since these latter do not include the transportation costs from B to A, as do the imports of A from B which Hilgerdt used to calculate his balances. This is a first difference between the data in the accompanyimg table and those in Hilgerdt's Table 44, his Diagram 6 or Condliffe's diagram. (We also exclude the balances within each region – arising from trade between its member countries – which Hilgerdt also excludes from his Diagram 6 but includes in his calculations of the total net balances for each Region in Table 44.) Both of our changes in computation lower the export deficits of the metropolis and increase the export surpluses of the tropics compared to those of Hilgerdt but constitute a better reflection of the structure and operation of the real trade imbalances between them.

However, for the 'minor' regions (excepting Argentina, which was treated like the foregoing 'major' ones), that is, for the U.S.S.R., Japan, China and other Continental Asia, and North Africa in columns 3, 4, 14 and 15, respectively, we used the export and import data as they appear in the tables of Annex III, 'World Trade, by Countries of Provenance and Destination'. The reasons for this change in methods of computation for the minor regions are the following: since the Annex III tables, like all others in Hilgerdt's work, are constructed in terms of the exports and imports of each country, computing the difference between them is much easier and time-saving than finding the exports to each country (imports minus transport costs, etc.) by looking for them among the exports statistics of each of its trading partners. This time-saving for the minor regions is justified by the consideration that their shares in total world trade and its imbalances is so small that the in-accuracies introduced by using their imports instead of exports to them should be relatively insignificant, especially inasmuch as the balances are rounded to the nearest $10 million anyway. Further-more, examination of the Annex III data on exports from one country to another and imports of the second from the first country (e.g. between China and North Africa) displayed some incon-sistencies (or misprints) which were sometimes also incongruent with total or sub-total trade figures. In those cases, the balance was estimated first by eliminating the incongruency and, if that was not sufficient to make the two countries' trade figures check with each other, by averaging out the inconsistency and then rounding to the nearest $10 million. Argentina, on the other hand, was treated like the major regions, that is computing the balance between exports to other regions and other regions' exports to Argentina.

We cannot aspire to clarify their position here, but in order to complete the circle of world trade and its imbalances we shall assign these countries to the other five regions anyway and use our best judgement about where they might reasonably be made to 'fit' best. Accordingly, observing the position of the U.S.S.R. (col. 3) between the regions of recent settlement and Continental Europe (col. 2) we assign her to the latter (col. $2+3+4 = 5$) to get 'All Continental Europe (and Japan)' in col. 5 and then 'All Europe' in col. 6, since like Europe, the U.S. and Dominions, the U.S.S.R. in 1928 is a net importer from the underdeveloped countries, and although like the Dominions she is also an importer from the U.S.A., albeit also from the rest of Europe. The case of Japan (col. 4) is still more doubtful, but we add it to Europe as well, to get 'All Continental Europe, U.S.S.R., and Japan' in col. 5, 'All Europe, U.S.S.R., and Japan' in col. 6. Though Japan has an import surplus from Europe, like the latter, she has an even bigger one from the underdeveloped countries even in 1928. China and other non-tropical Continental Asia (col. 14, excluding South and South East Asia) and North Africa (col. 15) are added to the 'Tropics' (col. 12, including South and South-east Asia) and Argentina (col. 13) to make up the 'Underdeveloped' region (col. 16). But both China and North Africa, unlike underdeveloped countries elsewhere, display an import surplus or export deficit in their trade with Europe and, indeed, with the world as a whole. It is not clear to what extent, for China at least, this anomaly is due to special export/import price differences or transport charges. Thus, the collapse of the residual category 'rest of the world' and the inclusion of China and North Africa among the underdeveloped countries significantly lowers the latter's export surplus-import deficit, as may be observed from the comparison of columns-lines 16 and 19, in which these countries are included, with columns-lines 17 and 18, from which China and North Africa are excluded from the underdeveloped countries and the world as a whole.

Throughout, export deficits = import surpluses or excesses (e.g. of Europe which imports more merchandise than it pays for with merchandise exports) are signified by + to emphasise the excess 'take' over 'give' and export surpluses-import deficits in what is conventionally called an 'unfavourable' balance deficits (e.g. of the

TABLE 5

Merchandise Export Deficits = Import surpluses (+) and Merchandise Export Surpluses = Import Deficit (−) of Five Major and Five Minor World Regions with Each Other in 1928

(in millions of current dollars)

Trade of With	1 Britain	2 Continental Europe	3 U.S.S.R.	4 Japan	5 All Continental Europe (2+3+4)	6 All Europe (1+2+3+4)	7 Recent Settlement	8 Argentina
1. Britain	x	− 730	− 60	+ 60	− 730	− 730	− 260	− 150
2. Continental Europe	+ 730	x	− 30	+ 50	+ 20	+ 750	− 820	− 300
3. U.S.S.R	+ 60	+ 30	x	− 10	+ 20	+ 80	− 50	− 20
4. Japan	− 60	− 50	+ 10	x	− 40	− 100	− 60	0
5. All 'Cont. Europe'	+ 730	+ 750	+ 20	− 40	− 730	x	− 930	− 320
6. All Europe	+ 730	+ 820	+ 80	+ 100	− 730	x	− 1,190	− 470
7. Recent Settlement	+ 260	+ 820	+ 50	+ 60	+ 930	+ 1,190	x	x
8. Argentina (subtracted)	+ 150	+ 300	+ 20	0	+ 320	+ 470	x	x
9. Dominions	+ 110	+ 520	+ 30	+ 60	+ 610	+ 720	x	x
10. U.S.A.	+ 630	+ 740	+ 70	− 90	+ 720	+ 1,350	+ 640	+ 110
11. U.S.A.-Doms.	+ 740	+ 1,260	+ 100	− 30	+ 1,330	+ 2,070	+ 640	+ 110
12. Tropics	− 200	+ 510	+ 40	+ 150	+ 700	+ 500	+ 60	0
13. Argentina (added)	+ 150	+ 300	+ 20	0	+ 320	+ 470	x	x
14. China	− 50	− 30	+ 20	− 50	− 60	− 110	+ 10	0
15. North Africa	+ 60	− 100	+ 10	0	− 90	− 30	0	0
16. Underdeveloped	− 40	+ 680	+ 90	+ 100	+ 870	+ 830	+ 50	0
17. (Under.-China-North Africa)	(− 50)	(+ 810)	(+ 60)	(+ 150)		(+ 970)	(+ 60)	0
18. (Total)	(+ 1,420)	(+ 1,320)	(+ 80)	(+ 220)		(+ 3,040)	(− 490)	(− 360)
19. TOTAL	+ 1,430	+ 1,190	+ 110	+ 170	+ 1,470	+ 2,900	− 500	− 360

Table 5 (*contd.*)

	Dominions (7−8)	U.S.A.	U.S.+Dom. (9+10)	Tropics	Argentina	China	North Africa	Underdeveloped (12+13+14+15)	Underdeveloped (12+13)	Total (with 17)	Total (with 16)
	9	10	11	12	13	14	15	16	17	18	19
1.	− 110	− 630	− 740	+ 200	− 150	+ 50	− 60	+ 40	+ 50	− 1,420	− 1,430
2.	− 520	− 740	− 1,260	− 510	− 300	+ 30	+ 100	− 680	− 810	(− 1,320)	− 1,190
3.	− 30	− 70	− 100	− 40	− 20	− 20	− 10	− 90	− 60	(− 80)	− 110
4.	− 60	+ 90	+ 30	− 150	0	+ 60	0	− 100	− 150	(− 220)	− 170
5.	− 610	− 720	− 1,330	− 700	− 320	− 60	− 90	− 870	− 970	(− 3,010)	− 1,470
6.	− 720	− 1,350	− 2,070	− 500	− 470	+ 110	+ 30	− 830	− 60	+ 490	− 2,900
7.	x	− 640	− 640	+ 60	x	+ 10	0	− 50	0	+ 360	+ 500
8.	x	− 110	− 110	0	0	0	0	0	0	+ 360	+ 360
9.	x	− 530	− 530	− 60	0	+ 10	0	− 50	− 60	+ 1,200	+ 130
10.	+ 530	x	+ 530	− 780	+ 110	+ 60	0	+ 610	− 670	+ 1,340	+ 1,270
11.	+ 530	− 530	x	− 840	+ 110	+ 70	0	+ 660	− 730	+ 1,340	+ 1,410
12.	+ 60	+ 780	+ 840	x	0	+ 100	+ 10	+ 110	+ 1,340	+ 360	+ 1,450
13.	x	− 110	− 110	0	x	0	0	0	0	− 280	+ 360
14.	− 10	− 60	− 70	− 190	0	x	− 20	− 120	− 100	+ 40	− 300
15.	0	0	0	− 10	0	+ 20	x	+ 10	− 10	+ 1,380	− 20
16.	+ 50	+ 610	+ 660	− 110	0	+ 120	+ 10	x	− 110	+ 1,810	+ 1,490
17.	(+ 60)	(+ 670)	(+ 730)	cx	(− 360)	(+ 100)	(+ 10)	(+ 110)	x	x	x
18.	(− 130)	(− 1,210)	(− 1,340)	(− 1,340)	− 360	(− 280)	(− 40)	(− 1,380)	(− 1,810)	x	x
19.	− 140	− 1,270	− 1,410	− 1,450	− 360	+ 300	+ 20	− 1,490	x	x	x

Table 5 (*contd.*)

Source:

League of Nations (Folk Hilgerdt). *Network of World Trade*, Geneva 1942.

Arithmetical balance of exports sent f.o.b, minus exports received (= imports minus freight + insurance) rounded to $ 10's of millions between Regions as defined in Source and Notes except where noted below.

Notes

Column/line categories are taken or constructed from the sources detailed below. Entries are rounded balance of incoming and outgoing exports only (except for columns 3, 4, 14, 15; as noted below) from Source Table 44 and from its Annex III, 'World Trade, by Countries of Provenance and Destination', pp. 106–71. References are to Regions 1–17 as defined by Source on pp. 11–13 and regrouped into Regions A-F by Source on p. 76.

Column/Line:

1   Region E = Region 16 (mainly United Kingdom and Ireland).
2   Region D = Regions 14 + 15 (Europe, industrial and non-industrial).
3   Region 13 (U.S.S.R.) = Part of Region F (Rest of World); export and import data, inconsistencies averaged.
4   Region 12 (Japan, Korea, Formosa) = Part of Region F; export and import data, inconsistencies averaged.
5   Sum of Columns 2, 3, 4 (All 'Continental Europe', including U.S.S.R. and Japan).
6   Sum of Columns 1, 2, 3 = 1 + 5 (All Europe, U.S.S.R. and Japan).
7   Region C = Regions 2, 4, 8, 17 (Regions of Recent Settlement = Canada, Australia, New Zealand, South Africa = British Dominions + Argentina, etc.).
8   Region 8 (Argentina, Uruguay, Paraguay, Falkland Islands).
9   Difference of columns 7 minus 8 (= Dominions = Regions of Recent Settlement minus Argentina, etc.).
10 Region B = Region 5 (U.S.A.).
11 Sum of columns 9 + 10 (U.S.A. + Dominions).
12 Region A = Regions 3, 6, 7, 9, 10 (Africa South of the Sahara, except South Africa; Latin America, except Region 8 + Argentina; South Asia = India, Burma, Ceylon; South-East Asia).
13 Same as Column 8.
14 Region 12 (China and other continental Asiatic countries, except India, Burma, Ceylon = mainly China = Part of Region F, 'Rest of World'); export and import data, inconsistencies averaged.
15 Region 1 (North Africa = Part of Region F, 'Rest of World'); export and import data, inconsistencies averaged.
16 Sum of columns 12, 13, 14, 15 (Underdeveloped Countries).
17 Sum of Columns 12 + 13, ie. 16 minus 14 + 15 (Underdeveloped Countries, not including China and North Africa = Tropics + Argentina).
18 Arithmetic Total of columns 1, 2, 3, 4, 9, 10 (= 6 + 11) plus 12, 13 (= 17).
19 Arithmetic Total of columns 1, 2, 3, 4, 9, 10 (= 6 + 11) plus 12, 13, 14, 15 (= 16).

underdeveloped countries which export more merchandise than they receive merchandise imports) are signified by − to emphasise the excess of 'give' over 'take' , in what conventional terminology calls a 'favourable' balance of trade.

Hilgerdt's (and Condliffe's) grouping of world trade into major regions – Britain, Continental Europe, Regions of Recent Settlement, U.S.A., Tropics and Rest of World – is largely retained, but has been modified in two ways. Argentina (col. 8, including Uruguay, Paraguay, and Falkland Islands) is removed, that is subtracted, from 'Regions of Recent Settlement' (col. 7) to give the British Dominions 'region' as Canada, Australia, New Zealand and South Africa. Though the retention of South Africa in this 'region' is also of doubtful accuracy, its relatively small share of the trade and the complications implied by its export of monetary gold does not seem to warrant the effort to separate it out for present purposes.

Though the trade balances computed in this way of the Dominions (col. 9) and of the United States (col. 10) are first considered separately, as they are by Hilgerdt and Condliffe, they are here subsequently added together to form the category 'U.S. and Dominions' in col. 11. Argentina (col. 8) for its part is then transposed to col. 13, in order to be subsequently added to 'Tropics' (col. 12) and other countries to form the 'Underdeveloped' region in col. 16 (and col. 17).

The other major modification of Hilgerdt's grouping is to divide up his residual Region F, 'Rest of the World' and allocate it to the other regions. Hilgerdt himself created this 'region' or 'group', accounting for about 10 per cent of world trade because its components did not fit well into the pattern of trade balances of the remaining 90 per cent. As he explained, 'A few words should be said of Group F, comprising the U.S.S.R., North Africa, and non-tropical Asia and not shown in [Hilgerdt's] Diagram 6 [of trade flows]. The U.S.S.R. with an excess of imports from the tropics, the United States and the regions of recent settlement, and an excess of exports to Continental as well as Non-Continental Europe, clearly enters that system between Groups C and D [regions of recent settlement and Continental Europe]. The position of the remaining countries of Group F is less clear . . .' (League 1942, 83).

For the period before 1928, that is for selected years between 1876 and 1913, we offer much more incomplete and inaccurate data on trade balances in Tables 6 and 7. Hilgerdt (League 1945, 100) himself prepared some estimates of merchandise import and export

TABLE 6

Merchandise Import (−) and Export (+) Balances Selected
Countries and Years 1881–1913

		Annual Averages in millions of current dollars			
		1881–3	*1891–5*	*1901–5*	*1911–13*
1. United States	R	+ 250	+ 197	+ 414	+ 343
	M	− 142	− 106	+ 41	+ 196
	B	+ 108	+ 91	+ 455	+ 536
2. U.K.+Ireland	R	−1,262	−1,291	−1,567	−1,990
	M	+ 755	+ 657	+ 717	+1,338
	B	− 507	− 634	− 850	− 652
3. Germany	R	− 332	− 586	− 879	−1,477
	M	+ 329	+ 357	+ 617	+1,158
	B	− 3	− 229	− 262	− 319
4. France	R	− 455	− 393	− 378	− 788
	M	+ 220	+ 251	+ 338	+ 461
	B	− 235	− 142	− 40	− 327
5. Italy	R	+ 21	− 2	− 46	− 196
	M	− 61	− 34	− 15	− 39
	B	− 40	− 36	− 61	− 235
6. Holland	R	− 100	− 101	− 126	− 252
	M	− 3	+ 3	− 33	− 9
	B	− 103	− 98	− 159	− 261
7. 'Continental Europe' (Sum B 3, 4, 5, 6)		−, 381	− 505	− 522	−1,142
8. 'Western Europe' (Sum B 2, 3, 4, 5, 6)	B	− 888	−1,139	−1,372	−1,794

Source: League of Nations (Hilgerdt), *Industrialization and Foreign Trade*, Geneva 1945, p. 100.
Note: R = Raw Materials, M = Manufactures, B = Balance.

balances for the years 1881–5, 1891–5, 1901–5 and 1911–13 in his
later *Industrialization and Foreign Trade* (League 1945, 100). These
data, however, are limited to some countries of Europe and the
United States, and most of them are reproduced in our Table 6. We
have retained Hilgerdt's notation of + for export and − for import
balances. Therefore the growing excess of imports of the United
States, similarly, is shown after + signs. Europe taken separately
(lines 3–6), and of 'Continental Europe' as a whole (line 7 = sum of
lines 3–6) and 'Western Europe' (line 8 = sum 2–6) are in his table

TABLE 7

Merchandise Export Deficits = Import Surpluses (+) and Merchandise Export Surpluses = Import Deficits (−) by Major World Regions, 1876–1913

(in millions of current dollars)

	1876–80				1896–1900				1913			
	A Exports	B Imports	C Imports Adjusted	D Balance	A Exports	B Imports	C Imports Adjusted	D Balance	A Exports	B Imports	C Imports Adjusted	D Balance
1. United Kingdom + Ireland	982	1,587	1,349	+367	1,230	2,011	1,770	+540	2,511	3,206	2,885	+374
2. North-west Europe	1,920	2,250	1,912	−8	2,990	3,585			6,402	7,717		
3. Other Europe	960	845			1,322	1,080			2,374	2,824		
4. Continental Europe (2+3)	2,880	3,095	2,630	−250	4,312	4,665	4,105	+207	8,776	10,541	9,487	+711
5. United States and Canada	700	520	442	−258	1,260	875	770	−490	2,836	2,431	2,180	−656
6. Underdeveloped (As., Af., Lat. Am.) and Oceania	1,448	1,860	1,581	+133	1,890	2,260	1,989	+99	5,036	4,885	4,396	−640
7. Totals		7,062	6,010	−8	3,693	9,811		+356	19,139	21,123		−211
8. x as % I			85%				88%				90%	

Source: Paul Lamartine Yates, Forty Years of Foreign Trade (London: George Allen & Unwin, 1959), p. 226.

Note: Imports are adjusted to exclude transport charges, etc.; reduce them to export 'equivalents' by applying the percentage relation of total exports to total imports (lines 7+8 in each year to the regional data.

shown after − signs. The excess of exports over imports of the United States, similarly, is therefore shown after + signs.

Since in this study Hilgerdt was interested in the relative expansion of the exports of raw materials (R) and manufactures (M), and particularly in the growth of the latter as part of the expansion of world trade and industrialisation, the balances (B) were not supplied by him and we have calculated them ourselves.

Table 7 summarises and adjusts import and export data for the years 1876–80, 1896–1900, and 1913 supplied by a more recent source (Yates 1959, 226) and constructs some estimates of merchandise export deficits = import surpluses (+) and export surpluses = import deficits (−) that are analogous, albeit much rougher and more inaccurate, to those presented for 1928 in Table 5. Since the source supplies export (columns A) and import (B), figures, and since the totals of the latter are in each year significantly higher than those and since import totals in each year significantly exceed export totals for the world, we 'reduce' the import data to export 'equivalents' (C) by applying the percentage of total exports-imports in each period, i.e. 85 per cent, 88 per cent and 90 per cent respectively, to the recorded imports in order to estimate 'imports adjusted' (C) to exclude transportation charges, etc. The balances between exports sent out (A) and exports (or adjusted imports) received (C) is then calculated in column D for each period. This procedure, of course, overreduces imports of relatively low-freight manufacture and underreduces those of the relatively high-freight raw. materials. In principle the arithmetic sum of all regions' (line 8, col. D) positive and negative balances should cancel out to a total of 0. This is the case nearly so, for the first period; but for the second and third we are left with balancing errors (in the data and /or our adjustments) amounting to about 4 per cent and 1 per cent of total exports, respectively.

Yates's grouping of regions, which we retain, except for the summation of "North-west" and 'other' Europe (lines 2 and 3) into 'continental' Europe (line 4) is similar to that of Hilgerdt – and therefore our tables for 1928 – except for the inclusion of Oceania and South Africa with Asia, Africa and Latin America, which we term 'underdeveloped' for the first two periods in line 6.

Bibliography

Abdel–Malek, Anouar. *Egypt: Military Society*. New York, Random House, 1968.

Aguilar, M. Alonso. *Teoría y política del desarrollo latinoamericano*. Mexico, Universidad Nacional Autónoma de México, 1967.

Amin, Samir. *L'accumulation à l'échelle mondiale*. Paris, Anthropos, 1970.

Aptheker, Herbert. *The American Revolution 1763–1783*. New York, International Publishers, 1960.

——*The Colonial Era*. New York, International Publishers, 1959.

Arrighi, Giovanni. 'Labour Supplies in Historical Perspective: a Study of the Proletarianization of the African Peasantry in Rhodesia', in Arrighi, G., and Saul, J. S., *Essays on the Political Economy of Africa*. New York, Monthly Review Press, 1973.

——Private Communication, subsequently rewritten for publication as 'Struttura di clase e struttura coloniale nell' analisi del sottosviluppo', *Giovane Critica*, 22–3, Milano, 1970; revised and enlarged version in *Problemi del Socialismo*, Roma, XIV, 10, luglio-agosto, 1972.

Ashworth, William. *A Short History of the International Economy since 1850*. London, Longman, 1962, 2nd ed.

Artesano, Eduardo B. *Rosas: Bases del Nacionalismo Popular*. Buenos Aires, A. Peña Lillo (ed.) 1966.

Bairoch, Paul. *Révolution industrielle et sous-développement*. Paris, 1963.

Baran, Paul. *The Political Economy of Growth*. New York, Monthly Review Press, 1957.

Barrat-Browne, Michael. *After Imperialism*. London, Heinemann, 1963.

Bertram, G. W. 'Economic Growth in Canadian Industry, 1870–1915', in Easterbrook, W. T., and M. H. Watkins, *Approaches to Canadian Economic History*. Toronto, McClelland & Stewart, 1967.

Bhatia, B. M. *Famines in India*. Bombay, Asia Publishers House, 1963.

Birnbaum, Norman. 'The Rise of Capitalism: Marx and Weber', in

Smelser, Neil J. (ed.), *Readings on Economic Sociology*. Englewood Cliffs, Prentice Hall, 1965.

Boeke, J. H. *The Structure of the Netherlands Indian Economy*. New York, Institute of Pacific Relations, 1942, and *Economics and Economic Policy of Dual Societies*. New York, Institute of Pacific Relations, 1953.

Box, Pelham H. 'The Origins of the Paraguayan War', *University of Illinois Studies in the Social Sciences*, Urbana, vol. xv, no. 3, 1927.

Bruchey, Stuart. *The Colonial Merchant. Sources and Readings*. New York, Harcourt, Brace & World, 1966.

——*The Roots of American Economic Growth, 1607–1861. An Essay in Social Causation*. New York, Harper & Row, 1965.

Buchanan, Keith. *The Southeast Asian World*. New York, Doubleday Anchor, 1968.

Cairncross, Alexander Kirkland. *Home and Foreign Investment 1870–1913*. New York, 1953.

Callender, Guy Stevens. *Selections from the Economic History of the United States 1765–1860*. New York, Augustus M. Kelley Reprints of Economic Classics 1965 (original ed. 1911?).

Cambridge Economic History of Europe. Cambridge, Cambridge University Press.

Ceceña, José Luis. 'La penetración extranjera y los grupos de poder en México (1870–1910)', *Problemas del Desarrollo*, Revista Latinoamericana de Economía, México, año 1, no. 1, Oct, Dec, 1969.

Chandra, Bipan. *The Rise and Growth of Economic Nationalism in India*. New Delhi, Peoples Publishing House, 1966.

Clairmonte, Frederick. *Economic Liberalism and Underdevelopment. Studies in the Disintegration of an Idea*. Bombay, Asia Publishing House, 1960.

Coatsworth, John. *The Stages of Economic Stagnation*. Ann Arbor, Michigan, Radical Education Project, 1966 (mimeo).

Córdova, Armando. *Inversiones extranjeras y subdesarrollo*. Caracas, Instituto de Investigaciones Económicas y Sociales, Universidad Central de Venezuela, 1968 (mimeo).

Condliffe, J. B. *The Commerce of Nations*. New York, Norton, 1956.

Cosio Villegas, Daniel. *Historia Moderna de México, el Porfiriato, Vida economica*. Mexico, Hermes, 1965, 2 vols.

Cox, Oliver. *Capitalism as a System*. New York, Monthly Review Press, 1964.

——*The Foundations of Capitalism*. New York, Philosophical Library, 1959.

Davidson, Basil. *The African Slave Trade. Precolonial History 1450–1850* (originally published as *Black Mother*). Boston, Atlantic-Little Brown, 1961.

Deane, Phyllis and Cole, W. A. *British Economic Growth 1688–1959. Trends and Structure*. Cambridge, The University Press, 1967, 2nd ed.

De Tocqueville, Alexis. *Democracy in America*. New York, Vintage Books, 1954, 2 vols. (original French ed. 1835, 1840).

Dike, K. *Trade and Politics in the Niger Delta*. Oxford, Oxford University Press, 1956.

Dobb, Maurice. *Studies in the Development of Capitalism*. London, Routledge & Kegan Paul, 1965, rev. ed.

Dowd, Douglas F. 'A Comparative Analysis of Economic Development in the American West and South', *Journal of Economic History*, xvi, December, 1956, excerpted in Harold D. Woodman ed., *Slavery and the Southern Economy, Sources and Readings*. New York, Harcourt, Brace & World, 1966.

Dutt, R. Palme. *India Today*. Bombay, People's Publishing House, 1949.

Easterbrooke, W. T. and Watkins, M. H. *Approaches to Canadian Economic History*. Toronto, McClelland & Stewart, 1967.

Emmanuel, A. *L'échange inégal*. Paris, Maspéro, 1969.

Engels, Frederick, *The Peasant War in Germany* (ed. including 'The Mark', 'On the History of the Prussian Peasantry', 'Decay of Feudalism and Rise of National States', and other manuscripts and letters). Moscow, Foreign Languages Publishing House, 1956.

Faulkner, Harold Underwood. *American Economic History*. New York, Harper & Brothers, 1960, 8th ed.

Ferrer, Aldo. *The Argentine Economy*. Berkeley and Los Angeles, University of California Press, 1967.

Florescano, Enrique. *Precios del maíz y crisis agrícolas en México (1703–1810)*. Mexico, El Colegio de México, 1969.

Frank, Andre Gunder. *Capitalism and Underdevelopment in Latin America*. New York, Monthly Review Press, 1967, 1969. London, Penguin Books, 1971.

——*Mexican Agriculture 1521–1630: Transformation of the Mode of Production*, manuscript 1966, Cambridge University Press, in press. Spanish translation, Escuela Nacional de Antropologia e Historia, Mexico, 1976.

Frank, Andre Gunder. *Latin America: Underdevelopment or Revolution.* New York, Monthly Review Press, 1969.

——'On Dalton's "Theoretical Issues in Economic Anthropology"', *Current Anthropology*, II, no. 1, Feb. 1970.

——*Lumpenbourgeoisie. Lumpendevelopment.* New York, Monthly Review Press, 1972.

——*World Accumulation 1492–1789.* New York, Monthly Review Press, London, Macmillan Press, 1978.

——*Reflexions on the Economic Crisis,* Barcelona, Anagrama 1977 (in Spanish).

——*The Contemporary World Crisis,* in preparation.

Frankel, S. Herbert. 'The Tyranny of Economic Paternalism in Africa', *Optima* (supplement), Dec. 1960.

Gabel, Joseph. 'Une lecture marxiste de la sociologie religieuse de Max Weber', *Cahiers Internationaux de Sociologie*, Paris XLVI, Jan.–June 1969. Reprinted in José Sazbón, ed., *Presencia de Max Weber*. Buenos Aires, Nueva Visión, 1971.

Geertz, Clifford. *Agricultural Involution. The Process of Ecological Change in Indonesia.* Berkeley, University of California Press, 1966.

Geller, Lucio. *El crecimiento industrial argentino hasta 1914 y la teoría del bien primario exportable.* Santiago, 1969 (mimeo).

Genovese, Eugene. *The Political Economy of Slavery.* New York, Pantheon, 1965.

Gerth, Hans, and Mills, C. Wright. *From Max Weber. Essays in Sociology.* New York, Oxford University Press, 1946.

Gough, Kathleen "New Proposals for Anthropologists" *Current Anthropology*, IX, no. 5, Dec. 1968. Revised as 'Anthropology: Child of Imperialism', *Monthly Review*, vol. 19, no. 1, March 1968.

Gouldner, Alvin W. *The Coming Crisis of Western Sociology.* New York, Basic Books, 1970.

Gray, Lewis C. *History of Agriculture in the Southern United States to 1860.* Gloucester, Mass., 1958, 2 vols.

Guerra y Sánchez, Ramiro. *Sugar and Society in the Caribbean.* New Haven, Yale University Press, 1964 (original Spanish edition, Havana, 1927).

Halperin Donghi, Tulio. *Historia contemporánea de América Latina.* Madrid, Alianza Editorial, 1969.

Hamilton, Alexander. *The Reports of Alexander Hamilton.* New York, Harpers, 1964 (original editions 1790–91).

Hamilton, Earl J. 'American Treasure and the Rise of Capitalism

(1500–1700)', *Economica*, Nov. 1929.

Hargreaves, J. D. *West Africa: The Former French States*. Englewood Cliffs, Prentice Hall, 1967.

Harlow, Vincent.*A History of Barbados 1625–1685*. London, Clarendon Press, 1926.

Harper, Lawrence A. 'The Effect of the Navigation Acts on the Thirteen Colonies', in Harry N. Scheiber (ed.), *United States Economic History, Selected Readings*. New York, Alfred A. Knopf, 1964.

Hartwell, R. M. (ed.). *The Causes of the Industrial Revolution*. London, Methuen, 1967.

——'The Causes of the Industrial Revolution. An Essay in Methodology', in R. M. Hartwell (ed.), *The Causes of the Industrial Revolution*. London, Methuen, 1967.

Hilgerdt, Folke. 'The Case for Multilateral Trade', *American Economic Review*, XXXIII, no. 1, Supplement Part 2, Mar. 1943.

Hill, Polly. *Migrant Cocoa Farmers of Southern Ghana*. Cambridge, Cambridge University Press, 1963.

Hinkelammert, Franz. 'Teoría de la dialéctica del desarrollo desigual', *Cuadernos de la Realidad Nacional*, Santiago, no. 6, Dec. 1970.

Hobsbawm, E. J. *The Age of Revolution 1789–1848*. New York, Mentor, 1964.

——'Lenin and the "Aristocracy of Labor"', *Monthly Review*, New York, XXI, no. 11, Apr. 1970.

Hoffmann, Walter G. *The Growth of Industrial Economies*. Manchester, The University Press, 1958.

Imlah, Albert H. *Economic Elements in the Pax Brittanica. Studies in British Foreign Trade in the Nineteenth Century*. Cambridge, Harvard University Press, 1958.

——'British Balance of Payments and Export of Capital 1816–1913', *Economic History Review*, 1852.

Issawi, Charles. 'Egypt since 1800: a Study in Lop-sided Development', *Journal of Economic History*, XXI, no. 1, Mar. 1961.

Jozyr–Kowalski, Stanislaw. 'Weber and Marx', *Polish Sociological Bulletin*, 1 (17), Warsaw, 1968, reprinted in Spanish in José Sazbón (ed.), *Presencia de Max Weber*. Buenos Aires, Nueva Visión, 1971.

Kaplan, Marcos. *Formación del Estado Nacional en América Latina*. Santiago, Editorial Universitaria, 1969.

Kindleberger, Charles P. *The Terms of Trade*. New York, Wiley, 1956.

Lacoste, Yves, Nonschi, André, and Prenant, André. *L'Algérie, passé et présent*. Paris, Editions Sociales, n.d.

Larraz, José. *La época del mercantilismo en Castilla (1500–1700)*. Madrid, Atlas, 1943.

League of Nations (Folke Hilgerdt). *Industrialization and Foreign Trade*, Geneva, 1945.

——(Folke Hilgerdt). *The Network of World Trade*. Geneva, 1942.

Leibenstein, Harvey. *Economic Backwardness and Economic Growth*. New York, John Wiley & Sons, 1957.

Lenin, V. I. *The Development of Capitalism in Russia*. Moscow, Foreign Languages Publishing House. Collected Works, vol. 3.

——*Imperialism, the Highest Stage of Capitalism*. Selected Works, vol. 1, Part 2, Moscow, Foreign Languages Publishing House.

Levin, Jonathan. *The Export Economies, Their Pattern of Development in Historical Perspective*. Cambridge, Harvard University Press, 1960.

Lewis, W. Arthur. 'Economic Development with Unlimited Supplies of Labour', in Aggarawala, A. N., and S. P. Singh, *The Economics of Underdevelopment*. New York, Oxford University Press, 1963.

Lipset, Seymour Martin. *The First New Nation. The United States in Historical and Comparative Perspective*. New York, Doubleday Anchor, 1967.

List, Friedrich. *National System of Political Economy*. Philadelphia, J. B. Lippincott & Co., 1856.

Lockwood, William W. *The Economic Development of Japan. Growth and Structural Change*. Princeton, Princeton University Press, 1954.

——'Postwar Trade Relations in the Far East', *American Economic Review*, XXXIII, no. 1, Supplement, Part 2, Mar. 1943.

Luxemburg, Rosa. *The Accumulation of Capital*. New York, Monthly Review Press, 1964.

Magdoff, Harry. *The Age of Imperialism*. New York, Monthly Review Press, 1968.

Manchester, Allan K. *British Preeminence in Brazil: its Rise and Fall*. Chapel Hill, The University of North Carolina Press, 1933.

Mandel, Ernest. 'L'accumulation primitive et l'industrialisation du Tiers-Monde', in Victor Fay (ed.), *En Partant du capital*. Paris, Editions Anthropos, 1968, and corrected version in *Pensamiento Critico*. La Habana, no. 36, Jan. 1970.

——'*Marxist Economic Theory*'. New York, Monthly Review Press, 1970, 2 vols.

Mannix, Daniel P., and Cowley, Malcolm. *Black Cargoes. A History of the Atlantic Slave Trade, 1518–1865*. New York, Viking Press, 1962.

Mantoux, Paul. *The Industrial Revolution in the Eighteenth Century*. London, Methuen, 1964 (original French ed. 1907).

Mao Tse-tung. "On Contradiction," in *Collected Works*. Peking, Foreign Languages Press, 1967, vol. 1.

Marini, Ruy Mauro. *La Dialectica de la Dependencia*. Mexico, Ediciones Era, 1973.

Martínez, Alberto y Aranda, Sergio. *La industria y la agricultura en el desarrollo económico chileno*. Santiago, Instituto de Economía y Planificación, Universidad de Chile, 1970.

Marx, Karl. *Capital*. Moscow, Foreign Languages Publishing House, 1959–62, 3 vols.

——*A Contribution to the Critique of Political Economy*. Chicago, Charles Kerr, 1904.

——*La misère de la philosophie*. Paris, Alfred Coste Ed., 1950.

Mauro, Frederic. *L'expansion Europénne 1600–1870*. Paris, Presses Universitaires de France, 1964.

——'Towards an Intercontinental Model. European Overseas Expansion Between 1500 and 1800', *Economic History Review*, XIV, no. 1, Aug. 1961.

Meier, Gerald M. *The International Economics of Development*. New York, Harper & Row, 1968.

Mintz, Sidney. 'The Caribbean as a Socio-Cultural Area', *Journal of World History*, IX, 4, 1966.

Mommsen, Wolfgang. 'Le sociologie politique de Max Weber et sa philosophie de l'histoire universelle', *Revue Internationales des Sciences Sociales*, Paris, XVIII, 1, 1965, reprinted in José Sazbón (ed.), *Presencia de Max Weber*. Buenos Aires, Nueva Visión, 1971.

Moore, Barrington, Jr. *Social Origins of Dictatorship and Democracy*. Boston, Beacon Press, 1966.

Mukherjee, Ramkrishna. *The Rise and Fall of the East India Company*. Berlin, Deutscher Verlag der Wissenschaften, 1955; New York, Monthly Review Press, 1974.

Myrdal, Gunnar. *Asian Drama*. New York, Pantheon, 1968, vol. 1.

——*Economic Theory and Underdevelopment Regions*. London, Duckworth, 1957.

Nehru, Jawaharlal. *The Discovery of India*. New York, Doubleday Anchor, 1960.

Nettels, Curtis P. 'British Mercantilism and the Economic Development of the Thirteen Colonies', *Journal of Economic History*, XII, 2,

Spring 1952, reprinted in William Appelman Williams, *The Shaping of American Diplomacy*. Chicago, Rand McNally, 1956, vol. 1, *1750–1900*.

Nettels, Curtis P. *The Emergence of a National Economy, 1775–1815*. New York, Harper Torchbooks, 1962.

Nicolaus, Martin. 'The Theory of the Labor Aristocracy', *Monthly Review*, New York, xxi, no. 11, Apr. 1970.

——'The Unknown Marx', *New Left Review*, London, 1968.

Nieto Arteta, Luis Eduardo. *Ensayos sobre economía colombiana*. Medellin, Oveja Negra, 1969.

Norman, Herbert E., *Japan's Emergence as a Modern State*. New York, Institute of Pacific Relations, 1940.

North, Douglass C. *The Economic Growth of the United States 1790–1860*. New York, Norton, 1966.

——and Thomas, Robert Paul. 'An Economic Theory of the Growth of the Western World', *Economic History Review*, xxiii, 1, Apr. 1970.

Palloix, Christian. *L'économie mondiale capitaliste*. Paris, Maspéro, 1971, 2 vols.

——'Imperialisme et mode de production capitaliste', *L'homme et la Société*. Paris, no. 12, 1969a.

——*Problèmes de la croissance en économie ouverte*. Paris, Maspéro, 1969b.

——'La question de l'imperialisme chez V. I. Lenin et Rosa Luxemburg', *L'homme et la société*, Paris, 15, Jan.–Feb.–Mar. 1970.

Parera Dennis, Alfredo. 'Naturaleza de las relaciones entre clases dominantes argentinas y las metropolis', *Fichas*, Buenos Aires, 1 año, no. 4, Dec. 1964.

Parsons, Talcott. *Sociological Theory and Modern Society*. New York, Free Press, 1967.

Parry, J. H. *The Age of Reconnaissance*. New York, Mentor, 1964.

——*The Establishment of the European Hegemony: 1415–1715. Trade and Exploration in the Age of the Renaissance*. New York, Harper Torchbooks, 1961.

——*Europe and a Wider World 1415–1715*. London, Hutchinson, 1949.

Preobazhensky, E. *The New Economics*. Oxford, Clarendon Press, 1965.

Quintana, Matías, in Quintana, Miguel. *Estevan de Antuñano*. México, Secretaria de Hacienda, 1957.

Ramírez Necochea, Hernán. *Antecedente económicos de la Independencia de Chile*. Santiago, Facultad de Filosofía y Educación, U. de Chile, 1967, 2nd ed.
Revilla Gigedo, Conde de. *Informe sobre las Misiones 1793 e instrucción reservada al Marqués de Branciforte 1794*. México, Editorial Jus, 1966. Colección México Heroico, no. 50.
Riad, Hassan. *L'Egypte nassérienne*. Paris, Ed. de Minuit, 1964.
Ribeiro, Darcy. 'The Culture-Historical Configurations of the American Peoples', *Current Anthropology*, Chicago, Oct. 1970.
Ricardo, David. *Principles of Political Economy and Taxation*. London, 1817.
Rodinson, Maxime. *Islam et Capitalisme*. Paris, Editions du Seuil, 1966.
Rodney, Walter. 'African Slavery and other Forms of Social Oppression on the Upper Guinea Coast in the Context of the Atlantic Slave-Trade', *Journal of African History*, II, 3, 1966.
Romeo, Carlos. *Comercio exterior, intercambio desigual, desarrollo económico*. La Habana, Ministerio de Industrias, 1964 (mimeo).
Rosa, José María. *Defensa y pérdidad de nuestra independencia económica*. Buenos Aires, Librería Huemul, 1964, 2nd ed.
Samuelsson, Kurt. *Religion and Economic Action. A Critique of Max Weber*. New York, Harper Torchbooks, 1961.
Santos Martínez, Pedro. *Historia económica de Mendoza durante el virreinato, 1778–1818*. Madrid, Universidad Nacional de Cuyo, 1961.
Sarç, Omar Celal. 'Tansimat ve Sanayimis' (The Tansimat and our Industry) in Issawi, Charles (ed.), *The Economic History of the Middle East 1880–1914*. Chicago, University of Chicago Press, 1966.
Sauer, Carl O., *The Early Spanish Main*. Berkeley, University of California Press, 1966.
Saul, S. B. *Studies in British Overseas Trade 1870–1914*. Liverpool, Liverpool University Press, 1960.
Shapiro, Meyer. 'A Note on Max Weber's Politics', *Politics*, New York, vol. 2, 1945, reprinted in José Sazbón (ed.), *Presencia de Max Weber*. Buenos Aires, Nueva Visión, 1971.
Schlesinger, A. M. *The Colonial Merchants and the American Revolution 1763–1776*. New York, 1918.
Schlote, W. *British Overseas Trade from 1700 to the 1930's*. Oxford, Oxford University Press, 1952.
Sen, Bhowani. *Evolution of Agrarian Relations in India*. New Delhi, People's Publishing House, 1962.

Shepherd, James F., and Walton, Gary M. 'Estimates of "Invisible" Earnings in the Balance of Payments of the British North American Colonies, 1768–1772', *Journal of Economic History*, XXIX, 2, June 1969.

Sheridan, Richard. *The Development of the Plantations to 1750. An Era of West Indian Prosperity 1750–1775*. Barbados, Caribbean Universities Press, London, Ginn & Co., 1970.

——'The Plantation Revolution and the Industrial Revolution, 1625–1775', *Caribbean Studies*, vol. 9, 3, Oct. 1969.

Sideri, Sandro. *Trade and Power. Informal Colonialism in Anglo-Portuguese Relations*. Rotterdam, Rotterdam University Press, 1970.

Sik, Endre. *The History of Black Africa*. Budapest, Akademiai Kiado, 1966.

Singer, H. W. 'The Distribution of Gains Between Investing and Borrowing Countries', *American Economic Review, Papers and Proceedings,* May 1950.

Smith, Adam. *An Inquiry into the Nature and Causes of the Wealth of Nations*. New York, Random House, 1937 (originally published in 1776).

Smith, Thomas C. *The Agrarian Origins of Modern Japan*. Stanford, Stanford University Press, 1959 (reprinted New York, Atheneum, 1966).

Sombart, Werner. *Der Moderne Kapitalismus*. München, Duncker & Humbolt, 1922, 5th ed.

Stark, Werner. 'Max Weber and the Heterogony of Purposes', *Social Research*, XXIV, 2, 1967, reprinted in José Sazbón (ed.), *Presencia de Max Weber*. Buenos Aires, Nueva Visión, 1971.

Stavarianos, L. S. (ed.). *The Epic of Modern Man. A Collection of Readings*. Englewood Cliffs, Prentice Hall, 1966..

——*The World Since 1500, a Global History*. Englewood Cliffs, Prentice Hall, 1966.

Suret-Canale, Jean. *Afrique noire. L'ère coloniale 1900–1945*. Paris, Ed. Sociales, 1964.

Sweezy, Paul., Dobb, Maurice, Takahashi, K., Hilton, Rodney, and Hill, Christopher. *The Transition from Feudalism to Capitalism*. New York, Science and Society, 1963.

Tawney, R. H. *Religion and the Rise of Capitalism*. New York, Mentor, 1945 (original edition 1926).

Thorner, Daniel and Alice. *Land and Labour in India*. Bombay, Asia Publishing House, 1962.

Torres Rivas, Edelberto. *Interpretación del desarrollo social centroamericano.* Santiago, Prensa Latinoamericana, 1969.

U. S. Bureau of the Census. *Historical Statistics of the United States. Colonial Times to 1957.* Washington, D.C., U.S. Government Printing Office, 1960.

Veliz, Claudio. 'La mesa de tres patas', *Desarrollo Económico*, III, no. 1–2, April-Sept. 1963.

Vilar, Pierre. 'Problems of the Formation of Capitalism', *Past and Present*, no. 10, Nov. 1956.

Vitale, Luis. *Interpretación marxista de la historia de Chile.* Santiago, Prensa Latino-americana, vols. 1 and 2, 1968, 1969.

Walton, Gary M. 'New Evidence on Colonial Commerce,' *Journal of Economic History*, XXVIII, 5, Sept 1968.

Watkins, Melvin H. 'A Staple Theory of Economic Growth', in Easterbrook, W. T., and M. H. Watkins (eds.). *Approaches to Canadian Economic History.* Toronto, McClelland & Stewart, 1967.

Weber, Max. *General Economic History.* Glencoe, The Free Press, 1950 (original German ed. 1923).

——*The Protestant Ethic and the Spirit of Capitalism.* New York, Scribners, 1958 (original ed. 1904–5).

Wheelwright, E. L. 'Australia and Argentina: A Comparative Study', *Radical Political Economy Collected Essays.* Sidney, Australia and New Zealand Book Co., 1974.

Williams, Eric. *Capitalism and Slavery.* New York, Capricorn Books, 1966 (original ed. 1944).

——*History of the People of Trinidad and Tobago.* London, André Deutsch, 1964.

Woddis, Jack. *Africa: the Roots of Revolt.* New York, Citadel Press, 1960.

Woytinsky, W. S. and E. S. Woytinsky. *World Commerce and Governments.* New York, Twentieth Century Fund, 1955.

Yates, Lamartine P. *Forty Years of Foreign Trade.* London, George Allen & Unwin, 1959.

Index

Abdel-Malek, Anouar, 155, 156
Accumulation, and production, 134–9; capital, 116, 139; capital and Karl Marx, 38–43; capital, historical process, 43; capital, Metropolitan, 71–5; capital, New England, 66; capitalist, 143; historical process of, xiii, 10, 43; Metropolitan 71–5, 189–90; world capital, 13, 21, 23, 78, 86, 87, 105, 129, 140, 170; world process of, xi
Adams, Brooks, 72
Adams, John, 67
Africa, 14, 17, 23, 77, 79, 113–19, 137, 142, 175; and imperialism 157–64; Britain in, 159; development of underdevelopment, in 160–4; economic development in, 158; peasant economy in, 162–4; settlement in, 159–61; slave trade with, 19–21; trade with, 21
Aguilar, M. Alonso, 140
Algeria, 33; development of underdevelopment in, 156
Ali, Mohammed, 154
Allard, General, 143
America, 14; development and underdevelopment in, 21–3, 25–69; linkages and industrialisation in, 115; see also Latin America; North America; South America; United States
Amin, Samir, xii, 5, 8, 9, 12, 103, 107, 109, 117, 133, 158, 159, 173
Arab world and imperialism, 154–7
Argentina, 49, 84, 117, 126–7, 132, 141, 167, 170, 174, 185, 186, 193, 196, 198
Aron, Raymond, 25
Arrighi, Giovanni, xii, 6, 7, 158, 159, 163, 164
Asia, 14, 17, 23, 77, 79, 113–18, 130, 175; and Europe, trade between, 17–19; imperialism in, 146–54
Asia Minor, 145
Asia, South-east, 149; development of underdevelopment in, 149–51; trading pattern, 190
Astesano, Eduardo B., 85

Australia, 11, 24, 33, 42, 43, 117, 120, 121, 126–7

Bairoch, Paul, 131
Balance of payments, 172
Baran, Paul, 4, 153
Barbados, plantation system, 50–1
Barrat-Browne, Michael, 182, 194
Bastide, Roger, 25
Beard, Charles, 63
Belgium, 29
Bendix, Reinhard, 25
Bettelheim, Charles, 4, 5, 107, 109
Birnbaum, Norman, 27
Boeke, J. H., 110, 111, 150
Bolivar, Simon, 82
Bolivia, 23
Bosch, J. van den, 151
Box, Pelham H., 85
Brazil, 20, 23, 44, 50, 52–5, 86, 96, 127, 132, 167, 170, 193
Bridenbaugh, Carl, 59
Britain, 29, 41, 44, 50, 117, 129, 156, 167, 174, 190, 194, 196, 198; and India, 87–91, 147–8; and India, trade between, 97, 191–3; and multilateral trade, 197; and Portugal, trade between 95–7; and United States, trade between, 68–9; colonisation policies of, 60, 63; foreign investment by, 195, 198; foreign trade from, 77; free trade in, 94; in Africa, 159; industrial revolution in, 78, 131; linkages and industrialisation in, 114–15; terms of trade for, 101–2; trade balances of, 192; trade growth in, 71–5; trade patterns of, 16; trade statistics, 177–89; trading system of, 175; underdevelopment by, 86
British Dominions, 103, 104, 116, 120, 174
Bruchey, Stuart, 30, 57–62, 79–81

Canada, 11, 23, 55, 117, 120, 121, 126, 183, 192, 198
Canning, George, 82

Capital, flow of, 194
Capital accumulation, 116, 139; and Karl Marx 38–43; historical process of, 43; Metropolitan, 71–5, 189–90; New England, 66; world, 13, 21, 23, 78, 86, 87, 105, 129, 140, 170
Capital goods production in the colonies, 113–14
Capital loans and peasant economy, 144–5
Capitalism, and colonial policies, 142–6; and internal market, 134; and Protestantism, 28–30; and puritanism, 58; exploitation by, 7; in Russia, 135
Capitalist accumulation, 143; world, 140
Capitalist development, 21, 23, 76, 78, 86, 87, 129, 140; and industrialisation, 11; world, 149, 152, 156, 164
Capitalist production, 38, 109
Capitalist system, expansion of, 19
Cardoso, Fernando Henrique, 85, 170
Caribbean, 19, 20, 23, 44, 47, 52–5, 60, 64–5, 115, 149, 167
Ceceña, José Luis, 169
Ceylon, 192, 193
Chandra, Bipan, 99, 191
Chile, xi, xiv, 23, 47, 83, 100, 167, 170
China, 18, 26, 88, 119, 130, 144, 146, 151, 152, 186, 192
Civil War, 80
Class structure and underdevelopment, production, 122–5
Climatic factors, 32
Coatsworth, John, 141
Cole, W. A., 74
Colombia, 49, 85
Colonial economies, 14
Colonial exploitation, 73
Colonial policies and capitalism, 142–6
Colonial structure, 6
Colonial trade, 15
Colonies, 5–11, 101, 106; capital goods production in, 113–14; development of, 36–7; exploitation, 24; settlement 24; underdeveloped, 11–12; underdevelopment of, 30
Colonisation, 24; British policies, 63; policy differences, 43–5; Spanish policies, 45–50; systematic, 42–3
Colonisers, motivations of, 35
Comparative advantage: and free trade, 94–101; theory of, 101, 105

Condliffe, J. B., 174, 176, 205
Córdova, Armando, 119, 168
Costa Rica, 49, 166
Cromer, Lord, 155
Cuba, 48, 86
Curtin, Philip, 20

Davidson, Basil, 20, 162
Deane, Phyllis, 74
Denmark, 104
Dependence, analysis of, xii, xiii
de Tocqueville, Alexis, 59
Development, 11, 12; and industrialisation, capitalist, 11; and underdevelopment in America, 25–69, 79–81; capitalist, 76, 78, 86, 87, 129; in Africa, economic, 158; in America, 21–3; in Argentina, 126–7; in Australia, 126–7; in Japan, 153–4; in Latin America, 82–7, 164–71; 'internal' v. 'external' determination, 2–7; internal market, 121–8, 130, 138; of colonies, 36–7; of underdevelopment, 44, 50, 138, 142; of underdevelopment in Africa, 160–4; of underdevelopment in Algeria, 156; of underdevelopment in Egypt, 154–6; of underdevelopment in India, 87–91, 146–9; of underdevelopment in South East Asia, 149–51; of United States, 124–5; structural theory of, 2; world capitalist, 149, 152, 156, 164
Development theory, vicious circle of, 1
Diaz, Porfirio, 167, 169
Dike, K., 157
Dobb, Maurice, 41
Dominions, 177–89, 190, 193, 196, 198
Dualism, 110–12
Dualist theory and underdeveloped countries, 111
Dutt, R. Palme, 191

East India Company, 75, 88, 90, 114, 149
Economic development in Africa, 158
Economic growth of North America, 79–82
Economic nationalism in India, 99
Economics of trade, 93
Economy, peasant, 150; and capital loans, 144–5; in Africa, 162–4; in China, 152
Egypt, 115; 129, 132, 144, 154–6
El Salvador, 166
Emmanuel, Arghiri, 5, 9, 12, 17, 30, 31, 40, 92, 94, 103–10, 173

England, 41, 129; *see also* Britain
Europe, 11, 24, 77, 130, 190, 192, 193, 194, 197; and Asia, trade between, 17–19; trade statistics, 177–89
European metropolis, 14, 23, 88
Exchange, questions of, 10
Exchange relations, 8, 10
Exploitation 4; periods of, 7, 11
Export balances, 199
Export statistics, 179–89
Export surplus of underdeveloped countries, 193
Exports, and import data, 208; of raw materials, 208; world merchandise, 195–6

Falkland Islands, 174
Faletto, Enzo, 170
Fanon, Frantz, 158
Farming, *v.* foreign trade, 58–69; *v.* slave plantations, 55–8
Ferrer, Aldo, 86, 122
Fei, J. C. H., 110
Feudalism, 41
Fieldhouse, D. K., 194
Fogel, Robert W., 79
Force, use of, 14
Foreign investments, 189–90; by Britain, 195, 198
Foreign trade, 39–40; from Britain, 77; *v.* farming, 58–69
France, 50, 78, 142
Frank, Andre Gunder, 5, 19, 84, 111, 141
Franklin, Benjamin, 66
Free trade, 75, 86, 131; and comparative advantage, 94–101; and Germany, 98; United States, 98; in Britain, 94; in Chile, 100; in Latin America, 83
Friedman, Milton, 37
Furnivall, J. S., 151

Gabel, Joseph, 26
Gallatin, Albert, 79
Gallman, Robert E., 79
Gandhi, Mahatma, 148
Geertz, Clifford 18, 149, 164
Geller, Lucio, 126
Genovese, Eugene, 123
Germany, 26, 95, 98, 129, 145, 182, 185
Gerth, Hans, 25, 26
Gough, Kathleen, 141
Gouldner, Alvin W., 25, 26, 27
Grant, Ulysses S., 79
Gray, Lewis C., 43, 52–3, 55, 56, 57

Growth, staple theory of, 112, 121
Guatemala, 166, 167
Guerra y Sánchez, Ramiro, 47
Guevara, Ernesto Che, 107

Haiti, 48
Halperin Donghi, Tulio, 84, 87, 169, 188
Hamilton, Alexander, 62, 98
Hargreaves, J. D., 20
Harlow, Vincent, 50
Harper, Lawrence A., 63
Hilgerdt, Folke, 173, 174, 175, 176, 181, 183, 185, 187, 188, 191, 195, 197, 199–205
Hill, Polly, 158
Hinkelammert, Franz, 131
Hirschman, Albert, 115
Hobsbawm, E. J., 70, 74
Hoffmann, Walter G., 131, 132
Holland, 40, 41, 50, 95, 150
Honduras, 166
Hong Kong, 192
Huntington, 32

Imlah, Albert H., 182
Imperialism: and Africa, 157–64; and Arab world, 154–7; in Asia, 146–54; in Latin America, 164–71
Import and export data, 208
Import balances, 199
Import statistics, 179–89
Import substitution, 128–30, 137
India, 18, 19, 23, 78, 114, 115, 119, 129, 130, 132, 175, 193, 198; and Britain, trade between, 97, 191–3; Britain in, 87–91, 147–8; development of underdevelopment in, 87–91, 146–9; economic nationalism in, 99; linkages and industrialisation in, 115; trade with, 72
Indonesia, 115, 150, 164
Industrial growth, 132
Industrial revolution, 70–91, 130–3
Industrialisation: and development, capitalist, 11; and linkages in America, 115; and linkages in Britain, 114–15; and linkages in India, 115; in Latin America, 84–7
Industry: infant, 128–9; shipping, 63
Innis, Harold, 112
International division of labour, 16, 75–8, 100, 101, 103, 111, 128, 130, 132, 137, 138
Investments: foreign, 189–90; foreign, by Britain, 195, 198; in underdeveloped countries, 198
Islam, 26

Issawi, Charles, 155
Italy, 29, 104

Japan, 24, 104, 120, 129, 132, 146, 153–4,
  192
Java, 23, 151
Jefferson, Thomas, 54
Jozyr-Kowalski, Stanislow, 26

Kaplan, Marcos, 84, 169
Kautsky, Karl, 25
Keiskammahock Rural Survey, 161
Kindleberger, Charles P., 103, 113
Knight, Frank, 37
Kolko, Gabriel, 30

Labour, international division of, 16, 75–
  8, 100, 101, 103, 111, 128, 130, 132, 137,
  138; migrant, 162
Labour exploitation by Spain, 45–50
Lacoste, Yves, 156
Landes, David, 73
Latin America, 19, 31, 77, 78, 79, 113,
  116–18, 129, 137, 149, 175; development
  in, 82–7,   164–71;   imperialism
  in, 164–71; industrialisation in, 84–7;
  liberal reforms in, 165–7, metropolis
  in, 168–70; role of state in, 169; trade
  in, 83
Lenin, V. I., 4, 115, 128, 134, 138, 141, 194
Leroy-Beaulieu, Paul, 43
Levene, Ricardo, 83
Lewis, W. Arthur, 110
Liberal reforms in Latin America, 165–7
Linkages, 112; and industrialisation in
  America, 115; and industrialisation
  in Britain, 114–15; and industriali-
  sation in India, 115; backward and
  forward, 113–21; final demand, 128
Lipset, Seymour, 59
Lisbon, 96
List, Friedrich, 92, 94, 95, 97
Lockwood, William W., 153
Lugard, Lord, 141
Luxemburg, Rosa, 135, 141–6, 147, 154,
  155, 161, 164, 167

Magdoff, Harry, 108
Manchester, 72
Mandel, Ernest, xiii, 8, 9, 13, 73, 78, 194
Mannheim, Karl, 25
Mannix, Daniel P., 15
Mantoux, Paul, 74

Mao Tse-tung, 2, 3, 6
Marcuse, Herbert, 25
Marginal productivity, theory of, 101
Marini, Ruy Mauro, 133, 138, 168
Market, internal, and capitalism, 134; in-
  ternal and external, 110–33; internal,
  development of, 121–8, 130, 138
Marshall, Alfred, 37
Martin, Margaret, E., 79
Martinez, Alberto y Aranda, Sergio, 12
Marx, Karl, 1, 2, 3, 14, 23, 25, 28, 38–43,
  54, 60, 71, 75, 88, 128, 134, 136, 137,
  141
Marx and Weber, comparison, 26–8
Marxism, 7
Materialist dialectics, 3
Meier, Gerald M., 103
Mercantile development in United
  States, 61–9
Mesopotamia, 145
Metaphysical outlook, 6
Metropolis, 5, 12, 101, 106; European,
  14, 23,   88; in Latin America,
  168–70
Metropolitan accumulation, 71–5, 189–90
Mexico, 22, 23, 35, 44–7, 55, 83, 85, 132,
  159, 166, 167, 169, 171
Middle East, 79, 142
Migrant labour, 161
Mills, C. Wright, 25, 26
Mining economics 45–7
Mintz, Sidney, 53
Mitre, Bartolomé, 127
Modes of production, 17–24, 30, 86, 128;
  capitalist, 109; transformation of, 77,
  140; transitions, 40–2
Mommsen, Wolfgang, 26
Moore, Barrington, 152
Mukerjee, Ramakrishna, 19, 90
Multilateral financing of trade, 16
Multilateral trade and Britain, 197
Multilateral trade balances, 189
Multilateral trade imbalances, 176–89
Myrdal, Gunnar, 92, 103

Napoleon Bonaparte, 157
Narodniks, 135
Nehru, Jawaharlal, 147, 148
Nettels, Curtis P., 61
New England, xiv, 22, 24, 44, 58, 59, 64,
  66, 129
New Guinea, 33
New World and Adam Smith, 33–7
New Zealand, 11, 24, 33

Nicaragua, 166
Nicolaus, Martin, 42
Norman, E. H., 153
North America, 190; economic growth of, 79–82
North, Douglass C., 62, 79, 124–5

Padmore, George, 161
Palestine, 11
Palloix, Christian, 3–4, 5, 74, 109, 133, 135
Panama, 166
Paraguay, 85, 129, 167, 174
Parera Dennis, Alfredo, 170
Parsons, Talcott, 25, 26
Payments: balance of, 172; circuit of, 177
Peasant economy, 150; and capital loans, 144–5; in Africa, 162–4, in China, 152
Periodisation, question of, 7–10
Perry, Commodore, 18
Peru, 22, 23, 35, 44, 55, 159; mining economies in, 45–7
Pimentel, Deustua, 83
Pinedo, Federico, 170
Plantation system: in Barbados, 50–1; in Brazil, 52–5; in Caribbean, 52–5; in United States, 52–5
Plantations, slave, *v.* farming, 55–8
Pombal, Marquis de, 95
Portugal, 29, 40, 82, 95–7, 129
Poverty of nations, 1
Prebisch, Raul, 92, 103
Preobazhensky, E., 7, 8, 9, 40
Production: and accumulation, 134–9; capitalist, 38; capitalist mode of, 109; class structure and underdevelopment, 122–5; modes of, 17–24, 30, 86, 128; modes of, capitalist, 109; modes of, transformation, 77, 140; modes of transitions, 40–2; of capital goods in colonies, 113–14; questions of, 10; raw materials, 115–121
Productivity: and wages, 107; marginal, theory of, 101
Profit: and trade policy, 136; and wages, 105
Protestantism and capitalism, 28–30
Puerto Rico, 48, 86
Puritanism, 30; and capitalism, 58

Quebec, 44

Radcliffe-Brown, A. R., 141

Ramirez, Hernán, 83
Ranis, G., 110
Raw materials: exports of, 208; production, 115–21
Reinsma, R., 150
Revolution, industrial, in Britain, 131
Rhodes, Cecil, 141
Rhodesia, 11, 164
Riad, Hassan, 153
Ribeiro, Darcy, 30, 31, 33, 59
Ricardo, David, 38, 92, 93, 95, 98, 136
Robertson, H. M., 25, 29
Rodinson, Maxime, 26
Rodney, Walter, 20
Russia, 121, 132, 135, 144

Samuelsson, Kurt, 29, 30, 58
Sanchez, Guerra y, 47
Santo Domingo, 48
Sarç, Omar Celal, 154
Sarmiento, Domingo Faustino, 85, 141
Sauer, Carl O., 47
Saul, S. B., 16, 102, 126, 131, 175, 182, 188, 190, 191, 193, 195, 196
Say, J. B., 97
Schapera, I., 161
Schlesinger, A. M., 63
Schlote, W., 101, 102, 182
Sen, Bhowani, 19
Settlement in Africa, 159–61
Seymour, David, 127
Shah, Said A., xii
Shapiro, Meyer, 26
Sheridan, Richard, 48
Shipping industries, 63, 67
Sik, Endre, 157
Simon, Herbert, 37
Singer, H. W., 103, 110
Slave plantations *v.* farming, 55–8
Slavery and slave trade, 15, 19–21, 51, 53, 54, 57, 66, 72, 124–5, 157
Smith, Adam, xv, 1, 3, 23, 25, 28, 33–7, 38, 42, 43, 44, 54, 59, 60, 72, 74, 75, 92, 93, 97, 106, 114, 134, 140
Smith, Thomas C., 153
Sombart, Werner, 28
Sorokin, P. A., 25
South Africa, 11, 103
South America, 192
Spain, 29, 44, 50, 78, 82, 104
Staple theory of growth, 112, 121
State role in Latin America, 169
Straits Settlements, 192, 194
Structuralists, 5

Suret-Canale, Jean, 159
Sweezy, Paul, 4, 41
Syria, 145

Takahashi, Kohachiro, 41
Tavares, Maria de Concepcão, 129
Tawney, R. H., 29
Technological gap, 130
Tergast, G. C. W., 151
Tertiary sector, growth of, 119
Torres Rivas, Edelberto, 166
Trade, between Britain and India, 97, 191–3; between Britain and Portugal, 95–7; between Britain and United States, 68–9; between Europe and Asia, 17–19; between West Indies and United States, 66; British system, 175; Caribbean, 64–5; colonial, 15; economics of, 93; for Britain, terms of, 101–2; foreign, 39–40; foreign, from Britain, 77; foreign *v.* farming, 58–69; free, 75, 86, 131; free, and comparative advantage, 94–101; free, and Germany, 98; free, and United States, 98; free, in Britain, 94; free, in Chile, 100; in Latin America, 83; Indian, 88–90; multilateral, and Britain, 197; multilateral financing of, 16; slave and slavery, 15, 19–21, 51, 53, 54, 57, 66, 72, 124–5, 157; terms of, 101–3; with Africa, 21; with India, 72; world, expansion of, 76–8; world, regions, 205; world, statistics, 200–8
Trade balances: of Britain, 192; of United States, 193
Trade growth in Britain, 71–5
Trade imbalance, 172; multilateral, 176–89; world, patterns of, 173–205
Trade patterns of Britain, 16
Trade policy and profit, 136
Trade triangles, 14–17, 67, 72
Transplanted peoples, 32
Transport charges, 186–7, 199
Trevelyan, Sir Charles, 89
Trinidad, 48
Turkey, 144, 192

Underdeveloped colonies, 11–12
Underdeveloped countries, 5; and dualist theory, 111; export surplus of, 193; investment in, 198; trade statistics, 179–89
Underdevelopment, 11; and class struc-

ture, production, 122–5; and development in America, 25–69; and development in United States, 79–81; by Britain, 86; development of, 44, 50, 138, 142; in Africa, development of, 160–4; in Algeria, development of, 156; in Egypt, development of, 154–6; in India, development of, 87–91, 146–9; in south East Asia, development of, 149–51; internal *v.* 'external' determination, 2–7; of colonies, 30; structural theory of, 2
Unequal exchange, 9, 12, 13, 18, 22, 24, 31, 78, 103–10, 117, 123, 173
United States, 11, 19, 20, 23, 31, 44, 55–8, 103, 115, 116, 117, 120, 174, 192, 193, 196, 197, 198; and Britain, trade between, 68–9; and free trade, 98; and West Indies, trade between, 66; development and underdevelopment in, 79–81; development of, 124–5; mercantile development in, 61–9; North-east, 58–69; plantation system in, 52–5; trade balance of, 193; trade statistics, 177–89
Uruguay, 117, 170, 174

Vitale, Luis, 84

Wages, 12; and productivity, 107, and profits, 105; and unequal exchange, 108
Wakefield, E. G., 43
Wallerstein, Immanuel, 5
Walton, G. M., 67
Washington, George, 54
Watkins, M. H., 112, 113, 120, 128
Watt, James, 70
Wealth of nations, 1
Weber and Marx, comparison, 26–8
Weber, Marianne, 25
Weber, Max, 25
Weber Thesis, 25–33, 58
Wertheim, W. F., 18
West Africa, 193
West Indies, 16, 48, 64–6, 72, 74, 192
Williams, Eric, 15
Woddis, Jack, 160, 161
World merchandise exports, 195–6
World trade: regions, 205; statistics, 200–8
Woytinsky, W. S. and E. S., 13, 18, 24, 76, 77, 182, 183, 195

Yates, Paul Lamartine, 208

Selected Modern Reader Paperbacks

The Accumulation of Capital by Rosa Luxemburg — $ 7.50

Accumulation on a World Scale by Samir Amin — 8.95

African Social Studies edited by Peter Gutkind and Peter Waterman — 6.95

The Age of Imperialism by Harry Magdoff — 5.50

Agribusiness in the Americas by Roger Burbach and Patricia Flynn — 5.95

The American Revolution: Pages from a
Negro Worker's Notebook by James Boggs — 1.65

Anarchism: From Theory to Practice by Daniel Guérin — 3.95

Armed Struggle in Africa: With the Guerrillas
in "Portuguese" Guinea by Gérard Chaliand — 2.95

Away With All Pests: An English Surgeon in People's
China, 1954-1969 by Dr. Joshua S. Horn — 3.95

Cambodia: Starvation or Revolution
by George C. Hildebrand and Gareth Porter — 3.25

Capitalism and Underdevelopment in Latin America
by Andre Gunder Frank — 6.95

Capitalist Patriarchy and the Case For Socialist
Feminism edited by Zillah R. Eisenstein — 6.95

Caste, Class, and Race by Oliver C. Cox — 7.95

China Shakes the World by Jack Belden — 6.95

China Since Mao by Charles Bettelheim and Neil Burton — 3.95

China's Economy and the Maoist Strategy by John G. Gurley — 5.95

The Chinese Road to Socialism: Economics of the Cultural
Revolution by E. L. Wheelwright and Bruce McFarlane — 4.50

Class Conflict in Tanzania by Issa G. Shivji — 4.50

Class Struggles in the USSR. First Period: 1917-1923
by Charles Bettelheim — 7.95

Class Struggles in the USSR. Second Period: 1923-1930
by Charles Bettelheim — 8.95

The Communist Manifesto by Karl Marx and Friedrich Engels,
including Engels' "Principles of Communism," and an
essay, "The Communist Manifesto After 100 Years," by
Paul M. Sweezy and Leo Huberman — 3.50

The Communist Movement. From Comintern
to Cominform by Fernando Claudin (2 vols.) — 11.90

Consciencism by Kwame Nkrumah — 2.95

Copper in the World Economy by Dorothea Mezger — 8.00

Corporate Imperialism by Norman Girvan — 5.95

Corporations and the Cold War, edited by David Horowitz — 4.50

A Critique of Soviet Economics by Mao Tse-tung — 4.50

Cuba: Anatomy of a Revolution
by Leo Huberman and Paul M. Sweezy — 3.95

Death on the Job by Daniel Berman — 6.50

The Debt Trap: The International Monetary Fund
and the Third World by Cheryl Payer — 5.00

Dependent Accumulation and Underdevelopment
by Andre Gunder Frank — 5.95

The Disinherited: Journal of a Palestinian Exile by Fawaz Turki — 4.95

The Economic Transformation of Cuba by Edward Boorstein — 5.95

The Education of Black People by W. E. B. DuBois — 3.75

The End of Prosperity by Harry Magdoff and Paul M. Sweezy   2.95
The Energy Crisis by Michael Tanzer   4.50
Essays on the Political Economy of Africa
   by Giovanni Arrighi and John Saul   6.50
Fighting Two Colonialisms: Women in Guinea-Bissau
   by Stephanie Urdang   6.50
The Geopolitics of Hunger by Josué de Castro   7.50
The Growth of the Modern West Indies by Gordon K. Lewis   6.95
The Hidden History of the Korean War by I. F. Stone   5.95
How Capitalism Works by Pierre Jalée   3.95
Huan-Ying: Workers' China by Janet Goldwasser and Stuart Dowty   5.95
Humanity and Society. A World History by Kenneth Neill Cameron   6.50
Imperial Brain Trust by Laurence H. Shoup and William Minter   6.50
Imperialism and Revolution in South Asia,
   edited by Kathleen Gough and Hari P. Sharma   6.95
Imperialism and Underdevelopment: A reader,
   edited by Robert I. Rhodes   6.50
Imperialism: From the Colonial Age to the Present by Harry Magdoff   5.00
Inside India Today by Dilip Hiro   5.95
Inside the Monster: Writings on the United States and
   American Imperialism by José Martí   5.95
Introduction to Socialism by Leo Huberman and Paul M. Sweezy   3.95
Karl Marx's Theory of Revolution. Part 1: State and Bureaucracy
   (2 vols. in one) by Hal Draper   9.50
Labor and Monopoly Capital by Harry Braverman   6.50
Labor Migration Under Capitalism: The Puerto Rican Experience
   by The History Task Force   6.50
Latin America: Underdevelopment or Revolution
   by Andre Gunder Frank   6.50
Law and the Rise of Capitalism by Michael Tigar and Madeleine Levy   6.95
Lenin and Philosophy and Other Essays by Louis Althusser   4.50
Lenin's Last Struggle by Moshe Lewin   5.95
Let Me Speak! Testimony of Domitila, A Woman of the Bolivian Mines
   by Domitila Barrios de Chungara with Moema Viezzer   5.95
Man's Worldly Goods by Leo Huberman   6.50
Marx and Modern Economics, edited by David Horowitz   6.50
Marx, Freud, and the Critique of Everyday Life by Bruce Brown   4.95
Marxism and Philosophy by Karl Korsch   3.45
Marxist Economic Theory by Ernest Mandel (2 vols.)   13.00
Maturity and Stagnation in American Capitalism by Josef Steindl   5.95
Mau Mau from Within by Donald L. Barnett and Karari Njama   7.50
Middle East Oil and the Energy Crisis by Joe Stork   5.95
The Military Art of People's War: Selected Political Writings
   of General Vo Nguyen Giap, edited by Russell Stetler   5.95
Monopoly Capital by Paul A. Baran and Paul M. Sweezy   6.50
The Myth of Population Control by Mahmood Mamdani   4.50
Notes on the Puerto Rican Revolution by Gordon K. Lewis   5.95
On the Transition to Socialism
   by Paul M. Sweezy and Charles Bettelheim   3.25
Open Veins of Latin America by Eduardo Galeano   6.95
Our Great Spring Victory by General Van Tien Dung   4.95

The People's Republic of China: A Documentary History of
   Revolutionary Change, edited by Mark Selden $10.00

The Political Economy of Growth by Paul A. Baran   5.95

The Political Economy of Race and Class in South Africa
   by Bernard Magubane   6.50

A Political History of Japanese Capitalism by Jon Halliday   8.95

Politics and Class Formation in Uganda by Mahmood Mamdani   5.95

Politics and Social Structure in Latin America by James Petras   5.95

The Poverty of Theory and Other Essays by E. P. Thompson   6.50

Pseudoscience and Mental Ability: The Origins and Fallacies of
   the IQ Controversy by Jeffrey M. Blum   5.95

The Ragged Trousered Philanthropists by Robert Tressell   7.50

Return to the Source: Selected Speeches by Amilcar Cabral   2.95

The Rise and Fall of the East India Company
   by Ramkrishna Mukherjee   6.50

The Scalpel, the Sword: The Story of Dr. Norman Bethune
   by Sidney Gordon and Ted Allan   5.95

Selected Political Writings of Rosa Luxemburg,
   edited by Dick Howard   6.95

Socialism in Cuba by Leo Huberman and Paul M. Sweezy   4.50

Studies in the Labor Theory of Value by Ronald L. Meek   6.50

The Sugarmill by Manuel Moreno Fraginals   10.95

The Theory of Capitalist Development by Paul M. Sweezy   6.50

The Third World in World Economy by Pierre Jalée   3.95

Toward an Anthropology of Women, edited by Rayna Reiter   6.95

Unequal Development by Samir Amin   5.95

Unequal Exchange: A Study of the Imperialism of Trade
   by Arghiri Emmanuel   6.95

The United States and Chile: Imperialism and the Overthrow
   of the Allende Government by James Petras and Morris Morley   4.50

The Watchdogs: Philosophers and the Established Order
   by Paul Nizan   2.95

Wasi'chu: The Continuing Indian Wars
   by Bruce Johansen and Roberto Maestas   6.50

We, the People by Leo Huberman   5.95

Women in Class Society by Heleieth I. B. Saffioti   6.95